Artists Handbooks
Making Ways

The visual artist's guide to surviving and thriving

edited by
David Butler
with additional work by
Richard Padwick

AN
PUBLICATIONS

AN Publications

By giving access to information, advice and debate, AN Publications aims to:

- empower artists individually and collectively to strengthen their professional position
- raise awareness of the diversity of visual arts practice and encourage an equality of opportunity
- to stimulate good working practices throughout the visual arts.

Acknowledgements

Editor	David Butler with additional work on 3rd edition by Richard Padwick.
Sub-Editor	Sharon McKee with additional work by Pat Wressel
Editorial assistance	Tracey Musgrove, Claire Veitch and Neil Sedgwick
Index	Susanne Atkin
Proof reader	Heather Cawte Winskell (100 Proof)
Picture research	Arabella Plouviez
Cover Design	Neil Southern
Design & Layout	Neil Southern & Richard Padwick
Printed	Mayfair Printers, Print House, William Street, Sunderland, SR1 1UI
Grant aid	The first edition recieved support from Northern Arts and the Arts Council.

ISBN 0 907730 16 7

AN Publications is an imprint of
Artic Producers Publishing Co Ltd
PO Box 23, Sunderland SR4 6DG tel 091 567 3589

Contents

1 • Introduction

Carol Pemberton

This book is for those of you involved in activities encompassed by the broad and blurred definition of fine arts – painters, sculptors, photographers, printmakers, film and video makers, and those artists and craftspeople who see their future in terms of one-off or small-scale production work. You are all concerned with constantly producing new work in response to personal change and development, rather than in response to consumer demand or expected profit. The authors in this book are concerned that artists should be able to gain some protection against those who under-value, under-use, under-price and under-estimate the contribution made by the visual arts.

Damon Burnard

To survive is *'to continue to live after the end or cessation of some thing or condition' (Oxford English Dictionary)*. That is what this book aims to help you do: to live as a professional artist after the security of education and the termly grant have been removed. To use the term 'professional' immediately raises the issue of what it means when applied to the visual artist. A definition that links professionalism with the provision of a livelihood would preclude most practising artists. Further more the linking of profession to the provision of a service for which there is a demand would be to over-vaunt the public response to much of the work you may do. A definition based purely on extrinsic factors: money, recognition, regular showings and critical acclaim won't do, because it decries the importance of personal intent and commitment. If you bridle at the thought your efforts would be dismissed as 'hobbyist' by the Inland Revenue because it has failed to provide a taxable profit, then it's an indicator that you invest in your work a value unrelated to monetary return and regard yourself as a professional.

Self-regard is one indication of professionalism, but to leave it at that would be to allow the Shavian definition of an artist to stand unchallenged, *'The true artist will let his wife starve, his children go barefoot, his mother drudge for his living at seventy, sooner than work at anything but his art'*.

This image of the ego-centred creator, oblivious to the needs of others and prepared to starve for his art may be romantic in the abstract, but I have yet to meet an artist for whom it was a career objective. Applied to any other profession it would be regarded as an indication of failure. This book is based on the belief that along with personal conviction, there are aspects of living as an artist that need to be considered so the individual can take some control of how his or her working life develops. It is a manual you can use to work out your own personal plan. The first chapter is *Looking at yourself,* because until you have thought through what being an artist means for you, reading the rest of the book will be worthy, but lacking in vitality. *Looking at yourself* is a base from which to direct yourself to those chapters that relate to your specific interests, and from which to devise your own support system.

A support system is what every artist needs. In Shaw's definition the sacrificial mother constituted the support system, for art college leavers it is often the bar job taken to earn money while things are sorted out. Nothing wrong in that, unless two years on the artist/bar person, has become the bar person who once went to art college. The movement from the first to the second position can be almost imperceptible, and only brought to consciousness when an old college friend is met, or you are asked if you still paint, photograph, sculpt. Having looked at the careers of a large number of artists over the five years after leaving college, what seems to differentiate those who carry on with their art from those who don't, is that the *stickers* don't make a separation between the continuance of their art and the support system needed to ensure it; a difference seen in these comments from two fine art graduates:

'It is hard, and I'm very poor, but being able to carry on doing my own work makes my life richer than any monetary system could offer.'

'Having to exist in a series of second rate part-time jobs... is becoming extremely dispiriting.'

In the first quote the speaker's self-image is related to being an artist, in the second the self-image has become tied in with the unskilled work leading to a questioning of the viability of continuing with art. I am not suggesting artists should be prepared to starve, that if personal needs are honestly recognised an appropriate support system can be sought. Perhaps the second speaker could have valued their work more highly if they had obtained a post-graduate vocational training that could then have acted as a support. It's different strokes for different folks, and the task of college leavers is to recognise the strokes they need if they are to continue their art with satisfaction.

This is not a book on how to make a fortune from the visual arts. If that's your prime goal you need read no further. But if you're wanting assistance to withstand the vicissitudes of committing yourself to the visual arts, and are willing to participate in the process of devising strategies that are right for you, then we believe this book will give you an informed starting point.

2 • Looking at yourself

Carole Pemberton   I am aware self-analysis is not an activity people are generally comfortable with, so if you are going to continue reading this section, I've got to convince you of what's in it for you. If you were sitting in my office, at this point you would probably have a list of pragmatic questions: who'll pay for me to do a travelling scholarship to..., who does a course in..., which RAB gives most money to...? All reasonable questions, but often totally unconnected to any sense of the individual and their personal strengths, weaknesses, commitments, fears. In time, you may decide to open up, to let me know how you are different from the ten other course members who also want to study overseas; we may eventually discover it's not a good idea for you to spend considerable time and money on applications when there are other more accessible ways of carrying on with your work. I won't be able to help you make that decision, however, unless you take the risk of thinking through your motivations. The problem was stated clearly by that ursine philosopher Winnie the Pooh: *'Here is Edward Bear, coming downstairs now, bump, bump, on the back of his head behind Christopher Robin. It is, as far as he knows, the only way of coming downstairs, but sometimes he feels there really is another way, if only he could stop bumping for a moment and think of it.'*

You are being asked to take time out to stop bumping along whatever path you are following to consider where it is leading, why and how you chose it, are there others more direct or enjoyable to travel along. To think through the path you want to follow as an artist and the system you will need to carry with you, moves you from being a passive to an active participant.

If so far you've been a passive participant you may recognise yourself in these statements: things will be OK when... 'I get a good degree'...,'The Royal College offers me a place'..., 'Someone discovers me'..., 'I get a grant'..., 'I'm offered a show in a West End Gallery'.

These statements assume either by just waiting, or by luck things will happen for you. They may. More likely they will not. Luck tends to happen when you've created the conditions in which the opportunity can

Life skills teaching,
B Hopson & M Scally.
McGraw Hill, 1981

arise. To live in expectation of something happening is a condition described by Hopson and Scally as 'pin-ball living', where like pin-balls we have no life of our own, but are set in motion by someone else, and bounce from place to place with no clear directions – sometimes hitting big scores, but as likely to go down the hole. The opposite to this is a philosophy with you as a force behind what happens, controlling *as far as you are able* possible outcomes. To do this implies:

• using your own feelings to recognise discrepancies between how things are and how you'd like them to be

• specifying desired outcomes and the action/steps needed to achieve them

• acting to implement goals

To act from a sense of personal power you must have thought through:

• what is important to you

• what would you like to happen

• what beliefs you hold that would support you

• what information you need

• what skills you have and additional skills you need to acquire.

If you don't know where you're going you'll end up somewhere else,
D Cambell. Argus,
1974

The process can be encapsulated in the phrase *'If you don't know where you're going you'll end up somewhere else'*.

Living out the life of a frustrated artist is a common and at times comforting stance – there are so many others around sharing the same ground, and so many very real economic, structural and bureaucratic obstacles to survival. But to take on the role of victim who has to accept the ways things are means you will be ill-prepared to notice chance even when it does appear. Carlos Casteneda wrote of using opportunity: *'All of us… have a cubic centimetre of chance that pops up in front of our eyes from time to time. The difference between the average man and the warrior is that the warrior is aware of this and one of his tasks is to be alert and deliberately waiting so that when his cubic centimetre pops up, he has the speed, the prowess to pick it up.'*

To recognise your cubic centimetre of chance, requires you to assess yourself in two ways:

• what have you learnt about yourself as an artist up to now

• what do you want to achieve as an artist in the future.

What have you learnt about yourself ?

Considering this question is important because it is a means of recognising the skills you have, the interests you hold and the values they embody.

Exercise

Think of occasions when you have experienced a sense of enjoyment and achievement from art activities which you have been involved in, eg:

- organising a painting event for children during a summer holiday
- seeing a piece of your work in a gallery
- mastering a particular technical skill
- campaign for greater council support for the arts in your town.

Having identified these, consider each of them and ask yourself:

- why it was satisfying to you?
- what does it tell you about the way in which you work best, your values and needs, and there any patterns?

In asking these questions you will be clarifying a view of yourself as an artist. For example:

- is recognition through your sales important to you?
- do you see your art as a social tool?
- do you want your work in public space, or owned by individuals?
- do you get enjoyment out of work being permanent or ephemeral?
- do you value critical attention or does your art need to meet only your own critical standards?
- do you need an audience?
- is involvement in administration and organisation of exhibitions or group studies as satisfying as doing your own work?
- is it important that issues related to gender, politics, race or sexuality be reflected in your work?
- do you need academic success in order to feel validated?

The satisfiers you identify will reflect the concept you hold of yourself, which differs for each of us.

Goal setting

The second stage of planning how to use the rest of this book is to decide what it is you want. Goal setting means to state how we would like to be. It is a way of rechecking our present interests, values and needs to see if we want to carry them forward, highlighting skills we may need to acquire and risks we need to be prepared to take. It is a direct means of confronting how large or small a part we want art to play in our future.

Goal setting exercise

One way of identifying possible goals is to allow ourselves the luxury of fantasising. Imagine there are no constraints in terms of time, money or commitment, and then construct for yourself:

A fantasy day

Write down (or close your eyes and think) what would be a perfect day. Where would you be, what would you do, who would you be with, what would be the major achievement? What part would work play in it?

Fantasy artist

Now close in on you as an artist during that day. Are you there at all? If you are, what are you doing, and does it seem to be a major or minor part of your life? Is the art for yourself; are you working with others; are you working to commission or for an exhibition? Try and get a sense of what it would feel like to be that artist.

Using fantasy to set goals can be a very powerful and direct way of acknowledging what we would like to experience. With an illustrator who was considering giving up her work for a 'safe' career, it was clear if she had the luxury of doing work for herself she could begin to value herself as an illustrator again; in her fantasy, far from a business woman, she saw an old lady showing her artwork to her family. Similarly, working with a photographer who had spent unhappy years as a salesman, his fantasy of being in Papua New Guinea looking at the proofs of a travel book he was co-producing encouraged him to enrol in the Enterprise Allowance Scheme. A year on, he had not reached Papua yet, but was the photographer for the local tourist department.

Declaring our fantasies also exposes conflicts which may be inherent in them, and recognises the self limitations or external restrictions which may exist. A fantasy of regular London showings implies a willingness to self-promote, the ability to develop a network of useful professional contacts, and an acceptance of being within reach of London. This may conflict with your assessment of your personal skills, your enjoyment of rural seclusion, and the greater importance domestic responsibilities have in your life at the moment. Recognising conflicts can allow us to rewrite the goals in a form that has meaning, allows for their achievement and incorporates longer-term planning. A more appropriate statement could then be, 'Right now I need to give time to the family, but in three years time I will... and in the meantime I can....'

Transferable skills

It is axiomatic that artists have transferable skills – limitations of the fine art market mean practically no artist pursues a linear career pattern which utilises solely those skills acquired at college. A survey of fine artists from Brighton Polytechnic found over a five-year period 80% had worked in art-related areas, jobs which required creative abilities, but were indirectly linked to the official course curriculum. Painters had become knitwear designers, film-makers, set designers; sculptors were arts administrators, architectural stonemasons and restoration workers; and printmakers community artists and art therapists. Each had gone through a process of identifying their particular skills and looking to see how they could be matched to the needs of the market. This is often slow and painful, and accounts for the apparently high unemployment and under-employment of art graduates in the first years after college. Unfortunately, art courses sometimes fail to acknowledge the hidden curriculum skills imparted over three years: self-discipline, time management, critical thinking, self-reliance, inventiveness, problem solving, working with others, living on a shoestring – abilities vital to surviving as an artist but which can be equally applied elsewhere.

Survey of Post College Experiences of Brighton Polytechnic Fine Art Graduates 1978-82. Brighton Polytechnic Careers Service, 1985

Skills exercise

Acknowledging skills is a means of acquiring greater confidence in achieving a goal, and of also opening up new possibilities.

List all the skills you have acquired over the course of your art education – technical, creative and personal. Stick at it – British diffidence often makes this a difficult task. Refer to the exercise on satisfying experience, or ask a close friend what skills s/he would say you had. Skills recognised by graduates from one art course included:

'I feel capable to make new connections and take new views of life around me. I also feel more able to make decisions for myself and feel independent in my thoughts.'

'As one who had difficulties in previous social communication, exercising my freedom of expression gave me an identity, social position and confidence in relation to my success.'

'The fine art course has the ability to provide students with an education which not only allows them to research a subject fully, but also gives them an attitude of self-discipline and self-reliance, which assists them in life no matter what they choose to do.'

Such apparently intangible skills are rarely spoken of, yet surviving as an artist can call upon them as directly as more creative abilities. The exercise may also highlight personal skills you feel you are lacking.

Technical skills

Recognising technical skills can suggest related work which could support your art activity, or conversely the exercise may have made you aware of deficiencies in your skills. When graduates were asked to list things they wished they had known or experienced before leaving, greater technical competence was a major complaint. It meant, for example, a photography major was unable to find work as a photographer's assistant because of limited experience in film developing. Easy to bad-mouth the college, but a more positive response would be to learn more about film development within a different part-time course.

The alleged non-vocationalism of fine art courses can cause considerable anxiety as to how graduates can compete in an increasingly specialised job market. It is true major organisations delineate roles, but it is equally true that in smaller organisations a variety of skills can be called for. If a national museum advertises in *The Guardian* for a graphic designer, it is only graphic designers who will be considered; but when a local museum advertises for a designer they will often expect a 2D designer, restoration worker, publicity officer, exhibition assistant and display designer rolled into one. In this situation the fine artist can come into their own. You can benefit also from the general ignorance of small employers. Very often little distinction is drawn between art and design disciplines, and you could be offered graphics work even though you last saw Letraset on your foundation course. Having watched the transformation of fine artists across disciplines, I have become convinced that confidence and *chutzpah* are prime survival skills.

Linked in with the issue of recognising, transferring and acquiring skills is the need to value the self. In the present educational climate, it is easy to be hooked into believing a fine art degree is a valueless commodity. It is irrefutable that a painter faces a chiller wind than a Business Studies graduate when leaving college, and the difficulties of finding a personally appropriate survival route are not under-estimated, but it is also important to recognise we can exaggerate problems through projecting our anxieties onto the *art system*. Each year when working in an art college I received letters from recent graduates who were angered by my enquiring as to what they were now doing. Their anger normally took the form of berating the art college, or decrying the art world and stating their decision to have no part of it. Fair enough if that's an honest statement, but often what I read into it was disappointment that nothing happened at the degree show, or a much-desired MA place wasn't forthcoming, and a lack of knowledge or confidence as to how to get started. By projecting our anxieties onto people and things we delude ourselves we are fighting when in reality we are fleeing. The artist who withdraws, when their fantasy self would like to belong, is failing to recognise and value themselves.

Assertiveness

Several contributors to this book make mention of the need to be assertive, and so I want to define what assertiveness is and suggest how it can help artists to survive.

Assertiveness is behaviour by an individual which is guided by strongly held beliefs such as:

- I have the right to be treated with respect as an equal by others (with regard to my sex, age, ethnic origins, work activity, etc)
- I have the right to deal with situations directly without making myself dependent on others' approval
- I have the right to ask for as much information as I need in order to make a decision
- I have the right to ask for what I want
- I have the right to change my mind
- I have the right to say no without feeling guilty
- I have the right to say what I feel and think without having to justify or apologise for it.

You may find it difficult to accept some of these *rights*. If you do, they probably highlight aspects of your behaviour with which you are uncomfortable. For example, if you don't accept yourself as an equal when dealing with funding bodies, commissioners or gallery owners, it will have an obvious effect on how you behave with them – you may be reduced to feeling like a child who has to accept whatever is meted out, or you may have an overwhelming desire to hit out at them before they 'put one over on you'. If saying no is a problem, you will probably overload yourself; agreeing to take part in activities because of not wanting to hurt others, or appear unpleasant. Being unassertive could also mean your career is directed by the will of others and not yourself, eg the craftsperson who becomes tied into producing work which is no longer enjoyable because of the pressure of retailers. If you found it easy to accept all the rights listed, ask yourself if you give the same rights to others. If you feel you are entitled to be treated with respect as an artist but wouldn't accord the same respect to the janitor who helps put up your exhibition, or the tutor who offers criticism, you are operating aggressively not assertively. We can only claim rights that we are prepared to give others.

I'm OK – You're OK,
Thomas Harris. Pan
Books

Assertion is based on the premise 'I'm OK – You're OK', that is I am equal, but no more or less equal than anyone else. When we are not being assertive we are moving from one of three other positions:

Passivity: I'm not OK – You're OK

When passive we feel we are dependent on others to decide what's best for us. Waiting to be discovered and relying on fate are common passive fantasies. We see ourselves as victims of unfairness without having to consider how we colluded in the outcome. 'I never said anything, but they should have known', is an example of how when we are passive we endow both ourselves with importance, and others with greater abilities than they possibly have. Passivity is strongly linked with a desire to be liked and to avoid conflict, yet ironically this response can cause resentment and lack of respect from others. When we are passive we hold onto our feelings and thoughts, so building up tensions which either eventually blow out – usually in a safe situation or with an inappropriate context (the 'kick the cat' or 'row over the washing up' syndrome) or we internalise the tensions as psychosomatic conditions.

Aggression: I'm OK – You're not OK

When we are aggressive we are feeling no more confident than the passive respondent, but we choose a different strategy, based on the premise 'get them before they get you'. Whilst using aggression can seem very powerful, it can leave us feeling we've lost control, looked stupid and wondering how to make amends. It leaves the recipients feeling angry and hurt, and if used habitually they will develop their own defence mechanisms: contact will be minimised, letters will replace face-to-face communication, they may look for ways of sabotaging activities, or plot how to 'drop' us in it. Since assertion and aggression are often confused it is important to be clear about the difference. When we are aggressive we view situations in win or lose terms with no room to compromise, we have an investment in the other person feeling bad, and will not be prepared to hear what they are saying.

Manipulation: I'm OK – You're not OK

Manipulation is indirect aggression in that we try to get our own way without being found out. Manipulation often starts from an apparent position of 'you're OK', in that flattery and friendship may be used to persuade us to comply with the manipulator's wishes, but if thwarted the iron fist in the velvet glove will be revealed. Manipulation is another means by which we hope to avoid conflict. In our society it is much rewarded as political behaviour and an acceptable 'female' ploy. When uncovered however it leads to the same feelings of resentment and defensiveness as aggression.

Assertion

Assertion differs from the three behaviours outlined above in that:

- it starts from a position of mutual respect
- it believes that open direct communication is preferable to games
- it doesn't automatically see situations in win or lose terms, but allows for compromise
- it separates out the issue from the person. As an assertive person I can lose on a particular issue but still respect myself as an individual if I've done my best
- it accepts responsibility for its own actions and doesn't expect others to make the world right for them.

In discussing assertion it is important to recognise there is nothing inherently wrong in any of the non-assertive behaviours, each has its place, but it is when we use them inappropriately and feel discomfort as a result that we need to consider whether an assertive response would be more satisfying and effective.

Recognition exercise

Consider these situations and your actual (or imagined) responses using the behaviour models of: assertion; aggression; manipulation; passivity.

- You arrive at a gallery as arranged to be told the owner is busy and can't see you.
- A piece of work is dismissed as 'unexciting' in a tutorial
- A meeting is being held to decide on exhibition space, and the space you had mentally stored for yourself is taken by a vociferous group member.
- When you receive your cheque for works sold at a craft gallery it is considerably less than you had expected, as publicity costs have been deducted from the fee.
- Your application for funding from your local arts board is rejected with no explanation.
- The tax inspector looks at your accounts and suggests it's 'just a little hobby'.
- Having sent a press release to your local newspaper, the reporter visits the show, only to report its tabloid sensational aspects.

You may find you have one preferred mode of behaving, or there may be some situations in which you are happily assertive, and others where it is difficult. Factors linked to perceived status, authority and the degree of intimacy in the relationship can control the extent to which we can allow ourselves to be assertive.

Becoming more assertive

Since, behavioural psychologists suggest, we learnt in our first years of life how to be passive, aggressive and manipulative, we can learn also how to be assertive. The basic assertive skills are:

Define your goal

Often we fail to obtain a satisfactory outcome because we didn't take time to think through what we wanted. For example, if as a sculptor I am unhappy at the way in which a piece of work has been placed on site I have a number of ways of expressing my dissatisfaction:

- I moan to my friends but do nothing (passive)
- I complain to the commissioners and ask them to do something about it (still passive as I'm leaving control with them – the 'something' relies on their commitment, interest and integrity)
- I write a letter telling the commissioners how incompetent they are and saying I'll never work with them again (aggressive – you've let off steam, have a temporary sense of satisfaction, but then what have you achieved?)
- I get a friend who knows one of the commissioners to express some concern at the siting of the piece (passive and manipulative)
- I'm on site at the time of installation to take charge of the process, so the problem doesn't arise (assertive)
- I contact the commissioners as soon as I'm aware of the problem, express my concern, make suggestions as to what could be done, and ask to speak with them about the issue (assertive).

The second to last solution is the most direct way of dealing with it, because it assumes I am responsible for my work and the way in which it is seen. But if it is not possible for me to have taken responsibility for the installation, the last solution is equally assertive because I have expressed my anxiety without loading blame, and stated my needs by making suggestions as to how the situation could be rectified.

Acknowledge

If we are going to be assertive not aggressive we have to be prepared to listen to the other person's point of view. This needn't change our goal, but if we don't give the other person clues that we are listening they will see us as being aggressive, and may also move into that position. In the case of the sculptor, asking the commissioner to respond to suggestions gives them an opportunity to offer information which may alter the sculptor's perspective and move toward a workable compromise. If however, having offered suggestions, the sculptor feels she is being stonewalled, she may want to use additional skills.

Broken record

A Woman in Your Own Right, Anne Dickson. Quartet Books, 1981

Broken record is a term coined by Anne Dickson to describe the necessity to repeat our viewpoint in order that it is heard. When an initial request is refused, people often withdraw because they feel they've failed. But often the request hasn't been heard, perhaps the non-listener's mind is tied up with other concerns, they have little investment in the issue, or to hear would involve extra work. Repeating it several times may be necessary before it is taken seriously. Also repeating it reminds us we are here to discuss X when the listener may be anxious to divert us into Y or Z.

Let's analyse what's gone on between the sculptor and commissioner so far:

Sculptor I'm ringing because I've just seen the way my piece of work has been placed on site and I'm concerned at its safety (assertive – issue is the safety of the sculpture not the failure of the installers).

Commissioner Oh I'm glad you've rung, there's some more paperwork I need from you before we can settle your fee (refusal to listen and attempt to hook).

Sculptor Thanks for mentioning it, I'll sort it out tonight (acknowledgement), but I'm really ringing because the piece is in danger of collapsing and I need to discuss how it can be stabilised (broken record).

Commissioner Well, all my workmen are busy right now, so there's nothing can be done for a while. But don't worry, it looked fine to me when I saw it. Very attractive I thought (double hook).

Sculptor I'm pleased you like it (acknowledgement), but I won't allow it to stay as it is. It needs to be more tethered to the ground, and I'd like to see you as soon as possible to discuss how it can be done (broken record).

Commissioner I'm up to my eyes in it right now dearie. I've far more important things than your sculpture to think about (Commissioner uses put down, indicating he is becoming aggressive).

Sculptor I know you're busy (acknowledgement, refusal to respond to the put down hook), but when can I see you? (broken record).

If the commissioner continues to block then the sculptor may choose to:

Switch gear

In this type of interaction the complainant often backs off, feeling embarrassed at being a nuisance. If the issue is important to you,

When I say no I feel guilty, Manuel Smith. Bantam, 1975

however, you must pursue it, otherwise you will be left with a feeling of failure that will knock your self-esteem. Manuel Smith suggests every opposer only has so many 'no's' in their repertoire and it is the assertors' task to have one more 'yes' in theirs. Just repeating your case may become fruitless if the opposer has a large investment in not moving. Authority figures are often over-endowed with a sense of their superiority and rectitude, which makes it impossible for them to listen to the rational content of what is being said. Eric Berne describes it as the *'Critical Parent ego state'*, ie they may be willing to be pleasant to you if you act as a compliant child, and punitive toward you if you show signs of resistance; they may find it difficult to respond to you as one adult to another.

Once it is clear the commissioner cannot recognise the danger of an unstable sculpture, the sculptor has to bring in a new strategy. This means switching gears to identify a person who could effect a solution.

Sculptor I know you're busy, but when can I see you?

Commissioner I'm not committing myself to a time to discuss one small bit of metal when I've got major policy meetings to prepare for (use of Critical Parent in put down).

Sculptor So you're saying you're not concerned that a considerable weight of metal could collapse and cause injury? (refusal to respond to put down. Use of questioning to elicit his position).

Commissioner I'm concerned, but it is unlikely, so it's not a priority.

Sculptor Well, to me it is a priority as my reputation is tied in with the work (assertive – owning of responsibility). As you have told me you're not willing to do anything now I'm going to contact...(switch of gears).

Commissioner You do that, but they won't say any different to me.

Sculptor Well, I'll keep going till I find someone who will take this seriously.

Pursuing an issue in this way can be mentally exhausting but the pay-off when we do respect our own opinion is enormous, and creates a confidence which gives us courage to take on greater challenges. Had the sculptor backed down s/he would have reinforced a belief s/he had no right to interfere or challenge 'experts' and reduced the likelihood of taking on any similar situation in the future; if the sculpture did collapse s/he would have been left with the guilt of 'if only...' This way, even if s/he fails to find someone willing to listen, s/he will know s/he has done his/her best and not failed her/his sense of self as an artist.

3 • Challenge & compromise

A sense of possibility

Colin Rose There is no role for me in the art world. I am that cherished commodity, the unknown artist. I pursue convoluted ideas that seem of little use to others, and with reason, the art world, commercial or otherwise is little interested in me, am I not a fortunate man?

I discovered books, films, theatre and above all, music at the same time as I realised I had creative ability. The elation of those discoveries and my sense of wonder at that sea of possibilities contrasted with the working class life I was heir to. Being an artist seemed heroic. Questions of income or career didn't enter into it. I still try to remind myself that the context for my work is the sum total of what I tried to encompass then, not just the narrow corner called painting I occupy now.

I paint full time often working well into the night. I worry little about producing an end result, five things a year is too many in a world overgrown with art. I work on a painting for as long as it requires. Ten years from start to finish is quite usual – it saves on the art materials!

I work on a relatively small scale, a gesture against overblown public rhetoric; and towards the primacy of the private experience – and they are easier to store.

The first 17 years after leaving college were tough. I sold three paintings and those for not much. I had (perhaps with a sense of misplaced class solidarity) moved to a depressed and low-cost area, reducing overheads but also reducing my contact with other artists and galleries. Constant poverty breeds self pity and in retrospect six or maybe more of those years were wasted but the alternatives seem even less healthy.

Isolation provided time to work but it also softened creative judgement and then work became a substitute for thought. Living at subsistence level in a derelict mining village without the means to get out, is a strained notion of freedom. To provide some income I took odd jobs, the most useful being as a building labourer which provided practical

Colin Rose, *Song to the Dancer*,
oil,1981-1991

skills which in retrospect have proved far more useful as a means of survival than my art school training. I did do some part-time teaching. I suppose I enjoyed it although I was a poor teacher then and I came to loathe sitting around in staff rooms with the time-servers who so often masqueraded as staff. But for the most part I got by, until by a process of osmosis rather than intention I began to acquire some support.

In the last few years I have again taken occasional teaching in a small art school and enjoyed the freshness of the students and the quaintness of the vegetating staff! I have done a few artist-in-residence schemes, most bruisingly at Drumcroon. In trying to explain or involve children in my vision, the simplifications I resort to destroy the purpose of that vision. I am an artist, not a cabaret turn. Yet when asked to stand up and perform I see the charlatan in my soul journey forth!

see 14 • Skill sharing

see 9 • Residencies

I admit to qualms when I hear my contemporaries being written about. To rise from oblivion to obscurity would bring worthwhile privileges to me, mainly of access – a very real consideration in our class and status ridden society.

By being out in the provinces, I have not established the contacts and contracts that I suppose are my due. On the other hand I have not had to devote time to that end and a decent living comes cheaper outside of metropolitan areas. I used to get angry at my lack of progress in the art world. Nowadays I smile ruefully. I enjoy my painting. I enjoy fighting and negotiating with my ideas and my agenda is my own.

There is probably a role for me as a footnote to culture.

Restraints & stimuli

Amal Ghosh I am a mural artist and a studio painter. Both impose certain restrictions and boundaries. Both are important to me. As a studio painter I have a freedom to work regardless of public response. Most of the time my painting is perceived, judged and dismissed by the host community as 'ethnic' or minority art. There are many restrictions in mural art, but once the difficulties of getting commissions are surmounted, this is not one of them. This is a point worth noting for artists who are members of minority

Amal Ghosh,
Treatment Room Mural, 1991.
Vitreous enamel on steel panels, each 90 x 100cm, overall size 180 x 900cm.
Eastman Dental Hospital, Grays Inn Road, London.

groups. The art, not the artist, is judged. The other side of this equation is that this is achieved by a loss of personal identity for the artist. The work becomes an integral part of its space. The challenges and compromises of architectural commissions cannot be isolated from each other but can be categorised for clarity and convenience.

Space

I have always liked architecture and believe art is an integral part of the total equation to the wholeness of the building. Most of the time the restraints imposed by a space are a creative stimulus. This realisation was a turning point in accepting the demands of an architectural space initially taking precedent over the development of my personal statement as an artist, then becoming an integral part of my personal development. Each space has a unique demand. When working at The Aumbry door for Manchester Cathedral I was aware of the room with its spiritual connotation and evolved a design which took on the essence of the period, the meditative nature of the space and my own understanding of the structure of the architecture. This approach in a different environment produced a completely different result in the Eastman Dental Hospital mural.

Materials

I have always tried to consider the most suitable material for both the proposed space and the design. I have found it essential to have a comprehensive understanding of a wide range of materials, including paint, mosaic, stained glass and vitreous enamel, and of the material constraints of particular kinds of sites. These are creative challenges.

Cost

see 11 • Project planning & fundraising

This relates to choice of material, nature of the design and the funding available. I try to decide on the minimum remuneration I can accept. I sometimes decide to cover only the cost of my subsistence and materials in order to do a commission in a preferred material that is more expensive but more appropriate. Balancing time, costs, size of design and choice of materials has been a major area of compromise and challenge.

The commissioning agents

see 10 • Commissions

This is shorthand for every one who has a possible say in influencing/ determining the finished work. I have only twice been involved with an architect from the outset, and have never been able to assume an architect will be involved in commissioning. I have rarely been in the position of submitting a design which was accepted in its entirety.

The Manchester Cathedral Aumbry design was the result of a series of designs. The Eastman Dental Hospital Mural had one section, which was important for the dynamics of the whole design, rejected by one art committee member on the grounds he could not literally identify it with any part of the hospital. It took many hours of work to resolve its replacement in the design. The Charing Cross Hospital Mural was commissioned by the Hospital with a design brief subsequently rejected by the elderly patients and the nursing staff, who were unanimous in demanding the narrative community recreation of Old Fulham.

My own feeling is that by compromising I am enabling the client to undertake some responsibility and credit for the commission. My satisfaction derives from using the environment as the starting point and stimulus for my own work.

Working collaboratively

Val Murray   I work with other artists on projects because I enjoy it and find it challenging and fruitful. The process of collaboration is fascinating in itself. Together with working in non-studio situations I find collaborating with others is one of the best ways of engaging with the here and now. I believe this engagement is an important part of my role as an artist.

Collaborations

see 12 • Strength in numbers   I work regularly with Those Environmental Artists (TEA – Jon Biddulph, Peter Hatton, Lynn Pilling and myself). We came together because of a

Those Environmental Artists, *Living Space,* Upper Campfield Market, Manchester, 1991. ***Photo:*** *Val Murray*

shared concern with ordinary things, context and accessibility. We started off by building separate installations in an old house. We have gone on to more fully collaborative and ambitious projects, always with a temporary and public outcome. We have developed a very trusting and supportive relationship. We are visual artists but recently expanded our scope by collaborating with a theatre company. New challenges stop the collaboration from standing still or getting cosy.

A challenging process

In a TEA project the main aims and strategies for achieving them in relation to a particular situation are determined early on. Ideas are pooled and discussed. We trust each other enough to be frank and respect each other enough to take criticisms seriously. At an early stage ideas take the form of visual proposals and responses. You can't talk your way to an art work – one danger when people work together. Some ideas are discarded or modified and new ones evolve. Materials and structures are explored through suggestions and experiment.

This interactive process gets rid of red herrings and unnecessary elaborations and stops you over-indulging personal obsessions. Far from leading to a weak compromise our collaboration produces strong, rich and focused work. It is the creative tension between mutual support and honest criticism, the individual and the group which makes it successful and takes everyone beyond what they would achieve on their own.

On a purely practical level collaboration is a flexible and effective use of resources. Individuals bring different experiences and skills are shared. Standards and expectations rise. We can tackle projects which would be daunting to an individual and get funding more easily.

Individuals and the group

In TEA everyone feels confident enough to put forward ideas. These may come from other work we each do. Varied input and strong individuals are necessary for a rich collaboration. I also work as an individual and sometimes develop things which originated in the group. Misunderstandings could arise from people doing their own in a collaboration thing or exploiting the group's ideas or products. We avoid this by a strong shared understanding and clear communication.

Potential pitfalls

I've been involved in less successful collaborations. They falter or produce poor quality work when people do not like or trust each other or do not respect each other's work and professional standards. Such a situation challenges your integrity, is frustrating and stressful. There has to be a clear understanding of expectations and commitment. Conflicts of loyalty and time can arise, especially if people are involved in other work. Inadequate communication is at the root of most problems.

Conclusion

The chemistry has to be right for collaboration to work. Laughing and eating are vital ingredients! With the right partners I find the process a fascinating evolution of creative ideas and team building. This model is not uncommon in other art forms and, based on my experience, I do not believe the individual artist working alone is the only route to creative output.

Taking control

Michele Weaver — Through the use of mechanical movement, I make sculptures and installations, using a simple narrative of action to describe emotions. The fact that I myself am constantly and furiously on the move, is by no means coincidental.

By wishing to concentrate on mechanical sculpture and avoiding static images, I have confused things considerably. When recently tackling the business plan for an Enterprise Allowance application (I was accepted as a self-employed 'arts worker'), I was bewildered by having to relate my work to a cash flow forecast. Moving sculptures are difficult to sell by 'normal' standards, with the added problem of needing to ensure a piece will function permanently. Sculptor Jim Whiting reputedly overcame maintenance difficulties of his complex mechanisms by having a team of assistants trained in their upkeep. Nice thought.

see 11 • Project planning & fundraising

Without my own team of assistants, I am faced with needing to achieve mechanical and electrical simplicity in my work, whilst acquiring the necessary technical skills for a creative vocabulary in the medium. If I approached exhibiting venues on an adequate scale and with the level of technical support capable of coping with fallible mechanisms, I would still need to take responsibility for the life span and efficiency of my work. Applications for funding and exhibiting are often confounded by requests for slides, which in my case are static representations of moving images. Videos are not always accepted.

see 4 • Training

see 16 • Publicity & promotion

I need sustained studio time in order to thoroughly investigate ideas, both technically and creatively, and given that selling and exhibiting can be problematic, how to fund my research, materials and time?

Arts workshops

see 14 • Skill sharing

I earn money by running workshops for a variety of groups and venues. Most requested are sessions in circus skills, accessible and enjoyable, and recreational arts such as mask, kite making and small group projects, mostly for children. The general scenario is being presented with hoards of babbling kids on a summer playscheme, and then having

Learning to juggle – Circus workshop run by Michele Weaver, **1989**

to engage them in constructive, creative and safe activity. There are many aspects to this work that do give me tremendous feedback and energy. It rarely provides any specific stimuli for my own work and eats into my time, but is usually well paid. The seasonal element can mean little work for months, then a long stint of manic travelling and crowd control, leaving the studio sadly abandoned but still generating rent bills.

Collaborative projects

My need is to direct my income earning time towards fulfilling and exploratory sessional work that feeds my sculptural practice with ideas and impetus rather than simply draining my energy. To this end I have joined a collaborative project, based in custodial institutions, and working towards the making of sculpture and devising of physical theatre in direct response to the experiences and feedback from thematic and structured workshops. The joining of physical theatre with my sculptures gives me an outlet for showing my work within performance, reducing the emphasis on gallery exhibiting. I now have the support of a co-worker and can organise my time efficiently around commitments to the project, personal studio time, and research, which complement my own sculptural

see 12 • Strength in numbers

motivations. Ironically my workload has increased, including the administration and fundraising. But, by concentrating on the positive aspects of the contact gained from facilitating arts workshops with specific client groups, I feel as though I have taken control.

It is down to choice making, by being 'fussier' over the use of my time and energies, I commit myself for the time being to a lower wage and considerable responsibility to project coordination. But now when I'm in the studio, I am fired by the collaboration, and personal elements of the workshops, rather than confused, distracted and exhausted by bread and butter work.

Compromise the ultimate challenge

Sally Penn-Smith On graduating in 1988 with a Degree in Glass, all I wanted to do was make a living from what I enjoyed doing most. Any artist's dream. The challenge was not just was I capable or was my work good enough, but what did I need to learn and do to achieve this.

Sally Penn-Smith, **blown and decorated glass**

My style of work involved (and still does) painting intricate patterns onto glass which is blown separately for me. At that time, I only designed and decorated one-off pieces, and to even contemplate making a paperweight would be 'prostituting my art'.

What should my next step be? I knew my vocation, but I did not know how to follow it – all of a sudden I was out of the education system and in the big wide world.

Then I started to explore what self-employment and business involved, on a course at Durham University Business School. I remember thinking 'I will try to learn the basics of running a business even though a scatty artist like me will not understand and besides I do not have to put into practice what they tell me anyway'. It seemed so cold and calculating having to identify my market, categorise my customer and to learn how to hard sell.

However, the more I learnt and understood, the more I adapted. I soon discovered that to get people and funders such as my bank manager to support me, I had to prove that I was not making glass just for the sake of it but that I knew how and where I would sell it, at what price and whether it would cover my costs. This was also very important because of the expense of my materials. Very quickly I was producing items that would sell, even the dreaded paperweights and I discovered that finding the compromise then became the ultimate challenge not sacrifice; to design something that I liked and would sell whilst still maintaining the uniqueness and quality.

A couple of years ago I decided to start approaching high quality shops so I had to adapt my image, the image of my business and the image of my work. This could be seen as compromise, but I saw it as a means to an end. In order to supply them I had to be on the same par as their other suppliers, that is to say professional. In the same way, because my work is unique, high quality and thus relatively expensive, I could not and would not sell it just anywhere – I became fussy too and that standard had to be maintained.

Today, I am far more eager to keep the individuality of my glass. I will not make something I do not want to, and should someone ask, as did a local company wanting some corporate gifts, the challenge then becomes to get *them* to adapt *their* ideas thus giving me a completely free hand to come up with a unique limited edition. By making them compromise, they get a far more exciting result. I know I could not achieve this without my business training and awareness.

I have to produce in batches now, but everything is hand-made and always will be. As I frequently remind my customers, I will always hand-paint each piece myself (from a design in my head rather than copied out each time from a drawing) and moulds will never be used in the blowing stage. This of course limits the quantity I can make and therefore fortunately rules out any mass-production.

In the future I hope to collaborate more with other artists and move back into making one-off pieces. But the burning question is can I still be an artist even though I have compromised so much and deal with things in a business-like manner? I see no reason why not, as long as I am happy.

4 • Training

Tom Smith Interviewing artists, I was amazed by the range of skills they required to survive. Incredibly, very few received any advice on essential survival skills whilst at college – even the basics of pricing work or preparing a CV.

Though many recognised the need to acquire new skills there was some confusion as how to go about this. The most common assumption was that they 'could find out for themselves' and there was a reluctance to consider formal training. This is surprising because properly organised training can be the quickest, safest and most efficient method of learning skills.

Training is available in many forms from individually-tailored programmes to a course at a local college. It should lead you step by step to the necessary level of competence, introduce methods of good practice, guide you in mastering difficult techniques and help you understand procedures including safe methods of carrying out dangerous tasks.

Most training should put you in touch with an instructor who has expertise and whom you can question. It provides a safety net, an advantage over learning from experience or trying to interpret complex information yourself. The training you seek will be specific to the problem you are trying to overcome but the skills learnt could be transferable to other purposes. Joining a course can also be a way to gain access to an informal network of contacts with engineering, building and business studies staff.

If you glance through the list below and think you have a poor grasp of some things, it is worth considering further training more carefully. Many artists and craftspeople spend far longer than is necessary trying to acquire these skills by other means.

Having decided on the need, you will want to identify the type and

see 2 • Looking at level of training. Firstly clarify exactly what you need – writing it down if
yourself necessary. Be prepared to be flexible as your plan might have to be

amended after speaking to an adviser or to fit in with what is available. Ask yourself the following questions:

- can I learn the skill more effectively than acquiring it through experience?
- at what levels do I need to start and finish?
- what are the benefits and disadvantages of the different methods of training available?
- what are the comparative costs?

What training?

Susan Jones   Some areas where you might need more training include:

- business – bookkeeping, budgeting, keeping records, using computers or word processors
- fundraising – making applications
- promotion and publicity skills – pricing, selling, documenting work in slides/photographs, designing publicity material
- communication – for interviews, sponsorship and fundraising, clients, purchasers, etc
- management – dealing with long-term planning, large projects, time management
- organisational skills – co-ordinating a group, working as part of a team, being part of a management group, running meetings, employing staff
- assertiveness, anti-racism, anti-sexism, equal opportunities, disability awareness, etc
- teaching skills – for adults, children, special needs groups
- new work practices – being an artist in residence, working to commission, etc
- career development – identifying goals and establishing plans of action
- learning new techniques or how to use new materials
- learning foreign languages to be able to work or promote your business abroad.

These skills may be acquired through taking short courses, daytime or evening classes over a period of time or through intensive workshops run by providers listed below.

In addition, one-off or occasional intensive workshops are sometimes offered by established arts organisations and these are generally advertised in *Artists Newsletter.*

Training providers

Organisations offering part-time training include:

Educational institutions
Further education departments offer short courses and classes generally throughout the year, with fees dependent on the qualification the course offers. Higher education institutions increasingly offer intensive summer courses which are advertised in the national press – or enquire at your local college. The Open College offers a wide range of technical and vocational courses on daytime television.

The Open University provides arts courses using a mixture of personal study, television programmes and summer schools.

Adult education, university extra-mural departments and other classes
Although these tend to be thought of as leisure classes, they can provide low-cost evening or daytime courses of value to artists.

Training and Enterprise Councils
see 19 • Benefits This network of autonomous organisations has taken over the work of the Training Agency. Amongst other schemes, they deal with training and advice for prospective Enterprise Allowance candidates.

Rural Development Commission
This organisation offers a range of short skill courses for those operating in rural areas.

Co-operative development agencies
In priority areas, local resource centres give advice and training to help the setting up of workers' co-operatives.

Arts administration courses
The Arts Council has helped to fund the establishment of four centres for arts administration training which offer a range of courses, some geared specifically to the needs of visual artists.

- **Arts Management at Northumbria University at Newcastle upon Tyne** – One and two-day courses for artists, makers, photographers and organisations including business, management and administration, fundraising, survival skills and working with local authorities. Details from Arts Management, Faculty of Art & Design, Northumbria University at Newcastle upon Tyne, Squires Building, Newcastle tel 091 232 6002.
- **Leicester Polytechnic Arts Training Programme** – short courses in marketing, fundraising, working with local authorities, management and business skills. In 1991 ran a course for artists working in educational settings. Details, Arts Training Programme, School of Performing Arts, Leicester Polytechnic, Scraptoft, Leicester LE7 9SU tel 0533 431011 ext 247.
- **Centre for Arts Management Liverpool** –courses for practitioners, managers and administrators involved in the arts, crafts, leisure and recreation. Contact Centre for Arts Management, Institute of Public Administration and Management, Roxby Building, Liverpool University, Liverpool L69 3BX tel 051 709 6022 ext 2748 for more information.

Other organisations providing courses for administrators and the voluntary sector, some of which are relevant to artists, are:

- **City University Department of Arts Management** – offers full-time courses in arts administration and management. Details from Department of Arts Policy and Management, City University, Level 12, Frobisher Crescent, Barbican, Silk Street, London EC2Y 8HB tel 071 628 5641.
- **The Management Centre** – offers courses and information on management and fundraising for non-profit organisations. Details from Management Centre, 9-15 Blackett Street, Newcastle upon Tyne NE1 5BS tel 091 222 1632.
- **Yorkshire Business in the Arts** – courses in management skills for arts organisation covering fundraising, financial management, marketing and promotion. Details from Yorkshire Business in the Arts, Dean Clough Industrial Park, Halifax HX3 5AX tel 0422 345361.
- **InterChange Training** – courses on management training, some of which are relevant to artists' groups and artist-run organisations. Includes management structures and constitutions, accounts and financial organisation, fundraising, marketing, printing, layout and design. Details from Training and Advisory Service, InterChange Trust, 15 Wilkin Street, London NW5 3NG tel 071 267 9421.

- **Directory of Social Change** – courses, like its publications, are aimed at the needs of voluntary and arts groups including fundraising, applying to trusts and companies. Details from Ann McLaughlin, Directory of Social Change, Radius Works, Back Lane, London NW3 1HL tel 071 435 8171.
- **National Council for Voluntary Organisations** – works with local agencies on a programme run from September to July of courses for voluntary organisations. Topics include managing meetings, taking initiatives, working in cooperatives and collectives and public relations. Details from Local Development Unit, NCVO Management Short Courses, 26 Bedford Square, London WC1B 3HU tel 071 636 4066 ext 2262.

Taking the initiative

If you find an ideal course for your needs whether in your region or elsewhere and can't finance it yourself, ask your local arts board or Arts Council if there are any grants available.

If a course you need isn't available, you could always look for others who need the same training and set about organising your own. Once you have mapped out the training course and what it involves, draw up a budget for the 'project' and investigate grants, awards and sponsorship.

Funding

see 11 • Project
planning &
fundraising

- **The Arts Council Personnel and Training Section** – offers individual bursaries once a year through the Transitions and Arts Access schemes as well as grants to arts organisations to run short courses or workshops providing they were of national or inter-regional benefit. The Visual Arts Department encourages the training of Black administrators and curators in the exhibitions field and has provided bursaries for administrators to gain experience with public art practice. Opportunities are usually advertised in the art press. Details from the Arts Council at 14 Great Peter Street, London SW1 3NQ tel 071 333 0100.

- **Career Development Loans**, provided by the major banks with the government paying the interest, are to finance courses and to improve skills. Further information from local enterprise and business centres.

- **The Graduate into Employment Programme** is government backed and enables participants to gain new skills through courses and placements. Details from Cranfield School of Management, tel 0234 751122 or local enterprise and business centres.

- **Rural Development Commission** – contact the Head Office at 41 Castle Street, Salisbury, Wilts SR1 3TP tel 0722 336255 or 11 Cowley Street, London SW1P 3NA tel 071 222 9134 for details of your nearest regional office and their training and advisory work.

- **Cooperative Development Agencies** – contact your local enterprise centre for details of your local agency.

- **Charitable Trusts** often provide funds for artists to undertake 'personal development', rather than training. The *Arts Funding Guide* lists those worth researching and the *Directory of Grant-making Trusts* gives the full picture. Also, look for advertisements in the art press.

see 26 • Further reading

5 • Exhibiting

Debbie Duffin with additional material by **Richard Padwick**

Why exhibit? Artist, Phil Nichol, gives four reasons:

- to show your work to the public – to exhibit is surely the reason behind working, without its exhibition the artwork can have no meaning or context

- to see your work – the exhibition provides a rare opportunity for the artist to see a bulk of his/her work, altogether, in good light, in neutral surroundings, and away from the cluttered and personal space of a studio

- to get known as an artist – an important function of an exhibition is for the artist to introduce himself/herself to fellow artists, critics, exhibition organisers and art administrators as well as the public

- to sell your work – sales are obviously important or essential to cover the costs of preparing the exhibition and to bring in some kind of income for your work as an artist.

Few galleries exist for the benefit of the artist. They provide an 'opportunity' or a 'platform' for contemporary artists to exhibit their work in public but it rarely goes much further than that. The principle responsibility of the public gallery is to provide a service for its community, those that live its catchment area and tourists. The private/commercial gallery exists to survive and make a profit. Each venue has its own constraints: the space, the availability of finances and staff, the requirements of the owner, who may be the local authority, an independent trust or an individual. These determine the nature of the exhibitions presented and the relationship between gallery and exhibitors.

Taking control

Many artists, not content with the traditional gallery structure, organise their own exhibition spaces or create their own exhibition opportunities, both as individuals and as groups. Such ventures are full of their own

When Ross and Cromarty Council hired in the Scottish Arts Council's exhibition bus they asked Ian Campbell to run it. After a very successful tour the council wanted to get their own bus, but as they never did, Ian Campbell decided to go it alone. The result was Magnus the Art Bus which Ross and Cromarty hire in. Ian runs the bus on a shoestring, doing exhibitions, workshops and theatre tours. Every two years he tours a new graduates exhibition which sells well. Sue Pirnie, the Highland Regional Council's Arts Officer uses the bus because 'It's the only way of getting artwork to small communities and provides a good environment for discussion and performance'. HRC is thinking of getting its own bus to tour alongside Magnus.

problems, constraints and compromises but the artist is usually more in control of their work and the way it is promoted and presented.

Studio exhibitions

Some artists choose to use their home or studio for an exhibition. Such ventures can be simply a display area within a studio or workshop kept clear from domestic or studio clutter, or 'proper galleries' with signposting, lighting, etc. The advantages of selling from your own space are that you remain in control of the list of customers (commercial galleries are reluctant to hand over the names and addresses of buyers to artists), you are not competing with other artists for exhibition slots or display space, and you lose no sales commission to a gallery. On the down side are the costs and energies required to publicise the space, of keeping it maintained and open, and dealing with the irregular 'disruption' of visitors, who may come out of curiosity and want to talk rather than buy.

Off-Centre Gallery, in artist Peter Ford's house in Bedminster, Bristol. The gallery is used to display his own work but also from here a number of thematic printmaking exhibitions have been organised, some of which have subsequently toured in the UK. The gallery specialises in East and Central European Art. This rose from Peter Ford having direct contact with artists from these countries.

Artists' studio groups occasionally organise open days, weekends or weeks when the public are invited into the artists' working environment – giving an insight into each artists' individual working processes as well as the work itself. The atmosphere of a studio is often more conducive to generating dialogue between members of the public and artist than the anonymity created by an exhibition space. On the other hand group studios avoid the over-personal and perhaps intimidating atmosphere of intruding into the 'private domain' of an individual artist's house or studio. Contacts and promotion of the group within the town rather than sales are the likely outcome.

Other artists' groups provide an exhibition space as part of their communal facilities. Used primarily to show the work of the artists in the group, and to provide a clean display space removed from the clutter and dirt of their studios, they are sometimes hired out to other artists. The cost of the space (rent, rates, etc) is usually shared amongst the artists in the group whilst the costs of mounting, publicising and invigilating the exhibitions are the responsibility of the exhibiting artist. As the rental costs continue to rise faster than inflation and suitable buildings for group studios become less available, a communal exhibition space becomes an increasingly rare luxury.

A few studio groups have taken the exhibition space one-step further creating to all intents and purposes a traditional gallery. The only difference, and perhaps it is a fundamental one, is that the control of policy and programming lies with artists not administrators.

Castlefield Gallery is an example set run by Manchester Artists Studio Association. It is physically separate from the studios and is not seen as a facility in which studio artists can exhibit as of right. It was set up to show contemporary art in a city, which at the time had poor provision and has established local authority and regional art board funding. The program is selected by a committee of artists.

Art weeks

'Art weeks' have recently developed to create a focus on artists and makers by coordinating the open days of both groups and individual

Prizes totalling over £3,000 were awarded to 18 Hertfordshire artists in the 1991 Hertfordshire Open Art Exhibition, a biennial show. Over 500 works were entered by 265 painters, craftspeople, photographers, designers, sculptors and video makers, and were judged in five sections. With only 76 works by 66 artists being selected for the exhibition, judging was tough.
Photo: Sheila Collingwood

studios throughout a particular town or county. Such cooperative efforts can attract grants or material assistance

Richard Layzell, *William's Crumbling Drips,* performance at Waterhouse Room in Reading Town Hall for Reading Art Week. One of the aims of the artweek was to use the international nature of live art to highlight the lack of gallery space in Reading.
Photo: Jim Harold

see 12 • Strength in
numbers from local authorities, the regional arts board and sponsorship from local businesses, and can attract local media attention.

Commercial
or subsidised

Traditional galleries fall roughly into two categories: those which operate commercially, running a business selling artwork, and those galleries which are subsidised in some way – for instance by a local council or arts association for instance – to show a programme of exhibitions.

Some commercial galleries exhibit and sell only contemporary art, whilst others deal in 20th century art as well as promoting and selling work by living artists. Their audience may be relatively small and specialised, although the gallery is usually highly aware of who their market is and the best way to keep them interested. Commercial galleries range from tiny spaces catering for local markets to those promoting a selected number of artists internationally. In the commercial sector, the financial arrangements between gallery and artists will vary, depending on whether the work is likely to sell and the 'risks' the gallery can afford to take. Selection of artists is largely based on whether the gallery thinks it can sell the work or develop a market for it.

Municipal or local authority galleries are subsidised by local or city councils, their main purpose is not to sell work but to provide a public facility, and most therefore, don't put selling high on their list of priorities. The degree of freedom and resources available to exhibition organisers or directors varies, as will the division of the exhibition costs. Increasingly, these galleries run educational activities – workshops, talks, residencies, etc – which not only engage the general public in the visual arts but also provide some income for the exhibitors and for other artists in the area. Most municipal galleries usually take care of the planning, administration and hanging of exhibitions.

The large number of independent, non-profit making galleries range from small local spaces to large galleries with national or international reputations. Most rely on a combination of public funds, private patronage and business sponsorship. Gallery policy differs considerably. It may be decided by a management committee or be the responsibility of the director or exhibition organiser. Don't assume that independent galleries will always take care of organisation and expenses involved, as this is dependent on the policy and budget of each gallery, and the status of the exhibition. The independent galleries are, however, significant. Unconstrained by commercialism they can provide opportunities for less established artists and are often in a position to take risks by showing issue-based, controversial or otherwise uncommercial work.

Artists & issues

Local councils often provide exhibition spaces, although these are often used for meetings, classes, conferences or other events. Policies lean towards the support of work by local artists or on local issues, although exhibitors are likely to have to organise and finance their own exhibition. More councils now organise associated educational activities – workshops and residencies – in conjunction with exhibitions.

Libraries, which have hundreds of visitors a day, are recognised as a valuable source of exhibition space for artists locally and facilities range from purpose-built galleries to hessian-covered screens in amongst the fiction shelves. They are often more suitable for small works or for two-dimensional work hung on screens or artwork which can be fitted into show cases. Here, the exhibition programme may not be exclusively visual arts, the organiser will have other responsibilities, and if the space is used for other events, an exhibition programme may not be a priority.

In library spaces, artists are usually expected to organise and pay for their show, perhaps paying a hire fee to use the room, although sometimes publicity and other help may be provided. Library space is less likely to be booked up far ahead and many applications are dealt with on a 'first come first served' basis. Libraries can provide a useful first opportunity and, in some parts of the country, a substantial visual arts programme is generated by a network of libraries.

Broadening audiences

Arts centre galleries and exhibition spaces are places where exhibitions are only one of a number of activities taking place. The exhibition audience is usually drawn from regular users of the centre, and where the gallery is in the foyer or restaurant the exhibition is unlikely to be the event that attracts them to visit.

Exhibitions are also shown in theatres, hospitals and other public places, often in small spaces, like foyers or bar areas, which are only suitable for small wall-hung work. The organisers here – theatre managers, publicity officers, art therapists for instance – are less likely to have a great knowledge of contemporary art and their choice may well be decided by which artists apply to show there.

At the same time there could be a limitation on the content of work suitable for showing in such 'public' spaces – no nudes, politically sensitive or violent images for example. A large audience may be guaranteed but like some arts centres, only a small proportion of visitors will come because of the exhibition. Organisation and costs are likely to be the artist's responsibility and selling work is usually not a priority.

Schools, colleges and polytechnics have exhibition spaces, ranging from small foyer areas to large purpose-built galleries. An artist's input into organisation and costs will vary and the audience is likely to be limited to those working or visiting the establishment for another reason. However, with the growth of programmes like artists in schools, exhibitions are often linked with fee-paid visits by artists, makers or photographers.

Hiring a gallery

Over the last five years, more and more galleries for hire have become available. These range from rooms within private houses to large warehouse-type spaces. Some take considerable responsibility for selecting work, organising shows and providing services, others simply let the space on commercial terms to the artist who has to organise, finance and invigilate the exhibition. Some take a commission on sales as well as a hire fee. Usually the audience for each exhibition changes with the artist concerned and attracting people through the door is likely to depend on the artist's own contacts and on their promotional skills.

Attitudes & specialisations

These are general characteristics not hard-and-fast rules. A commercial gallery may for instance, be prepared to show work for which the market is small and look for funding to support a particular exhibition. Many subsidised galleries are putting a greater emphasis on selling work and this may therefore, affect the choice of work exhibited.

Some galleries have developed clearly-defined policies or specific aims – to promote the work of a particular group, nationality, race or sex – whilst others specialise in photography or ceramics, or a particular subject matter or style of work.

There are those which concentrate on thematic or mixed shows and others who prefer to promote solo shows. Some are especially interested in the work of young or unknown artists whilst others only wish to show the work of the internationally-known, although in both cases, they may wish to show the best work they can.

Some spaces can only accommodate small two-dimensional work while others welcome installations or large-scale work. A community setting might only show work with subject matter of local relevance, an innovative private gallery may pride itself on a policy of showing 'experimental' work.

Making an informed choice

see 26 • Further reading

Don't waste your time making overtures to a gallery which doesn't generally show work like yours. If you select galleries showing work of a similar nature, subject matter or concerns to yours, your chances of success are much greater. Use the *Directory of Exhibition Spaces* published by AN Publications to locate the galleries that might be suitable to you.

How do you decide on the type of gallery to look for? The best results will occur if you match up the work you make and your aims and needs with those of the galleries you approach. Start by building up a

see 6 • Selling

picture of yourself and your work by answering these questions.

Why do you want to show your work?

If your main aim is to sell, you need a commercial gallery or certainly one which makes positive efforts to sell work on show. If you make 'installation' work the physical nature of the space is of primary importance and you need a gallery which is enthusiastic about your ideas. If you are predominantly interested in what a gallery can do to promote your work, then obviously you need a gallery with an extrovert approach to publicity.

What kind of audience do you wish to attract?

To reach a local audience or serve some social function, choose a local or community-based space. And if the aim of an exhibition is to attract those who can offer you work, for example in education, you may look towards showing in a school, community centre, or polytechnic.

What kind of work do you do?

It is easy to define your work as large or small, abstract or figurative, two or three-dimensional, but how do you define your subject matter or your overriding concerns? Can you identify how your work relates to others, and thus what kind of audience might take an interest in what you are doing? Is your work based in an established tradition or are you working in a relatively new area?

At what stage in your career are you?

If you haven't shown before you may have more chance of success with a small local venue which is committed to showing less established artists whilst if you've already had some shows, you'll need a gallery which will provide you with a more challenging experience.

If you've only been in group shows, try to find a small friendly gallery that will guide you through the experience of a first solo exhibition. But with several small solo exhibitions on your CV, you can afford to be more ambitious and aim for a small group or solo show at a more prestigious gallery. Consider, also, the advantages of getting together with other artists and making a group application to a gallery either for a one-off show or one which is suitable to tour to a number of galleries.

How do you feel about your work at present?

Are you confident or going through a period of doubts and/or changes in your work? Would you feel happy about exhibiting at short notice should the opportunity arise, or do you need time to develop new ideas or images?

Galleries work to very different time scales, some up to eighteen months or two years in advance, others may offer space much sooner, and a few can offer a slot at very short notice. Are you after an exhibition in the near future or one in two years? The answer to this affects where you apply!

In which part of the country do you want to exhibit?

If the kind of gallery you are looking for happens to be just round the corner, then planning and holding an exhibition is easier, providing the gallery wants to show your work. However, most artists, particularly those working outside big cities, must look further afield.

If you are seeking to show at a gallery outside your area, however, you'll need to pay particular attention to the respective financial and organisational responsibilities of artist and gallery and to be sure, for instance, that the gallery will organise or pay for transportation of your work.

Having used the *Directory of Exhibition Spaces* to make an initial choice of where you could apply, don't just rely on what's in print. Find out as much as you can about each of the galleries you've shortlisted.

For instance, ask other artists who've exhibited, telephone each gallery and ask for more details, visit and look at publicity for previous and current exhibitions and find out about future plans. This not only helps you to build up a picture of the gallery, but demonstrates to the gallery that you have a professional approach.

Look carefully at each gallery's application procedure and find out how work for exhibitions is selected. If the book doesn't tell you, ask. Most galleries operate their particular system for very good reasons, and since most of them receive far more applications than they can cope with, it is worthwhile making it as easy as possible for them to consider yours. In 1986 for instance, Ikon Gallery in Birmingham got 200 applications from artists, and Darlington Arts Centre 300.

Your chances of serious consideration are greater if you know what the gallery does, that your work is relevant and if you supply the information they ask for in a well-presented application.

see 16 • Publicity & promotion

Most galleries ask for slides or photographs and a curriculum vitae (CV), and many also require a more extensive written application or proposal. Some prefer postal applications, others ask you to make an appointment with a folio. Some look at applications at any time, others only on particular days; some look at applications at regular intervals, perhaps twice a year.

Selection may be made by the director or exhibition organiser although often there are also selection committees. Some galleries clearly only handle a limited number of artists' work and do not welcome unsolicited applications.

Application checklist

- Avoid just turning up at a gallery with your work, it's very unlikely to be looked at on the spot.
- Make sure you have all the material necessary for making applications because you will need several sets of good quality slides and/or photographs (if you can't take them well enough yourself employ a professional), as well as copies of a typed curriculum vitae and statement about your work.
- Applications should be addressed to the current contact, check for out-of-date names beforehand as part of your initial homework.
- Send all the information asked for. Your application is likely to fall by the wayside if a gallery is expected to chase you for omissions.
- Don't send *more* than is requested. It takes time to look through applications and the gallery doesn't usually need more than eight to ten slides or sheafs of additional information to gain a good idea of what you do.

- Pack slides in flat plastic sheet holders as these are more likely to be looked at than those in boxes. Label the sheet with your name and address and the number of slides sent.

- On an accompanying sheet give details of each work, dimensions, medium, date and title and mark which way up slides and photographs should be viewed on an accompanying sheet.

- Make sure you label everything you send with your name as it's very easy for slides, photographs or loose sheets to become separated from the covering letter in a busy office.

- Even if the gallery doesn't ask for a written application, send an accompanying letter.

- Explain why you are interested in exhibiting with the gallery. Point out anything of particular interest whilst keeping your letter short and to the point, as most people won't read more than one side of an A4 sheet.

- Type your application unless your handwriting is exceptionally good. Include a daytime telephone number or indicate where messages can be left.

- Keep a copy of your application and a list of slides submitted.

- Be patient, don't telephone the gallery after only a couple of weeks, many don't acknowledge applications and it will always take some time to go through a large number of applications and make a selection, especially if you are applying in response to a specific deadline. You might, however, telephone to check it has been received.

Success or failure?

Your application may be turned down for any number of reasons. The gallery may not like your work; it may not fit in with what they are doing; they may already have selected work similar to yours and be trying to provide a balanced programme; it may be that they did like your work but had to select from many such applications or they could just be booked up for the next eighteen months. If you are given a reason, make a note of it as it will be useful with future applications to that gallery or others.

If a gallery says they can't do anything at present but apply again in six months, follow this up, and invite them to your other exhibitions in the meantime.

Seeing the work

If a gallery is interested in your work they will usually want to see actual artworks. This could mean either taking work to the gallery or a studio visit. When preparing a folio to take to the gallery, select around ten to fifteen works which you feel give a comprehensive view of what you are doing. Don't include too many works which are very similar, but on the other hand, you don't want to give the impression that you skip from style to style.

Present work well by mounting drawings or prints or using a display folio with plastic leaves. Ideally, ask someone else to have a look at it to check that the selection is coherent and makes a good impression. It is also worth practising talking through your folio to someone, to check that *your* presentation is coherent. You might want to take along a framed work providing it isn't enormous, as well as press cuttings, reviews and catalogues. Don't forget to take a diary so that you can make a note of future meetings or time-schedules for an exhibition.

A studio visit puts a gallery director on your home ground, so make the most of it. Tidy up sufficiently to make sure that work is seen at its best. Try to give an impression of how your work would look in a show – lay it out with enough space between each piece.

If your studio is difficult to find, give directions or a map, put up signs for the day, or arrange to meet at the gate or front entrance. Prepare for a late arrival and allow plenty of time for the meeting even if it might not be needed.

Although a decision is unlikely to be made on the spot, ask for an idea of how long it will be before you know. Be patient, but follow up if you haven't heard after several weeks.

Making arrangements

Before finalising arrangements with the gallery, make sure you are happy about the balance of responsibilities. Do you feel that the arrangement is a fair exchange, can you fulfil your part of the bargain, and, importantly, can you afford the exhibition?

As a rough guide if a gallery states that all organisation and costs are the responsibility of the artist, you would expect to pay little or no commission on sales, perhaps 10% maximum. If these responsibilities and costs are shared you might expect to pay 15-20% commission, if the gallery will bear most of the responsibility and costs, with you framing and transporting the work, you might expect to pay 30-40% commission on sales. If the gallery takes full responsibility, pays all the costs and will promote your work widely as well, you would expect them to take 50% and occasionally 60% commission.

Beware of the gallery which expects you to bear too many of the costs and takes a high commission, especially if it is for hire. But if the gallery is prepared to shoulder all responsibilities and overheads, commission will be higher accordingly as the gallery will be doing a great deal to promote and sell your work whilst your responsibility will only be to make the work.

Once you are happy with the agreement, put the details in writing, sending one copy to the gallery and keeping one for yourself. The best way of making an arrangement is to use a written contract, either the gallery's or one of your own. The National Artists Association at the time of going to press, was about to publish a model exhibition contract.

It is important that both sides agree and the terms for the exhibition are clear from the outset. Having a contract or letters of agreement will minimise misunderstandings and problems later on.

Contract checklist

see 23 • Contracts **Practicalities**

- What space is allocated to the exhibition? Are there show cases, plinths or other display materials for you to use? What kind and how many lights are there? What hanging system does the gallery use?
- Who selects and installs the work – you, the gallery staff or jointly? The exhibition organiser is responsible for the way the exhibition looks and must be able to justify the exhibition to the public? Ideally selection and presentation should be a joint activity.
- Who transports the work and who pays for it? Who packs the work for transporting? Make a checklist of the work sent. Use a delivery note.
- If your work needs framing, who will provide or pay for the frames? Are there restrictions on fixing to walls or floor? Will you be able to hang the exhibition at the weekend or evenings?
- Who is responsible for insurance cover, both in transit, on exhibition and in store?

Sales

- What commission does the gallery charge, does it include VAT? Establish whether the commission is deducted from or added to your sale price – it should be quoted as a percentage of the asking price. Avoid stating 'prices are negotiable', few potential buyers will do so! Say whether the prices are inclusive or exclusive of frames.
- When will you be paid for sales?

Publicity

- Will there be a poster – how many will be printed/distributed, who will design the poster, do you have to supply a photograph? Will the gallery discuss the poster with you before it is printed? Will they send you a proof of the design for approval? How many copies will they let you have?
- Will there be a catalogue? What format will it be and how many will you get? Can you write a good statement? What is the deadline for information/photographs for inclusion?
- Will you have to deal with press releases or the gallery? There should always be a press release which gives sufficient information for newspapers and periodicals to cover the exhibition briefly. Differently 'angled' releases should go to the local and regional press and to the art press. All will have different deadlines and if you are responsible for press contacts find these out well in advance.
- If the press do visit the show, they may only see picture value in the situation if a 'girl' is draped around a work – be warned! Don't expect national coverage but send the information to all the national critics nevertheless. Contact your regional arts board (RAB) for a good press list.
- Will the gallery have a private view? Will you have to provide the wine or beer? Will there be a separate press view? What commitment will be required of you? How many preview cards will the gallery let you have for your own use? To how many addresses on your mailing list will the gallery send preview cards?

Gallery events

- As many galleries have a programme of lectures, seminars, or workshops with their exhibition programme, check whether you have to give a talk or slide show. Have you got enough good slides, can you talk to the general public, colleges and schools without too much problem?
- Do you want to suggest a complementary workshop to run with the exhibition?

The exterior of the Norwich-based Contact Gallery, which has made an important contribution to the provision of exhibitions in the town.

Costs & fees

Mounting any exhibition is an expensive business for both gallery and artist. Artists holding an exhibition in public galleries could be eligible for Exhibition Payment Right fee. This is intended not to help artists or galleries to cover some of the exhibition costs but to recompense artists for allowing public access to their work. It operates patchily in England and Wales, not at all in Scotland and only in very selected galleries in Northern Ireland. The scheme offers an artist about £250 for a solo and £125 for a two-person exhibition, though the actual amount varies from region to region and gallery to gallery. The participating galleries (and not every gallery does participate) pay the fee directly to the exhibitors – the galleries seeking a percentage of the fee from their appropriate regional arts board. Check with the gallery whether, and how much, you will receive under this scheme and when it will be paid. If the gallery does not operate the scheme, ask why not and persuade them that they should!

6 • Selling

Commercial galleries

Debbie Duffin   Generally commercial galleries are independent from public subsidy and must be self-financing. Most earn an income through sales of work.

A small commercial gallery like Lamont Gallery in London's East End, runs on a shoestring and the gallery's income is precariously tied to such unpredictables as interest rates. Work will be modestly priced, outgoings low and publicity and organisation correspondingly modest.

At the other end of the scale a gallery whose publicity and reputation is worldwide and whose premises must reflect their image, will have high outgoings and may only show and sell work by internationally known artists whose work commands high prices.

The buyers

A commercial gallery must be able to create, develop and sustain a market for the work it sells. Some galleries, like the Lamont Gallery, cater to a local market who want something for their home, which friends will admire and which may have to go with the decor. Many of these buyers spend small amounts and purchases will be occasional.

Many galleries sell to collectors who buy art more regularly. But their interests and finances are variable. Some collect as a hobby, others make it big business with huge investment at stake.

Commercial galleries like Art For Offices in London's Docklands, cater to the corporate sector, ie businesses, hotels and restaurants, who want large numbers of works.

Selecting work

Although commercial galleries receive many slide applications, artists are rarely taken on in this way. Most work closely with a limited number of artists who may stay with them for long periods of time. The gallery may occasionally take on a new artist usually through recommendation. This can seem 'unfair' and it is important to understand the reasons. Every time a gallery makes a decision to select or reject an artist's work, a risk is being taken which can affect its' survival. Even taking work on sale or return is a risk – if the work doesn't sell, time and space is taken up by unprofitable works.

Looking at the work of new artists is a time consuming business. The gallery may look at slides, make studio visits, receive artists at the gallery and go through portfolios. In many cases the work is not suitable and postage, phone calls and travel add to overheads. Most look for new and interesting work, but the time available to devote to this may be limited. Recommendation is more reliable from someone who knows both artist and gallery.

Commission

For the artist who works for years on a low income and feels emotionally attached to the work, the issue of commission is an emotive one. It can seem hard to part with 50% of the asking price. However, as Simon Edmondson (who shows with Nicola Jacobs Gallery) put it: 'I don't know enough people who could afford to buy my work at half the selling price. Without the gallery I couldn't make a living from my work.' With the right gallery the artist has a far better chance of selling.

The commission can vary considerably between galleries and between artists with the same gallery. It is important there is a fair balance between commission and responsibility taken by the gallery, it can range between 30% and 60%. A small gallery may take works from many artists for a one-off exhibition on a sale or return basis, the artist having to frame and transport the work, with no regular relationship and little responsibility for promotion of the artists' work. In this case the commission should be no more than 40%.

Gallery & artist

Galleries are run differently and have different kinds of relationships with artists. Many handle the work of a small number of artists and work closely with them on a regular basis. Others show many artists occasionally, with little contact between shows or keep examples of large numbers of artists' work permanently on show.

Some artists have exclusive arrangements with one gallery over a long period of time, during which a working relationship is developed. This has many benefits and the artist may show with other galleries and sell through them, but all arrangements will be made through the main gallery. Some artists show and sell through more than one gallery and some have no regular agreement with a commercial gallery but sell work through a number of galleries which take work on a sale or return basis.

Yourself

see 2 • Looking at yourself

How can an artist who would like a gallery begin to work towards this aim? Try to put your work into some perspective.

- Is your work based in an established tradition or a relatively new area?
- Can you identify potential audience or clientele?
- Is your work saleable, durable and well presented – if not can you make changes you feel are acceptable?
- Regardless of your age, how resolved is your work? The development of an artist's work is individual.
- Have you shown with other kinds of galleries? This may help in negotiations with a gallery and show you take your work seriously and others do too.
- Is public recognition important or are you content to sell behind the scenes? Not all galleries provide sufficient exposure for an artist.
- How do you feel about possibly having your work categorised and parting with it? Can you work consistently and be prepared for deadlines at short notice?
- How do you feel about someone else making decisions about how, when and where your work is shown?
- How well can you communicate/negotiate – would you be able to talk to a gallery which had lost or damaged a work and firmly insist on payment without losing your temper?

Research

Begin by looking at a wide range of galleries, the artists they show, the work they sell, exhibitions they mount. Make further visits to those of interest and ask yourself if you can see your work fitting into the programme.

Select a few and find out about their attitude to approaches from artists. Ask to be put onto the mailing list, make your interest known by talking to the owner or receptionist – whoever is visible at the gallery.

When you feel you have gained a good knowledge find out if they look at new work, if they are making visits or looking at slides at present or in the near future. It may be easier to begin with smaller galleries, those newly set up or ones like Art for Offices that handle the work of many artists and look at applications regularly.

Applications

see 5 • Exhibiting

Making direct applications is one way to try to attract attention. Check they are looking at new work, make sure your application is in a convenient form and present your work at its best.

Make sure you have good 35mm slides. If you can't take them yourself hire a professional. Enclose a letter saying a little about your work, explaining why you would like to show with the gallery and if you can honestly enthuse about the gallery do so, but briefly.

see 16 • Publicity & promotion Include a typed CV, a list of your slides and examples of press cuttings or catalogues of previous shows. But don't send too much – it won't be looked at. Don't expect an immediate reply and resist temptation to phone before the gallery has had time to look at your work but after a couple of months phone to ask if they have had time to look at your slides.

Other approaches

As so few artists are taken on through application or direct approaches, it is sensible to look at other ways in which you might attract attention.

Most find artists' work through recommendation – how might you make it possible? There are no guarantees but the more people who know your work the more likely you are to be recommended.

There is no knowing who might be the 'contact' who eventually recommends your work. Begin with the people you know – friends, artists, colleagues, ex-tutors, galleries you've shown with. Regularly widen the circle of people who know your work. If someone shows an interest, invite them to your studio or next exhibition. You could make it a regular habit to open your studio, initiate a joint studio show with others.

Every time you make one new contact you open up many potential ones. Part of the art of developing contacts is knowing when to invite or follow up a suggestion and when not to – this can only be learnt by trial and error.

Another way for galleries to find artists is seeing their work at other galleries, so develop an exhibiting career in other spheres. Exhibiting anywhere will widen your audience but it is important to show with artists whose work you respect and galleries you feel good about.

It is particularly useful to take part in mixed shows whenever you can, the audience is far greater and many gallery directors visit them.

Commitments

see 5 • Exhibiting If you do begin to show and sell work through a commercial gallery make sure you are clear about the division of responsibilities – who will deal with transportation, framing, insurance and press photographs. Find out how commission is worked out, how this will affect the pricing of the work. Ask how long sale payments will take and whenever you leave work with a gallery ask for a receipt stating the title and medium of the work, its selling price and make sure it is dated and signed. Galleries differ in whether or not they provide a detailed written contract, but it is always worth asking if a written agreement of some kind can be provided.

Selling from a shop

David Butler Research shops by using the Crafts Council's shops/galleries map, talking to other artists, looking in local listings, etc. You should visit a shop to see if it is right for your work. Shops, unlike many galleries, want to have artists approach them. They are usually keen to see work, though

Collective Gallery is an artist-run gallery in Edinburgh. Their policy and guidelines states they:
• **promote young, emerging, less established artists... by providing a rent free exhibition venue...**
• **improve access to... visual arts by producing an... exhibition programme... organising educational activities... encouraging collaboration... supporting community action**
• **provide a forum for exchange of information and ideas... encouraging local and Scottish-based artists to participate in the growth and activities of the gallery...**
Work for the shop is selected by a committee drawn from the management committee and staff. They meet at least four times a year.

you may need to ring for an appointment. When Julia Linstead and Sally Penn-Smith took their glass to Walmgate Gallery in York they suggested how the glass should be displayed. They thought the gallery might be put out by this but in fact found them very open to ideas. It showed the artists knew what they were about.

Work left at a shop should always have a delivery note or you should get a receipted list from the shop. Some shops may buy work outright. The shop then owns the work but if they are not paying on delivery you should include on any documentation (invoice, delivery note, etc) the words, '(artists name) retains ownership of the work until purchase price is paid in full'.

Most shops will take work on sale or return, or consignment. Legally you are then lending work to the gallery who are operating as your agent. Sale or return needs a lot of follow-up. Don't rely on the gallery to tell you when a sale is made. Keep in touch with them regularly to collect your money and replace sold work. If work is not selling talk to the shop about it. It could be the work, the price, the way work is displayed. Find out and do something about it. Most importantly don't leave work with a shop if it's not selling. The shop will stop promoting it, regular customers will get bored with it and maybe another shop will sell it straight away. Follow through like this means keeping a list of outlets with information on the work they have got, prices, when it was delivered, owner's name, etc.

It is important to remember that a shop has to have a reasonable mark-up on price to cover its overheads and make a profit. This cannot come out of your price it has to go on top otherwise you will end up selling work and losing money. But this means the price of your work could increase by 30% to 100%. You have to be prepared for this. Talk to the shop about pricing, keep looking at your pricing policy and monitor your sales.

Sale or return checklist

Richard Padwick

For use when work is consigned to a gallery, shop or agent on a sale or return basis.

- name/address/tel of Artist
- name/address/tel of Agent
- list of Work consigned to the Agent by the Artist detailing title, medium, size, edition number if relevant, retail price, whether the Work is consigned ready framed and whether the frame is included in the retail price, and whether the prices are inclusive or exclusive of VAT
- whether the Artist and Agent are VAT registered or not
- how, when, for how long and where the Agent will make the Work available for sale (eg can the Agent lend the Work to other agents or display it on other premises)
- what is the Agent's commission on sales
- how and when the Artist will be informed of and paid for sales

see 24 • Copyright & Moral Rights

- the Artists retains Copyright in the Work
- artist asserts Moral Rights in the Work
- limitation on the Agent's use of reproductions of the Work
- the Agent to inform the Artist of the names and addresses of the purchaser for the purposes of arranging access to the Work for photographing and loans for exhibitions
- the Agent to adequately maintain the work and have adequate insurance or agree to indemnify the Work against loss, damage or theft whilst it is in the Agent's care

- the Agent to inform the Artist immediately of any loss or damage and not to effect any repairs without the agreement of the Artist
- signed (on behalf of the Agent)
- signed (Artist)
- date.

Commission & VAT

Richard Padwick Most galleries whether private or public will charge commission for selling work. This is normally worked out as a percentage, but beware what is it a percentage of? Usually the commission is a percentage of the retail (asking) price, but it can also be quoted as a percentage mark up on the price the artist wants for the work. Very different figures result. A 33.3% commission deducted from the retail price is equivalent to a 50% mark up on the price the artist wants for the work. Check which system is being used.

VAT further complicates how the retail price is established and there is much confusion over how VAT should be applied. VAT is only chargeable in the following circumstances:

The gallery is registered for VAT but the artist isn't

- *Gallery acts as a sale or return agent*

The gallery at no point owns the work as in most temporary exhibitions or sale or return arrangements. The gallery should add VAT only on the commission it charges the artist. The purchaser is charged no VAT as the artist who is the person actually selling the work is not VAT registered.

Retail price	£500.00
Gallery commission (40% of £500)	200.00
VAT on commission (17.5% of £200)	35.00
Gallery charges the artist	235.00
Artist receives	265.00

The gallery accounts to the Customs and Excise for £35 VAT charged on its commission.

Note this method is only accepted by Customs and Excise if there is a contract between gallery and artist which makes it clear that the gallery is selling the work as an agent of the artist and that the customer understands this arrangement. If this is not done the gallery must charge VAT on the full retail price of the work as in the example below. This is a clear disadvantage to the customer as it increases the price of the work and is a disincentive to sales.

- *The registered gallery buys a work from an unregistered artist and then resells it*

The gallery charges VAT on the full retail price:

Retail price inc VAT	£587.50
VAT on Retail Price (17.5% of £500)	87.50
Retail price exc VAT	500.00
Gallery Commission (40% of £500)	200.00
Artist receives	£300.00

Both gallery and artist are VAT registered

- *The gallery acts as an agent selling work on behalf of an artist*

The artist (or the gallery on the artist's behalf) charges VAT on the full retail price. The gallery adds VAT on the commission it charges the artist for acting as a selling agent.

Retail price inc VAT	£585.50
VAT on retail price (17.5% of £500)	85.50
Retail price exc VAT charged to customer	500.00
Gallery commission (40% of £500)	200.00
VAT on commission (17.5% of £200)	35.00
Gallery charges the artist	235.00
Artist receives	350.50

The artist receives £585.50 less the gallery's commission and the VAT on the commission, ie £350.50. Out of this the artist has to account to Customs and Excise for the VAT on the retail price, ie £85.50. The gallery accounts to Customs and Excise for the VAT on the commission, ie £35.

- *The gallery buys a work from a registered artist and resells it*

Retail price inc VAT	£585.50
VAT on retail price (17.5% of £500)	85.50
Retail price exc VAT	500.00
Gallery commission (40% of £500)	200.00
Gallery buys from artist)	352.50
VAT on artist's price (17.5% of £300)	52.50
Artist's price	300.00

The gallery accounts to Customs and Excise for the VAT on the full retail price, ie £85.50 (17.5% of £500) but this is offset by the VAT the gallery is charged by the artist, ie £52.50 with the net result being £33. The artist accounts for VAT chargeable on the sale of the work to the gallery, ie £52.50 (17.5% of £300).

Craft fairs

Kathryn Salomon Advantages to exhibiting at a craft fair include selling work directly to the public, so making a greater profit than through a gallery or shop and getting paid straight away. Craftspeople also appreciate the chance to 'network' with fellow makers.

The standard of work is very mixed at most craft fairs. Craftspeople working to a high standard participate in fairs where quality is more variable if sales potential is good. There are simply not enough fairs with exclusively top quality work.

Local craft fairs, touring fairs nationally, trade fairs in Britain, and exhibiting abroad represent different types of market. Varying levels of resources (human, financial and time) are needed to pursue them. Start with small local events where outlay is low and mistakes can be easily forgotten. You can only really judge a fair by seeing it for yourself. A craft fair which is good for work retailing at £20-£30, may be unsuitable for work selling for £200-£300. It must be both right for you and capable of producing worthwhile sales, particularly if the fair is far away.

Find out about advance publicity, visitor numbers and if possible, the previous year's sales. Visitor numbers don't mean everything, it's a buying public that counts. Looking at the last catalogue helps to assess the standards and the competence of the organisers. If it lists exhibitors' addresses you can contact them for their opinion.

Be professional

see 16 • Publicity & promotion A methodical approach to ensure existing customers know you are exhibiting, and making and keeping new contacts is fundamental. Mail your client list and, for an important fair, mail the press. Develop a system for recording potential new customers, perhaps a book at the fair to jot down details of people interested in your work to follow up later.

Pricing levels must be calculated so you don't undercut your trade customers by pricing too low at retail craft fairs.

Postcards, leaflets and/or business cards are useful, some form of printed literature is a must. All aspects from loss of production time in preparing for, attending and following up the fair, promotional material, postage, packaging materials and transport must be considered.

Accommodation, with the average London hotel costing £70 a night, can be more expensive than the stand. Electricity, hiring extra chairs, tables and lights can prove expensive, lighting can be particularly expensive abroad. Other costs include security and insurance of work in transit and during the show.

In short, a professional, systematic approach is necessary to ensure the craftsperson exploits all opportunities to the full. The necessary steps may appear time-consuming and away from the craftperson's real work of producing craftwork, but making the most of all opportunities and attending fewer unproductive fairs means more time spent producing.

Southern bias

There are far more opportunities for selling better quality and higher priced work in London and the south of England than the north.

Craftspeople living outside London create their own selling opportunities by joining craft guilds which organise small local fairs and sometimes hire marquees at larger events and then rent space to members. The Rural Crafts Association also rents marquees and arranges space for craftspeople at shows. There are advantages to showing at large agricultural events, the craftsperson is 'tagging on' to a large, well publicised event 100,000 people can pass through. Craftspeople could create other opportunities. Some of the fairs with the best standard of work are organised by art centres or groups of craftspeople. The Tent, in Edinburgh at the time of the Festival, is an example.

Abroad

It makes little sense to spend great effort in exhibiting abroad if there are still many worthwhile opportunities to be exploited at home. It can take greater energy and hard work to sell to an unknown market. Contacts need to be made in advance. Taxes and customs duty need careful investigation.

It is necessary to work out why you want to export and consider what methods are most cost effective. One maker had 2,000 colour brochures printed to take to a fair abroad and brought the majority back. He mailed them to every gallery in the back of *Crafts* magazine and in the selected gallery index and received many orders. The money spent on publicity literature was more productive than exhibiting abroad.

see 26 • Further reading

How easy and inexpensively products can be transported is crucial. Small pictures or toys will be far less expensive than large pots or furniture. Aesthetic taste varies in different parts of the world, work may sell in one country and not another simply because of national taste. It is essential to understand the market, calculate costs and assess the risks.

Group stands (provided by the Crafts Council or another body) at fairs outside the EC reduces costs and the bureaucracy involved.

Trade fairs

Liam Curtin with introduction by **Kathryn Salomon**

Trade fairs can be regional, specialist or international. They all require a greater financial outlay for stand, equipment and other facilities than a craft fair. It's important to choose the right fair.

Wholesale selling requires a different approach to that for retail customers. Many store buyers expect to order identical items against a sample, as crafts are essentially unique pieces this can be a real problem. Buyers may cancel orders if deadlines are missed.

Exhibiting needs to be planned well in advance. Every aspect of the fair from transport, the stand, printed literature, the product range and the price must be considered. A professional sales technique needs to be cultivated.

The trade show is an up-front situation. The buyers all have big badges which say 'Buyer', the exhibitors have big badges which say 'Exhibitor'. This saves you talking to other exhibitors when you should be chatting up the buyer. If the trade show is a suitable market place for your work it would take months to do the same by visiting shops and galleries with samples.

The stand and situation should give you confidence but problems occur when you actually begin to engage with buyers so here are some examples based on experience!

What they say

- *'What's your minimum order?'* Probably a good idea to have one but it's always possible to negotiate.
- *'What are your delivery dates?'* Be realistic and also leave space for someone who's desperate to have it for, say, Christmas.
- *'How do you get the work to us?'* Say if prices include delivery.
- *'Would you like an exhibition at our gallery?'* Be careful – they might just be after sale or return, but if you're interested ask if there's a fee, if they pay for transport, what publicity they do, etc.
- *'Who else do you sell to in our area?'* You can always offer different shops different lines and patterns.
- *'How much is that piece?'* You don't always have to answer straight away particularly if they are pointing at the most expensive piece. Introduce them to the whole range of prices it's better than having them walk away moaning it's too dear.
- *'What's a good selling line?'* Obviously the one you want to make a lot of and not one you're sick of doing.

The Northern Ireland Craft Development Organisation's (Craftworks) stand at a trade fair.
Photo: Nicky McGarry

- *'Would you give us an exclusive in our area?'* NO, NO! Not unless they are prepared to make huge and regular orders. There may well be a better customer around the corner.

What you say

- *'Where are you from?'* This is better than 'Can I help you', which can just get a 'no'.
- *'Have you seen our work anywhere before?'* Gives you a chance to tell or it may imply they should have!
- *'Do you like the work?'* Very upfront but if they do they will want to talk to you more. It also gives you the chance to sell it to them.
- *'What sort of shop or gallery do you have?'* Gives you a chance to work out whether you're ever likely to want to sell to them.
- *'Do you think this would sell in your shop?'* This searches them out a bit but don't forget selling to them is a mutually rewarding deal, they sell it and get the same money as you do.
- *'Would you like to see a price list/catalogue?'* Only give expensively produced publicity to those that really need it – beware of students!
- *'Do help yourself to all the publicity material.'* You might say this to a buyer who you recognise to be representing a shop you would like to sell your work to.

- *'Would you like to make an order?'* Upfront again! There is a time to hurry things along as there are buyers walking past your stand right now who may be too tired to come back!
- *'Have you got a card?'* Anyone who is at all interested won't mind giving you their card which you can staple into your notebook or writing their name and details directly into your notebook – this gives you a mailing list at least!

The trade show is a very equal situation, they have to buy something, you have to sell something, neither is degraded and so mutual respect abounds. Just be yourself and make sure the work can sell itself.

Art fairs

Tony Warner

see 12 • Strength in numbers

In late 1989 sculptor Steve Vince heard there were still some spaces left at the ART 90 art fair at the Business Design Centre in Islington. He asked me to bring in a few artists who were less directly commercial than those he was already in touch with and days of chaos ensued. Each put in a share of the expenses and supplied photographs and copy for a small booklet to be distributed at the fair. The stand cost £1,200, plus another £40 for each lamp illuminating the nine square metres. Transport was extra, with labour and accommodation thrown in for free by the artists. Most of the artists had other commitments, and were not able to help with the hanging. Two of the group had the dubious pleasure of having to hang all of it themselves. This was mitigated by having a trial run in one of the artists' studios, where a similar space was mocked up with the artists present.

Steve took a video player and monitor to play the videos many of the artists had of their work. In the end this was a dead loss. The videos could not be seen, their commentaries operated just as background noise and the flickering screen acted as a distraction.

As for the event itself, the results were mixed. Some did very well and anybody who sold anything more than got their money back. Prices ranged from £200 to £1,450. To put that in perspective, the RAAB Gallery sold a Rainer Fetting picture for $47,000! The artists from the 'less commercial' area were pleased when, despite lack of sales, their paintings turned up as a major part of the advertising for the following year's fair. At least two people managed to make connections with London galleries.

All through we kept a visitor's book, which I later copied for artists to use as a private view list for future exhibitions. Several of these people came back to our stand the following year. On the debit side, the stand itself was a mess. Artists got down to London to help out when they could, which meant there might be one person on the stand at one time and eight at another! Being marooned on the stand meant that lunch was taken in public and the remnants took some time to be cleared away. When customers came back for a second or third visit they were not recognised by the new person on the stand and sales were lost. Finally, because everybody had paid towards the costs they insisted, quite rightly, that their work was hung. Every square inch of wall space, and some above stand level, was crammed with work.

In the end, though, everyone agreed it had been worth the effort and that somehow it should be done the following year.

Selling from the studio

David Butler and Oliver Bevan

If you sell from the studio on a regular basis you may want to specify times for people to visit. This will depend on your working pattern and studio location. You might sell mainly to tourists and open only in the summer. There may be a lot of early evening visitors to the location of your studio so you only open then. Regular hours are important both for prospective customers and your own working routine. It also means having permanent display space in or separate to the studio. But selling from the studio doesn't have to mean setting up a 'shop'. Many artists open their studios only once or twice a year, mailing to regular and now buyers.

Be careful with pricing. Buyers often expect to pay less on a studio sale. This can be an advantage – you have keen buyers. But don't be tempted to undercut a realistic price. It is better to try negotiating on payment in instalments (write it into your bill of sale and/or get pre-dated cheques). Most importantly, if you sell a lot through shops, you should charge the normal shop price, otherwise you'll be undercutting the shop and they may refuse to take work in the future. Charging the shop price on a studio sale of course means a bigger profit as there is no discount/commission to come off the price. Another advantage is that usually the buyer will take the work with them, so no delivery costs.

Setting up

Clean the place up, but not beyond recognition; non-artists find studio equipment and evidence of the work in process not only fascinating, but also illuminating. It reassures the visitor of the source of the work and may well provide a subject for conversation in the first few minutes, leading naturally into a consideration of the work you intend to show. If you have catalogues, a folder with CV, etc leave it prominently on a worktop. Decide well in advance what you are going to show.

If you are showing large paintings, stack them in the order you wish them to be seen. I prefer to do this with the backs facing out so each canvas can be turned round and presented for full, undistracted attention, like turning the leaves of a huge book. With small work, a temporary exhibition can be created, it is a good idea to have a few works well displayed at the outset so the visitor does not arrive to a blank space. These can be moved when the main stacks are shown. It is essential to have a system for restacking what has already been seen. A 'shortlist' stack of work to be seen again saves a good deal of confusion. Getting the work out, especially large canvases in a small space, is a kind of performance and all the moves must be plotted. This avoids wasting time and, from the artist's view, visitors seldom allocate enough time to do justice to the occasion.

You will be expected to say something about your work. Very few people are prepared to trust their eyes alone, so what you say is extremely important. The first stage is to ask yourself what someone unfamiliar with your work would like to know. This is not the same as what you would like to tell them. A few clues to link your work with other aspects of your life and interests are worth any amount of technical jargon in persuading a stranger to look more searchingly.

7 • Earning from reproductions

Simon Stern   Illustration in Britain is thriving. We have the most developed industry in the world which is divided into fairly distinct areas, each with its own fee levels and culture.

Greetings cards & wrapping papers
Swamped by semi-amateurs, this is poorly paid though a few earn a lot at the popular end of the market. At the posh end (eg 'Artists Cards') exposure may compensate for lack of money. Designs are seldom commissioned; clients expect a selection from which to choose. Many expect to buy complete copyright, which is not recommended. Sell a licence for a limited period, eg two years (designs seldom last longer than one season).

Prints for the framing industry
A large, chaotic and varied market. It pays to put in research. Go to your local poster shop and look at the catalogues. Payments are very variable, sometimes royalties, sometimes lump sums. Again, limit the rights you sell, never sell complete copyright unless offered an enormous sum.

Children's books
Ranges from picture books through children's novels to educational publishing. For a picture book you will need a story and two or three specimen double page spreads to present to a publisher, who may then offer a contract. Don't expect to get rich. Payment is by royalties, with an 'advance' averaging about £3,000, and this may be all the money you see. Only best-sellers make real money, and they are extremely rare. It is quite likely you will not find a publisher, since it is not easy to create a good picture book. If you *have* produced one, look for a conventional publisher, rather than a book packager (see 'Pitfalls' below).

Educational publishing can be regular work but illustrations must be made to a tight brief. Competence, reliability and stamina are required. Payment is generally a lump sum, and not generous for the work involved. Some publishers ask for complete copyright. Resist.

If you can draw children in black and white fairly fast, children's novels may be the best option. They don't take up months of time and they offer creative satisfaction. Publishers generally require one or two pictures per chapter and pay about £750.

Magazines
The professional illustrator's bread and butter. They have tight deadlines and require the ability to make an appropriate image for the text. In this enormous market fees are in the region of £150 for a spot illustration, £250 for a quarter to half page, £450 for covers.

Book, CD & cassette covers
The type of work used is quite adventurous in the up-market book trade, as a glance at paperback racks shows. Fees are £500 to £800 and deadlines usually reasonable.

Design
Commissioned by companies specialising in brochures, company reports, product labels and other forms of non-media advertising. Fees vary; typical are £250 for a spot brochure picture, £650 for a brochure cover, £800 for a product label. Deadlines are tight, but the illustrator can often produce his/her own image and a surprising amount of work is adventurous. Agents handle much of it. Define what use the image is to be put to, and sell only those rights. Resist attempts by some design groups to obtain complete copyright for 'administrative convenience'.

Advertising
This is where the serious money is. Tight deadlines and briefs are the norm (work is often from an art director's rough already approved by the client). Typical fee for a black and white image for a newspaper advertising campaign is about £1,500. This market, mostly handed by agents, requires a high level of professionalism.

Portfolios & promotion

see 16 • Publicity & promotion

Illustrators usually typecast themselves by evolving an individual style. You need a portfolio with a few pieces of illustration (not fine art) consistent in style and in the area of work you are seeking. To get work in cards and wraps, prints, books and book covers call round with your portfolio, if you are in London. Have something to leave with the commissioner; photocopies will do, though for colour work printed cards are better.

For magazines, design work and advertising you need to spend about £800 on promotion in one of the paid-space annuals. This takes courage but pays off, and is the only realistic course for artists who live outside London.

Some pitfalls

Agents
Most are reputable, a few are not. Look out for agents who want you to assign them copyright, or whose contracts do not allow you to withdraw work from them on reasonable notice. Contact artists already on the agent's books. If in doubt, get advice.

Book packagers
(Companies who produce books up to the manufactured stage, but do not sell or distribute). Again, a few are dubious. Always have a contract before starting work and get advice on book contracts (below).

The copyright rip-off
see 24 • Copyright It is very disadvantageous to assign copyright to a commissioner. A number of companies try to get you to do it. Don't.

Fees & royalties

The question most often asked about a proposed fee is 'Is it fair?'. More useful questions are: Is it acceptable in terms of time spent, publicity gained, or some other consideration? Is it the 'going rate'? Does it reflect the value of the creator's work to the buyer?

Fees vary enormously according to the use to which the work is to be put and the market strength of the creator. An image for a greetings card may fetch £100 to £150; the same image used in advertising, £1,000 to £1,500. Rates differ because the greetings card industry is over-supplied with willing artists and sells in a competitive environment; whereas advertising is supplied by a smaller number of specialists, usually represented by agents, and operates in an environment where the cost of creating the image are as nothing compared to the costs of buying advertising space.

Types of fee

Flat fees

Flat fees are suitable where the licence is limited, eg an edition of calendars for a company to send to clients at Christmas. To the artist, the advantages are certainty about the amount and reasonably quick payment. Even if the proposed use is open-ended, a flat fee may be suitable, eg if there are a lot of contributors payment of royalties to all, each requiring negotiation of a long and complicated contract, may be a practical impossibility.

A flat fee may be for initial use, eg fabric, with possible further uses if the design is a success, eg wallpaper. Where the initial fee is for one season, with a possible extension, a repeat flat fee may be negotiated. This can be: a percentage of the original fee (a wasting asset because of inflation, so unsuitable for long-term agreements); 'to be agreed' when the occasion arises (flexible but uncertain); or, if the original producer is selling on rights to a third party, a percentage of the sum received (eg in the case of a book cover for the UK edition, where a USA publisher buys the right to use it on the USA edition). This is halfway to a royalty, the most complicated form of payment.

Royalties

Royalties give the creator a continuing stake in a product's success. Payments, usually expressed as a percentage of the retail (published) price or wholesale price (actual amounts received), address the inflation problem. Royalties expressed as 'x pence per copy' are only suitable for short term agreements. If the original producer/publisher has the right to sell on rights to others, the creator gets a substantial proportion of 'rights' sales.

A proportion of royalties are usually paid in advance as a lump sum which should be about half the royalty value of the first printing/ manufacture. Advances are customarily not returnable, even if sales never cover them, and may be the artist's only payment. Thus the artist is assuming some of the risk (advances are usually less than flat fees) as well as standing to gain from successes. Royalties, therefore, are not suitable where there is no potential to sell a lot of copies, eg in the case of a (genuine) limited edition, or a seasonal design.

see 23 • Contracts When entering royalty agreements always seek expert advice, or read up on the subject. They often involve long-term relationships, and are complicated documents. Be aware of snags:

- payment should be based on retail price, or 'actual amounts received', never on amounts received less cost of manufacture

- the publisher/producer should undertake to publish/produce within a defined period
- rights should revert to the creator if the product goes out of print/out of production
- the creator's accountant should have the right to inspect the accounts of the publisher/producer
- there should be set times for payment
- the creator's copyright should be declared on the image/product
- the artist should have confidence in the probity of the publisher/manufacturer.

Royalty is usually between 5% and 20%; 10% is standard for books, but they are always negotiable. In sales of rights the creator should get at least 50%.

Check list

For use when the copyright owner (normally the artist) permits a gallery, agent or publishing company to reproduce a piece of work:

- name/address/telephone number of gallery/agent/publisher and of the artist
- details of the work(s) to be reproduced (title, media, size, date)

Use

- form of reproduction (eg poster, postcard, calendar, book)
- method of reproduction (eg four colour process lithography, duotone)
- size of reproduction
- number of copies of the reproduction (ie print run)
- other details of the product in or on which the work is to be reproduced
- is the product to be sold (if so how and at what price) or given as a gift (eg business Christmas cards)?
- is there an option for the publisher to increase the print run or to reprint and under what terms?
- is the publisher required to return the work, transparencies, plate, negatives, etc after the agreed number of copies are printed or licence ended?

Area

- where is the reproduction being marketed; UK, Europe, USA, World, etc − it may be appropriate to define the area in the licence

Duration

- the licence must state how long the publisher has the right to reproduce the work without having to come back to the artist to renew or renegotiate the contract

Exclusivity

- is the licence exclusive or non-exclusive? An exclusive licence gives the client the sole right to make use of the image within the other terms in the licence

Attribution

see 24 • Copyright & moral rights

- the artist should assert moral right of authorship; the licence should state the agreed form of accreditation to appear on every copy
- the licence should state every copy will bear the copyright symbol © together with the artist's name and date of first publication

Integrity of reproduction

- will the work be reproduced in full without cropping, superimposition of text, image, symbol or other mark, or does the agreement permit this (in which case full details should be given)?
- the artist should have the right to view proofs and refuse permission to publish if the quality of reproduction is unacceptable

Fees

- Is the artist paid royalties on sales (ie an agreed percentage of the wholesale or retail price)? If so what is the percentage?
- or is the artist paid an agreed lump sum?
- or is the fee a combination of royalties and flat fee?
- how and when are payments to be made?
- has the artist the right to a regular detailed royalty statement?
- signed (on behalf of the publisher)
- signed (artist)
- date.

8 • Working with people

Barbara Taylor Sculptor John Maine has been working in Lewisham since December 1988. Employed as a member of the Lewisham 2000 team on the planning, design and management of the new town centre, he has been called upon to comment on other developments in the Borough and on one occasion to work with local residents on shaping their park. When

John Maine,
Bridge & Banks,
part of a
community
project to develop
a local park in
Deptford, London,
1991

Fairview New Homes PLC were building housing in Deptford, part of the local park was taken in and replaced by another section of land. Residents were asked what they wanted in the park and when they called for a wild area Maine was asked to work with residents, acting as interpreter and enabler. There had to be water for a wild garden and Maine was able to suggest that a path could lead over the pond. He worked on site, edging the pond with stone and building a bridge and the site was left for residents to develop, for example local schools have come in to plant and help to keep the area clean. A spin off to working on site was the chance to talk with residents on an informal basis, more naturally than 'public consultation'. Ideas about the town centre scheme have been aired.

There is not a gallery in the Borough, other than that at Goldsmiths College, so artists utilise billboards, shops, parks, restaurants, community centres and the street.

The Waterfront Festival in Sunderland, the town's first community arts festival had an unusually strong visual arts element for such an event with a programme organised by artist-run Arts Resource. The organisation used its embryonic artists register to commission new work, exhibitions and demonstrations. The festival site was signposted with commissioned seafront banners. There were also pavement and graffiti artists and groups of artists making large scale sand sculptures on the beach. Even more unusual, the festival included a 12 hour long performance event by David Butler, Gilly Rogers and Helen Smith.

Artists connected with the Bromley by Bow Community Centre are holding a three month festival of art, crafts and entertainment at Tobacco Dock Shopping Village in Wapping entitled 'Where Art Meets Community' during summer 1992. At the end of the festival exhibitors will move to the Bow Centre to take part in the East End Open Studios and Arts in Education Festival. Although the Centre involves a wide variety of local community activities the artists can make contact with an even wider range at Tobacco Dock.

The Avenues Project in Gateshead is an ambitious community or public art project, depending on the viewpoint. Keith Alexander led the project as artist in residence with Gateshead Libraries and Arts and involved over 500 people including children and special needs groups in furnishing a house bought by Northern Rock Housing Trust. At least 40 objects were made including wrought iron chairs, mirrors, ceiling roses and a carved and stained fascia. Seventeen other artists from the area were involved in making different works.

Gainsborough's House in Sudbury has, as other galleries, been criticised for not doing enough for local people. The Gainsborough portraits inspired June Freeman to work on an exhibition, a portrait of the town and its people. Photographer Janine Wiedel and Freeman worked together on text and images which form the exhibition and a book. The exhibition uses people's own photographs and Wiedel's portraits. There is a tension between snapshots, studio portraits, Wiedel's work and the text. A photograph of operators in the textile factory wearing earmuffs has the caption 'They used to measure deafness in yards. They'd ring a bell and you walked away until you couldn't hear it any more'. During the exhibition the local arts centre ran the Photography Roadshow when people were invited to bring in photographs and join in a discussion

Stranded, a collaboration between choreographer/ dancer Rosemary Lee and maker Caroline Broadhead, was commissioned by the South Bank Centre in 1991, as part of the Ballroom Blitz programme. The commission, a nine day residency was performed by nine professional dancers and nine children.

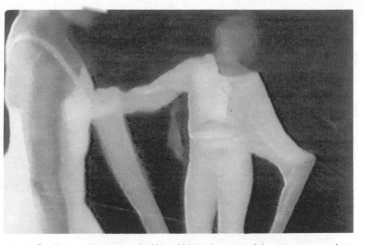

about Sudbury with a panel of local historians, and there was a project with schools.

Caroline Broadhead divides her time between making jewellery in partnership with Nuala Jamison under the label C&N and in making clothing or body pieces. She worked with choreographer Rosemary Lee on the Ballroom Blitz, a week long festival of dance at the South Bank. The open gallery space at the Festival Hall is used and many different groups and people participate in workshops and performances. Broadhead worked with Lee several months before on the ideas for the dance, then worked at the South Bank for nine days devising and making costumes for nine dancers and nine children. Open rehearsals involved improvising with dancers using her dresses and culminated in a performance. Broadhead found the experience exciting but time was short – especially as costumes could not be cut until the dancers were fixed. The performance won a London Dance and Performance Award.

Woodcarver Jeremy Turner spent 13 weeks working at Restore, a rehabilitation workshop in Oxford for people who have suffered psychiatric illness. The residency had a very definite purpose to feed into the workshop production of toys and other wooden items for sale through a catalogue. Turner was employed for his woodcarving skills but more to encourage ways of thinking and doing. An interesting aspect was that Turner had to work very slowly to gain the members' confidence and it was a visit to an exhibition of East African sculpture at MOMA that brought out the energy and commitment of the group. More people started to attend his sessions and worked on large drawings to loosen up. They then attacked large lumps of wood with great energy and little experience of the tools. The scheme opened up people's ideas to the

The Sea Chest with musicians Dawn Wrend **and** Steve Riley. *Photo: David Cross*

effect an outsider could have on the workshop but it needed longer to develop the potential of the ideas.

The Sea Chest, a joint Eastern Arts and Shape East initiative, is another illustration of how artists have worked with disabled groups. The Chest brings together different elements designed to give pleasure and stimulate activity and reminiscence among people who suffer from a visual impairment. The Chest is carved wood, the lid incorporating a jigsaw. Inside there are puppets, toys, sound machines, musical instruments. Special music was commissioned from Jane Wells, Composer in Residence at The Wells Centre in Norfolk. 'The chest proved a catalyst producing interest, energy and joy amongst staff, patients and relatives' (Ian Southgate, Aylsham Hospital) but it was also made in part by organisations which bring together artists and disabled people. The chest was carved and made by Rowanwood Workshops, a cooperative business making sculptured panelling, furniture and jigsaws which employs people with differing degrees in learning difficulties. Street Forge Workshops who made toys employs four disabled workers, and is part of a larger project employing 25 disabled workshops covering pottery, computer skills, market gardening and jewellery-making among other skills.

The under-representation of the work of South Asian artists and the lack of any visual arts provision for the large Asian community in the West Midlands led artists to meet with the West Midland Exhibition Curators/Promoters Forum and develop the idea for South Asian Visual Arts '93. During June, July and August 1993 there will not only be a series of exhibitions to showcase the range of contemporary visual arts practice but also public art commissions, educational projects, artist placements, debates and workshops. There is a possibility of publishing a catalogue documenting the art of South Asians living in Britain. In order to ensure the programme reaches the South Asian community the Festival Researcher has to identify community venues and groups. The programme has not been prescribed, rather effort is being made to gain a wide range of submissions and ideas from South Asian artists and groups to ensure work and marginalised communities are involved.

Among many artist projects in hospitals Andrew Sheridan spent two months at St Margaret's Hospital in Durham, using an empty ward as a studio. His aim was to encourage elderly patients to paint and draw whilst keeping his own visual record of his time there.

Brenda Whormsley, artist in residence at Clatterbridge Hospital on the Wirral, took a different approach and organised 'Dawn to Dusk' where artists were invited to visit the hospital to produce images of life in the wards, kitchens and corridors. As a result ten artists came and produced a body of work. An exhibition was toured to libraries and hospitals in the area. Whormsley's project is long term and she has had time to settle into the life of the hospital and have some effects on it. After 18 months she had completed murals for two departments and planned

Nancy Willis, **artist in residence at Hammersmith Hospital.**
Photo: Gina Glover

others. She has brought in students, runs activities for patients and staff and produces a newsletter to keep everyone informed.

A logical extension of this type of work is to see more opportunities for artists who are disabled. The residency at Hammersmith Hospital was specially designed for an artist who is disabled and who has practical experience of the hospital environment. This was not only to provide the opportunity for an artist but to demonstrate disability need not be a deterrent to being a professional artist. Nancy Willis was the first and spent a year making work for permanent display.

Whilst projects in hospitals are relatively common it is rare to see them in special hospitals that care for those who are not only mentally ill but an extreme danger to society or themselves. One obvious reason is security but the idea has become more established in the USA. The first in Britain was at Park Lane Special School in Liverpool, initiated by Ruth Richardson at the hospital, the Tate Gallery Liverpool and Rosemary Christmas of Merseyside Exhibitions. Woodcarver Christine Kowal Post and painter Frank Linnet worked in the hospital for eight months.

There are good recreational facilities at the hospital but a tight security and routine. It is the routine which makes personal expression difficult. The artists had to come to terms with practical limitations such as the need to hold all workshops indoors even in sweltering heat and to begin with no tools could be used which might be dangerous such as knives or string. By the end of the project the group who took part had made progress, developed a cooperative feeling and trust, had built self-esteem and confidence. For their part the artists felt their attitudes had been changed. Kowal Post remarked she felt vulnerable on occasions, particularly as a female but felt it was a privilege to work with people who showed such commitment in difficult circumstances.

Artists work in the community in a slightly different way when working together to raise money or make social and political points. Artists in the Lewisham Visual Arts Festival held an open exhibition outside the local hospital with 15% of income from sales going to the Hospital's Life Line Appeal. Artists for Nuclear Disarmament organise activities in support of their cause. In 1992 their second exhibition is to be held at Swiss Cottage Library with work by over 100 artists of national and international repute including Elizabeth Blackadder, Felix Topolski and official war artists. All work is donated and proceeds of sales go towards CND's current campaigns.

9 • Residencies

Daniel Dahl By providing opportunities for direct contact with artists and active participation in the creation of art, residencies and placements improve the public's understanding of art. For artists, they provide an opportunity for direct contact with their audience.

Artist-centred residencies

- *Transferred-studio:* one of the most common types where an artist transfers his/her studio to a new site, eg gallery, library, arts centre, factory, community venue, hospital, school, etc. The artist's work proceeds more or less as before and the artist may only be required to give a few lectures (eg in a university), or considerable contact with a public may be involvod.

see
10 • Commissions
- *Commission:* here the intention is the production of artwork for a specific site rather than interchange with the public, but it may involve public participation and some artists believe the public must be involved if such a commission is to win acceptance.

People-centred residencies

see 14 • Skill sharing
- *Community:* where artists as 'animateurs' assist in the creation of work which is the community's rather than the artist's. Such a residency might be based in a housing estate or school.

Other site-related residencies place less emphasis on working with the people connected with the site.

- *Consultation:* here an artist, attached to a large, often governmental institution, makes a creative contribution by perceiving new possibilities and making connections across conventional demarcations. Other residencies and placements, influenced by this, define the artist's work as suggesting courses of action rather than making art objects.

Lucy Glegg **(right), artist in residence at Bletchley Community Hospital, May 1991**

• *Interchange:* balances the interests of artist and public and could include elements from other types, such as a commission. Learning is the main emphasis. People build up a relationship with the artist and his/her work, through the way the project relates to their lives, their work place, or their activity. An artist may make a sculpture in response to a work place or community situation. Or people may make their own artwork alongside that of the artist.

The key to success lies in identifying the residency or placement appropriate for you. Making the right decisions means thinking about the sort of artist you are, and what you want out of a residency.

If the residency has specific requirements, show that your art practice is relevant. If you've had little to do with the public, it will be hard to be a convincing candidate for a residency in a school or hospital.

Look critically at yourself and your practice. Would this residency make a mutually beneficial match? The prospect of working as an artist might seem overriding, but is it a good idea to let yourself in for a period of what might become hell? If you feel it's your duty to take an uncompromising stand over artistic standards rather than create accessible work, do not apply for interchange residencies. The more interchange is involved, the more the situation will demand a response from your work. You will achieve far more where there is a creative balance between your interests and those of the project's audience and participants.

see 2 • Looking at yourself

If you are interested in the commission type, look for advertisements, but make sure it is really your kind of work they have in mind. Ask for further details if the brief isn't clear.

see 10 • Commissions

If it's the money you need, apply for everything. But don't be downhearted if you don't get anywhere, particularly if you haven't got a track record. Residencies of the transferred studio type generally go to well-established artists. Check out the organisation's policy on appointing less-established, new or unknown artists.

'National' residencies are advertised in the art press, eg *Artists Newsletter* and *The Guardian's* Creative and Media section. Others may be advertised regionally if organisers want applications only from their area. Contact regional arts boards who not only organise residencies and placements, but may also fund schemes run by others.

see 25 • Contacts

The interview

Questions to expect

Don't assume all interviewers are acquainted with art. Give clear, simple explanations of your work; your ideas for the residency and what you hope to achieve; how you will fit in, both as an individual and as an artist; about possible strategies, how you plan to operate, how you will introduce yourself, etc

Questions to ask:

- although it might be difficult, you must find out what the organisers expect the residency to achieve, especially if the brief is unclear
- how will the fee be paid? What does it cover, eg removal expenses, materials, rent?
- is the studio secure and are contents insured? What about access and the possibilities of displaying work?
- are there specific expectations, ie do they want you to produce a mural or other piece of work?
- must the residency be undertaken in one continuous block or can you take a holiday or go back to your own studio to 'take stock'?
- what happens if things go disastrously wrong? What sort of back-up is there? Even one person to discuss problems with is better than being expected to cope single-handed
- check that the ownership and rights of any work produced rests with you, unless there is a clearly stated commission element, or the host is being offered 'first refusal'.

Organising your own

Some artists organise their own residencies as a natural extension of their practice. Others want to create a means of 'employment', a way for artists to work as artists. There are, therefore, alternative approaches:

- look at the artist and work, then find the residency or placement to suit, or
- look at the residency or placement, then find the artist to suit.

Finding sites

Although it is possible to start 'cold', by approaching a site, it's better if some groundwork is done first. Once a relationship has been established, developing it into a residency becomes easier. Artists can get together to canvass for residencies by contacting selected sites and persuading them to host a project. A simple, well-produced leaflet is be a good idea.

see 12 • Strength in numbers (Groups need not be studio-based. Many are formed specifically to create work for artists).

Ideas for sites:

- hospitals, health centres, homes, institutions
- galleries, museums, libraries
- prisons, probation hostels, community service units
- schools, colleges, nurseries, universities
- commerce & business: offices, institutions, shopping centres
- industry, not just factories but service industries, farming, etc
- government: local & national departments, police, armed forces
- trades unions
- communities: housing estates, community projects
- outdoor situations, eg lakes, forests, etc.

Negotiating
Although easiest if a relationship already exists, a 'cold' approach can be successful if properly handled. Be prepared for:

- unfamiliarity with art, especially contemporary art practice: it's no good being contemptuous of people who think painting is all portraiture
- the assumption that the artist will profit financially from the residency or placement
- the assumption that it's a sort of 'commission' situation: explain that it's the artist who's being financed, not the work
- the need for adequate facilities. People often have the vaguest ideas about how artists work, in terms of work space, display space and types of access. Although the artist needs access to the public, s/he also requires privacy. (Define 'access' and 'interaction' or people may think you are going to 'perform', or give demonstrations)
- expectations about the artist's 'allegiances', eg that they represent management, rather than workers
- dealing with unacceptable or inappropriate responsibilities.

Don't sweep problems under the carpet for the sake of short-term gain.
see 2 • Looking at yourself For instance, the host should understand that an artist's work will not always be celebratory: it can be critical and penetrating. Show them the sort of work you do, and the sort of artist you are. Be ready to explain what residencies and placements are, how they can function: documentation from others is useful. Explain that residencies can take many forms. Find

out about restrictions that might affect freedom of movement. The Official Secrets Act, for instance, governs all work carried out in a factory dealing with armaments.

A clear agreement

see 23 • Contracts

You must end up with a clear agreement in writing: put down as much as possible when exchanging letters. You need to ensure the site really has agreed to host the residency and they agree on its aims and nature. See 'Contracts & conditions' at the end of is chapter.

The next problem is funding. Remember to explain that obtaining this can be a lengthy process, possibly as long as a year!

Funding residencies

see 11 • Project planning & fundraising

Whether drawn up by organiser, host or artist, a realistic budget is needed, incorporating all costs, including 'in kind' contributions. As many arts boards now offer only 50% of project costs, showing the monetary value of in-kind contributions ensures arts funders can contribute the maximum possible. The placement budget should not be confused with a separate one for a related commissioned work or with costs of a related but off-site exhibition.

Placement costs checklist:

- organiser's fees and expenses for preparatory work, management and follow up
- recruitment costs – advertising, interview expenses
- artist's fees for preparatory work (including percentage of the total fee payable if the project does not proceed beyond the feasibility stage) and for working on site
- materials and services
- artist's accommodation costs, expenses, travel
- fees for trainees or apprentices
- fees/expenses for the project's support group
- promotion and publicity internally and externally to the press, media and interested parties
- transport of artist's work, equipment or materials on to the site
- display or exhibition costs
- insurance charges specific to the project
- photographic documentation of the placement (you may need a professional photographer)

- written documentation and photocopying of report to funders, press and media, other interested parties
- costs involved in proposals to extend the residency
- 10% contingency to cover unforeseen costs.

Fund-raising campaign

Get the site to cooperate in a fundraising campaign, especially if it can be viewed as a 'worthy cause', eg a hospital placement. A leaflet can be useful, and the host may pay for the printing or produce it 'in house'.

Since it is unlikely you will attract the full amount from one source, you will have to find joint funding. Here, problems can begin afresh. Other parties may wish to have their say in the project. Every funding body has its own policies and parameters, and conflicts of interest need to be resolved in the planning stages.

You may prefer to create a steering committee of representatives from each party. This can be essential for resolving differing expectations and identifying common ground. This committee could remain throughout the residency and provide important support.

As a rule, allow ten months to organise and raise funds for a six-month placement. Of the overall budget, you might look to raise between a third and a half from the host organisation.

Consider the implications of working within RAB guidelines. Those who fund residency and placement schemes require a say in the choice of artist. In making decisions about public funding, they must be publicly accountable. The usual stipulation is that the post must be advertised and the artist chosen by their panel. There are instances where the RAB has 'taken over' the scheme, and, despite the groundwork done by an artist or group of artists, the residency once advertised has been given to another applicant.

Have as many alternative sources of finance as possible, reducing reliance on RABs. It may be possible to apply for money for a project under 'awards to artists', but they usually fall far short of the sum needed to finance a residency or placement of any length.

For further details on findraising and funding sources see 'Project planning & fundraising'.

Contracts & conditions

Placement contract checklist:

see 23 • Contracts • name, address and telephone number of: the artist; the site and the contact person there; the organiser or agency (if appropriate)

- brief for project including aims and objectives
- artist's employment status
- number of hours a day or days a week for which the artist is contracted and whether these are in blocks or for specific periods
- attendance 'on site' expressed as a number of hours/days or percentage of the overall time, and the time allowed for the artist's own work
- dates of commencement and completion
- artist's fee: preliminary work and 'feasibility stage'; whether it covers preparation, on-site attendance and preparation of a report
- schedule for payment
- budget for materials, travel, other expenses including how those funds are made available to the artist
- specific requirements of the artist, eg groups or situations with which they must work and allocation of placement time to them
- arbitration procedures
- grounds for terminating the contract, how termination would be effected and how termination affects the artist's fees

see 22 • Insurance

- insurance cover for public liability, personal accident, sickness, equipment and materials and art work
- use of facilities and how they can be accessed (io limitations on use, from whom permission should be gained, etc)
- terms of use of any services, ie accommodation, studio and workshops plus a description of any restrictions on access, etc
- details of the roles and functions of the support group and how often it meets, who is responsible for managing it, etc
- whether the artist must present an on-site exhibition as an integral part of the residency. (If held off-site, an exhibition contract should be drawn up between artist and gallery using the model contract under production by the National Artists Association)
- details of conditions with which the artist must comply ie writing a report, documenting the project, attending meetings or events
- description of who is responsible for first aid and health and safety
- description of evaluation techniques to be used
- provision for review of aims/objectives and extension of the project
- ownership of preliminary and on-site work, and of finished work(s)

see 24 • Copyright & moral rights

- copyright in all work produced during the residency remains with the artist, or detail who owns copyright in the case of works jointly produced

- artist to assert his/her moral rights in the work produced during the residency
- signatures of the parties contractually involved
- date.

Preparation

In your application and interview you will have indicated how you would approach the residency. Once selected, you can spend more time on preparation.

Try to get permission to visit the site in advance. (For a surprising number of artists their first day is also their first visit.) Experience gained before you start is invaluable in planning your approach. You can check physical arrangements (workspace, access, etc) are adequate.

Informing people about yourself and the reasons you are there can begin before you officially arrive – talks to the workforce, an interview with the press. If there is an in-house bulletin or journal, get something published in it and arrange publicity to coincide with when you start.

Starting: the first contact

It is essential to present yourself and the purpose of your residency as soon as possible. Early feedback can be invaluable. Consider introducing yourself through your best representative, your work, by holding an exhibition. Put it where it's most accessible, or move it around if the site's large. Be on hand to talk to those coming to look at it. Arrange a get-together to introduce it. Distribute a leaflet or handout in the form of a bulletin – this could be produced regularly throughout the project. On a large site, a letter describing the project, asking for help and publicising the exhibition might elicit a response from people with whom you want to become involved. A questionnaire could make people aware of their participatory role. Their response might not only highlight problems at an early stage, but give you ideas or inspiration!

see 16 • Publicity & promotion
In letters, leaflets or bulletins, say something about your work and the residency. To dispel myths about artists, you may need to explain employment status and income-earning ability in general. Spell out what you'll get: your expenses, who is providing funding, etc. Say how you want people to be involved and ask for suggestions. Misunderstandings over role and status can develop into enormous problems.

Establish working relationships with other artists in the area. Asking their advice and making use of their local knowledge shows you value their opinion and regard them as an important source of support. They may have spent years building up a relationship with the community, the local authority, arts boards and businesses. They will be reassured to find you plan to enhance their position, rather than breeze in, cause

Claire Quest, details of *Window into Wood,* a 30' sculpture built in larch and poplar during a 12 week residency in Bourne Wood, Lincoln. The residency began with a quick sculpture to alert people. Armed with a list of potential participants and advice from her support group, the central four weeks was spent working with groups, planning the layout, organising materials and building the frame for a permanent sculpture. Although well-thought out the role of coordinating the community groups and events was time-consuming and she felt that it would have been better for this role to have been done by someone else.

a furore, and breeze out. Local artists may, after all, have been the pressure group through which your residency was established.

Operating the residency or placement

How do you build on your initial contact with people? How do you deal with their curiosity and, hopefully, enthusiasm? They won't give you their full attention when they're working, so use the lunch or tea breaks. Prepare regular displays or exhibitions about the work and its progress. Give regular bulletins or handouts. Consider opening the studio, some enjoy a flow of visitors as they work; others need a time to concentrate and a time to talk. Decide which you want and publicise it. It could be open at break times or after work.

Consider working the same hours as the workforce. Strolling in at 10am after people have already been at work for two hours may not impress!

You may like to establish regular meetings with a contact group, made up of representatives from the site, or of the committee that selected you, or both. It could prove crucial if things go wrong and your relationship with people on site shows signs of breaking down.

Maintain relations with the local press: they will be only too pleased to publish interesting material. What's best: a 'scandal' story about your project emanating from an enraged community charge-payer, or features explaining the purpose of the residency?

If stimuli from the site prove overwhelming, you may need to get away to 'process' the material. You risk being an 'absentee artist', but if it is vital, discuss it with your contact group, and negotiate a mutually beneficial arrangement. Residencies where the artist is 'on call' every day for three months don't address this problem. Consider the advantages of eg dividing a three-month residency into three blocks with space in between, even if you are paid only for the time you spend on site.

Concluding the residency or placement

see 5 • Exhibiting Even if not expected, mount an exhibition. It gives people the opportunity to comprehend what you were doing and how they contributed. The site is the logical place, but organisers tend to put exhibitions in galleries – where people may not go. Write a report, even if organisers/funders don't ask for one! If possible, get it published so others can benefit from your experience.

10 • Commissions

Peter Fink A public art project offers a unique opportunity to shape a new social role for yourself and your work. This new role centres on the social and creative demands of such projects, as well as on active leadership from you the artist.

You need the will to take your work out of the confines of your studio and the gallery system and, more crucially, skills to deal with social and economic realities on their own terms, without sacrificing artistic integrity. Evidence of artist-initiated projects shows tremendous potential to be explored and developed in partnership with others, eg local government, development agencies, industrial concerns, community groups.

While these projects can be realised only with the involvement and energies of others, it is essential you have a clear-cut ability to act as principal developer, negotiator, finance director, construction supervisor and publicity agent. Convincing leadership will provide aesthetic and philosophical coherence over the time from initial idea to full realisation.

Analysis of completed projects shows the biggest difficulty in getting a project off the ground is not financial, but the credibility gap between contemporary art and the general public. Your first hurdle is bridging this through lobbying and education, and by the establishment of the project in the public perception, in partnership with those who see 11 • Project planning & fundraising support you and your ideas. Practicalities such as fundraising and planning permission can only be tackled once your proposal is backed by a solid organisational structure.

Winning a commission

An increasing number of commissions are advertised in art magazines and newspapers, such as *Artists Newsletter* and *The Guardian*, as 'open competitions' or 'open submissions for limited competitions'. In the first case you are expected to produce a full submission without any fee. In the second you are expected to submit documentation of your work

Ian Beesley, *Pirelli General – Western Esplanade – Southampton.* When Southampton Art Gallery closed for refurbishment the City Arts Team launched a series of events in alternative spaces. One of these was the Pirelli Project sponsored by Pirelli when they relocated to Eastleigh. An exhibition of local landmarks past and present, 'Altered Estates', toured venues such as the General Hospital. Darrel Viner was commissioned to make a kinetic sculpture in the disused Pirelli Cable Works using found materials from the site. Ian Beesley was commissioned to photograph the old empty factory and machinery at Western Esplanade and the new Pirelli factory at Eastleigh. He produced a portfolio of forty black and white photographs which are now in Southampton's City Art Collection. The Pirelli sponsorship attracted further funding from Southern Arts, Hampshire County Council and Business Sponsorship Incentive Scheme.

see 16 • Publicity & promotion

(usually slides). On this basis a small number are invited and paid to develop their ideas. These are judged in a limited competition by a jury. Such competitions may not even be advertised, you may be invited directly by the client or selection jury. The shortlist is usually compiled from RAB, Crafts Council or gallery index, or a survey show.

Critics of competitions claim time and effort expended by artists in unsuccessful submissions is difficult to justify. Yet there is sufficient demand for competitions by organisations and clients to counter this criticism. When entering a competition it is useful to ask:

- how can I present my ideas and work as on the one hand unique and on the other right for the brief?
- how can I make my presentation visually and conceptually as effective as possible?
- how can I communicate my professional competence?

Selectors face an enormous task when assessing large numbers of submissions, so help them see beyond the presented image towards the core idea of your proposal by carefully chosen captions and descriptions.

Direct commission

In most negotiating situations the first impression is probably the most important. First meetings are crucial for the establishment of confidence between you and the client. Success helps create an atmosphere of constructive engagement which automatically optimises your chances. Ensure you have done the necessary preparation. Know enough about the person or organisation you are dealing with. Run through your presentation and check where and when your meeting is to be.

If meeting in your studio make sure you have organised a clean, quiet place to make your presentation without interruptions. Preliminary meetings are by no means a one-way business – they give you the opportunity to assess the client and help decide if you want the job. If in doubt about commission or client, do not be afraid to reject the offer as this might in the longrun save trouble. But it is advisable to give yourself time to think your position through. Better than blunt refusal might be to renegotiate the client's original concepts and expectations.

Commissioning process

It is important to be aware at all times of the whole context of the commissioning process, taking into account the social as well as practical implications of your work. Many artists think their responsibility is to do their bit in the studio and that consultation with the community, planning permission, maintenance and so on are someone else's concern. As a result, commissions may run into troubles later, facing dramatic rejection at planning permission stage or persistent vandalism after their unveiling. The main stages of any commissioning process are the design/idea and the contractual/realisation stages.

Design/idea stage

Having received from or put together with a client a commission brief, you are ready to engage in the crucial stage of winning or securing a contract for its realisation. A workable brief should answer the following:

• who are you dealing with?

- what does the client expect?
- where is the commission to be located?
- has the commission got a theme, subject, etc?
- what are the social circumstances related to it?
- what is the proposed budget and expected timetable for its realisation?
- what are the specific limitations of the commission?
- where and from whom can you obtain additional information?
- how much time have you to sort out the details of your submission; what form should it take; what sort of fee should you receive; where and when must you deliver your submission?
- when and by whom is the commission awarded?
- who is the final owner of the submission material and its copyright?

see 23 • Contracts As in the next stage of the commissioning process you should obtain a clear-cut, legally binding agreement on most of the above areas.

Having considered the answers to these questions it is prudent to form a clear picture of what it is possible to create within the brief and start working as normal on exploring ideas. With the investigative idea stage completed, decide on the format of your presentation to make it as effective as possible. A good presentation should clearly communicate your ideas, rather than be over-elaborate and flashy.

Contractual, realisation stage

Having secured or been offered a commission it is essential that this stage of your involvement is fully supported by a legally binding document before you start working or spending any money.

Its main function is to protect the interests of everyone involved, to delineate mutual obligations as well as make clear-cut provisions for possible difficulties later, eg cancellation due to unforeseen circumstances or destruction of the commission by fire in your studio or during transit.

In the case of most small commissions and at design idea stages, contractual agreements take the form of letters of intent signed by both parties, whilst in the case of a complex architectural commission the agreement will be a hefty legal document. A solicitor should draw up the final version of any agreement and it is advisable to take independent legal advice before signing on the dotted line. Most contractual agreements should deal with:

Blue Field, an installation by House Artists for Brooke Lodge, an elderly people's ward at Guy's Hospital. The installation hangs at light level, two feet below a false ceiling and it comprises 14,000 aluminium 'butterfly' shapes, painted blue and suspended by wire from forty-eight steel frames. The frames are suspended from beams concealed above the false ceiling. The work covers an area of approximately 2,800 square feet, and was worked on and completed over a period of almost seven months. The £15,000 installation was funded by the Friends of Guy's. House Artists Cooperative, a North London based group, was formed in 1990 by artists committed to the development of public art. Its permanent members are Martin Charter, Andrew Marchant and Lawrence Sullivan.

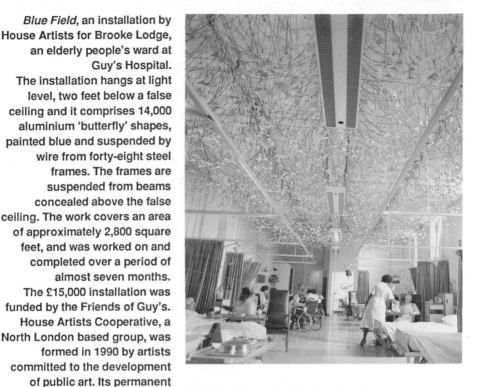

Identification of the involved parties

• you – your tax and VAT status during the commission.

• the commissioner's name and address. In some cases this might prove difficult, for example, where the RAB is providing incentive funding, the local authority the site but no funds, and an industrial concern the remainder of the funds as sponsorship. The agreement must clear this matter up, by for example establishing a new entity such as a trust to act as a commissioner

• agent – name and address. This clause should also specify on whose behalf the agent is working

Description of the commission

• title

• medium, materials, method of fabrication

• subject matter

- a clause guaranteeing fidelity of the commission to the accepted proposal and a clause preventing further editions of the original
- a clause specifying a need for a mutual consent to any changes

Fees

- is the fee inclusive or exclusive of VAT?
- does the fee cover the cost of delivery of the work to site, installation and the cost of related ancillary works, eg flood lighting?
- a timetable of stages of payment and the definition of these stages – you might be paid 50% of the budget on the date you start work, 25% when the complete work is seen and approved by the commissioner in your studio, 20% when installed, 5% might be held by the commissioner for one year against hidden defects
- the specification of any other payments due to you such as incidental expenses during installation

Insurance

see 22 • Insurance

This clause must establish who is responsible for obtaining the insurance cover and to what level of indemnity to avoid under-insurance. The usual insurance cover consists of:

- all risk insurance while the commission is being made – protecting you, for example, in a situation when you have already spent most of the materials budget and had a fire in the studio in which you lost all the purchased material
- your personal accident insurance
- public liability insurance – during the installation phase this insurance is absolutely essential but is also available during other stages – the level of indemnity might vary, as for example, during installation you should have a higher level of indemnity than during the period when you are working in your studio.

Timetable

This clause needs to specify:

- the date when you can start working
- the date when the commission should be ready for inspection, delivery and installation
- the date for the completion arrangements.

Yanina Temple, *Fabric Wall Hanging,* The Stroud & Swindon Building Society

The precise identification of all these dates is related to other possible clauses which, for example:

- protect your interests in a situation where you finished on time but the commissioner has not made the site available, did not obtain planning permission and you as a result incur storage costs
- protect the commissioner's interests in a situation where money is lost as a result of your late delivery and which deal with the subsequent penalties you would incur in these circumstances.

Responsibilities of the involved parties

- a guarantee by you to exercise diligence and skill in the execution and installation of the work
- the need for further guarantees, for example, from fabricators and material suppliers
- an indemnity clause protecting the commissioner from any loss or damage from your negligence or wilful acts of omission
- responsibility for obtaining planning permission where necessary – clarification of the need for planning permission and the actual planning process is often one of the most difficult hurdles. Great care should be taken when dealing with this process
- responsibility for provision for access to the site and of for its readiness for installation
- responsibility for the ancillary works
- responsibility for an increase in cost due to circumstances beyond your control.

Termination of the agreement

- determination of ownership of the partly or fully finished commission if the agreement is terminated by you, for example, due to illness, or by the commissioner for whatever reason.

Completion arrangements

This section should determine:

- formal acceptance of the work
- transfer of responsibility from you to the commissioner for the finished commission in areas such as insurance
- an acknowledgement clause specifying that the commissioner will at all times acknowledge you as creator, as well as specifying the wording on the plaque
- the period during which you are responsible for any hidden defects.

After-life provisions

This section needs to specify mainly the maintenance provisions:

- who is responsible for maintenance? In some cases, you as an artist can contract this from the commissioner for a yearly fee
- who is responsible for producing a maintenance manual? This must contain all technical data such as type of material used, method of fabrication, etc as well as a timetable and procedures to be used in maintaining the work.

Copyright and moral rights section

see 24 • Copyright & moral rights

Whilst copyright clauses are directly related to the protection of your legitimate extended economic rights, moral rights are concerned with the protection of the integrity of the finished work as well as of your personal integrity as the maker. Clauses dealing with moral rights should include protection against acts of distortion, mutilation or modification of the finished commission. Such a clause is linked to another giving you right of first option to repair any damage so that the work can continue legitimately to be considered as your creation. With, for example, a permanently-sited outdoor sculpture, you may wish to stipulate that you be consulted if the original siting needs to be changed.

Concluding clauses

This section usually involves clauses dealing with:

- proper law – specifying, for example, the contract is governed by the law of England and Wales and may be changed only by a further mutual agreement signed by everyone involved

- arbitration – specifying settling of disputes related to the contractual agreement shall be done in accordance with the Arbitration Act.
- signatures and addresses of involved parties.

Some artists see consultation as a trendy procedure devised by bureaucrats to justify expenditure on bland, populist works. Some consider the issue best left to community arts and that even the broader social issues surrounding public art shouldn't be an immediate concern.

But this attitude is frequently the strongest contributory factor in the creation of bland, non-communicative commissions, where the private world of the artist evokes no resonance in the public domain. It is consultation in varied forms that offers potentially exciting clues as to how to start creating this. Research and consultation enable you to gather information about a place and its people and incorporate this into your work, making it site-specific in more than the architectural sense.

Permission

Most permanently-sited public works of art require planning permission. Check with the planning authority if your work requires it, or if it is among the small number of exceptions (including murals which are not for advertising or direction-giving purposes). If permission is needed, you or the commissioner will need to complete an application for either outline or full planning permission. The application is lodged on a standard form to the local authority, which has jurisdiction over the proposed site. In a full planning application you will be required to support the information with a complete set of visual and technical documentation of the proposed work.

If you only intend to test the reaction of the authority to an idea, apply for outline planning permission. This, if granted, means the authority in principle has no objection to a proposal being considered for a location. Before proceeding with actual installation or work on site, you need full permission, which can only be granted for a specific project.

Once an application is lodged, the authority must give a decision within eight weeks, unless an extension is agreed. This stage is usually preceded by an informal meeting with the planning officer, giving the opportunity to discuss the finer points of detail of your commission as well as any impact of a particular planning policy on your project.

To help ensure the commission is considered in as objective and informed a manner as possible during the committee stage make sure:

- the proposal is well represented visually and its technical details well explained

- your professional background and past work are well documented
- any public, ACGB or RAB support for your commission is well known to committee members
- the planning officer is well acquainted with the details of your proposal before the actual meeting.

The experience of artists with the planning process has been mixed. Although many commissions proceed smoothly, a high number do not. Some are not realised at all; others are delayed by up to several years. Whilst refusal is expressed in terms of planning law, in most cases the overriding factor is the desire of councillors to block a potentially controversial project. This commonly found instinct may also be fuelled by aesthetic prejudices. Be aware of and efficient in using DoE policy statements. DoE circular 22/80 (para 19) and Development Control Policy Note 10 *Design,* make it clear aesthetics are subjective and the purpose of the Planning Acts is not to give elected representatives power to censor public access to the enjoyment of contemporary art.

If faced with refusal, you can appeal to the Secretary of State within six months. The Secretary looks into the project, hears you and the planning authority, and may or may not hold a public enquiry. After the investigation s/he takes the final decision. A number of artists have appealed successfully but it can be time, energy and expense-consuming.

11 • Project planning & fundraising

Susan Jones with additional material by **Helen Smith**

Raising funds can be a long-winded and time-consuming process and there is no formula for success. But if you are as creative with fundraising as you are with doing your own work, you may be surprised at what you achieve.

Different situations demand different types of proposals and proposals fall largely into three categories:

- artist initiated – artist makes a proposal to a venue, collaborator or funder
- response to a defined brief – project initiated by an organisation or individual who defines how they want an artist to contribute and an artist makes a proposal in response
- response to a broad brief – project initiated by an organisation or individual who defines broad parameters for an artist's contribution, and the artist develops a proposal which includes elements of the first two points.

One difference is that proposals in response to an advertised brief may have budget guidelines within which to work and an initiated proposal may be seeking funding.

Aims & purpose

Making a proposal is the opportunity to capture the imagination and interest of future partners or funders. It needs to anticipate and answer all the questions listed below which the receiver of the proposal is likely to ask about the project:

- who is involved?
- what is the project about and what will the end result be?
- when will it happen?

- where will it happen?
- who will benefit from it?
- why is it of interest?
- how can it be achieved?

The detailed explanation should cover the headings and points listed below. This is not only for the benefit of the recipient, but also to help the artist to think it through and make sure the project is feasible, practicable and viable.

Who, when & where

- details of artist(s)
- anticipated date
- who else will be involved
- venue or location
- a summary of the project idea.

Aims

- why you want to carry out the work
- who the project's audience is
- what the benefits will be to you, the community or others involved
- how the project relates to other work
- what the outcome of the project will be – exhibition, environmental improvement, etc.

Practicalities

- outline of how it will be carried out and time-scale involved
- breakdown of costs and possible sources of income
- supporting statements from people who will be involved

see 16 • Publicity & promotion

- details of the experience and skills you have to undertake the project – digested from your CV
- good visual documentation of related work and how this proposal will be realised.

Resources

- workshop space, public space needed
- any planning or other permissions needed
- water and electrical services and access requirements
- materials and equipment needed
- transport requirements

- insurance – personal, equipment and public liability
- time-scale for ordering/locating resources

Consultation

Mural Project in a school
Two artists were asked by a school to propose a large-scale permanent mural project to involve children, staff, parents and the local community. The school's contribution – materials, scaffolding and documentation – was costed at a third of the overall budget of £4,000. The second third was raised from district council's arts budget and the remainder from the local projects budget of the regional arts board. They also received in-kind sponsorship from a local industry.

If you invest time in developing a proposal, put time into researching where to send it and to whom to send it.

Involve potentially interested people in the early stages of developing the proposal. In this way the concept can remain intact whilst specific issues such as site, time-scale and costings can develop on a mutually acceptable basis. This method of locating who is interested in a self-initiated project reduces the risk of spending a great deal of time working up an idea no-one is interested in.

Retaining the integrity of your proposal is crucial. How much you are prepared to adjust your proposal to fit guidelines is a question only you can answer and each project will be different. Consult the following:

- RAB officers – not just artform officers but others who may be interested. Use RAB knowledge of regional events, sites, organisations who may be interested in your work, knowledge of potential funders, assistance on marketing your proposal and developing budgets
- local authority arts officers – for knowledge of opportunities and contacts, events that link with your proposal, budgets or resources you might access
- education arts advisers – for knowledge of artists in school programmes, INSET training needs
- organisations or agencies dealing with similar projects to discuss collaboration and avoid duplication
- other artists, makers or arts organisers for the same reasons.

Purpose

An application for funding for a proposal needs to answer these questions:

- what do you want the money for? – to refurbish a studio building, mount an exhibition, produce a video for broadcasting, carry out a residency or commission, set up an art week, etc.

Group Exhibition
In 1991, an artists' group organised an exhibition in a regional gallery. The cost of transport, producing publicity and running workshops throughout the show was £2,250. Fundraising began a year in advance. The gallery paid for transport, publicity and private view to the value of £925, the amount they would normally spend themselves. The regional arts board's exhibitions scheme gave a grant of £1,500 and of the six trusts approached for sponsorship, Sainsbury's gave £200. Because they had 16 images to print, the group negotiated a much cheaper rate with a postcard printing firm and the postcards on sale with the show made a little income for artists.

• how much money do you need? – this helps to establish a realistic budget
• when do you need the money? – this helps to determine the time-table for fundraising
• what are you offering in return and to whom? – this helps to determine which organisation(s) you should apply to, as different organisations have different policies and priorities

The first question is different from 'what funds are there available for which I can apply'. It demonstrates you understand that successful projects occur when your interests coincide with an organisation who may be able to help fund a project's realisation.

Funding sources

Local authority
Arts activities may be funded by almost any department including:
• Recreation & Arts – sometimes called Tourism, Leisure, etc
• Arts & Libraries
• Architects
• Parks & Cemeteries
• Planning
• Social Services
• Education Authority
• Rates Department – discretionary or charitable Uniform Business Rates relief for studios, workshops, etc
• Economic Development – may provide access to funds for training projects
• Urban Programme – a scheme administered through the local authority for the Department of the Environment who provide part of the funds for a project, the local authority providing the rest.

Other sources
see 26 • Further reading
The Arts Funding Guide provides information on major sources of funding from public, charitable and business sources, including more details on those listed below. *Who does What in Europe*, published by

Steve Tanner, *Poppy Pollacks*, 1992. This photographer recently won a Prince's Trust travel award to St Petersburg, Russia under their 'Go and See' scheme which enables those under 26 to visit other countries to make contacts to generate further work on business opportunities.

the Arts Council, contains a wealth of useful information on potential funds from sources in Europe.

Arts councils

The Arts Council of Great Britain's current visual arts schemes include 'Special Projects' from the Visual Arts Department for exhibitions, conferences, research and publications of 'national importance'; Video Awards for Black arts projects and Film & Video production awards in conjunction with Channel 4 and BBC; Training Bursaries, New Collaborations for across artform projects, also the International Initiatives Fund. Contact individual departments for leaflets. Contact the Welsh and Scottish Arts Councils for their current schemes.

British Film Institute

Funds for film and video development and production.

Crafts Council

'Setting up' grants for individuals, subsidy for touring exhibitions.

Regional arts boards

Each of the boards covering England has policies and schemes to assist the development of visual and media arts in their area. The three regional arts associations in Wales initiate and develop specific projects.

British Council

Some grants for established artists to exhibit abroad, also helps young film-makers' work to be seen in international festivals.

Charitable trusts
Research those whose policies fit your needs. Contact the regional Charity Information Bureau.

Sponsorship
Business, industry locally and nationally – can be linked to government money through the Business Sponsorship Incentive Scheme which matches sponsorship from a business sponsor with a grant. Leaflet from ABSA (Association for Business Sponsorship of the Arts).

Tourist boards
Discuss projects with them which might be publicised or financially assisted.

Trades unions
Have funded some arts and media projects in the past.

Other voluntary or community projects
May be able to raise funds for a collaborative project because they are more established, have access to different sources, etc.

Urban development corporations
All have arts policies, and some offer awards or grants to individuals.

Department of Trade and Industry
Schemes include product development and marketing assistance.

Rural Development Commission
Capital grants towards conversion of redundant buildings in rural areas.

Health authorities
May fund projects in hospitals or outside in the field of mental health.

Training and Enterprise Councils
Some have funded training programmes for voluntary arts organisations.

European Social Fund
Some arts organisations in the 'assisted' areas of high unemployment have obtained funds for training or employment projects. Information pack from National Council for Voluntary Organisations.

'In-kind' funding
This can be a valuable addition to cash grants. If given goods or services, estimate their monetary value, and itemise this within your project budget. For example:
- under 'Expenditure': Photography – £300

- under 'Income': J.B Bloggs Photographic – £300.

You could be offered:

- materials – paint, wood, framing, etc
- services – photographic, construction, publicity, etc
- equipment and furniture
- old stock or seconds
- a discount on list prices
- secondments of staff with specialist skills
- temporary workspace
- temporary living accommodation.

Drawing up a budget

A budget for a small or medium-scale project is likely to include some of the following:

- fees to artists – use the regional arts board's guidelines and don't under-value your time and expertise
- cost of overheads and administration
- cost of hiring equipment or facilities
- materials
- insurance
- display or setting up costs
- transport costs
- promotion and publicity costs
- technical help
- documentation – textual, visual
- a 10% contingency to cover unforeseen costs.

Providing you work out an overall budget in the early stages, you will have an accurate picture of the costs involved. You can then look for funds from appropriate places. Joint funding – where a project is funded from several sources – is more likely to be successful than one which aims to get all the money from one source.

Seek specialist advice on setting out financial information, as your application is likely to be judged by people such as business people, accountants, local authority officers or board members of a charitable trust.

Fundraising to study abroad

An increasing number of artists are seeking funds to study abroad. An artist, who had been out of college for two years, was offered a one-year post-graduate course at a European art college starting in September 1991. She had almost a year to raise £3,000 needed to undertake the course.

The college would provide accommodation. She applied at the beginning of 1991 to two charitable trusts – neither application was successful. In June, she made a successful application for part of the costs from her regional arts board who offer travel awards of up to £1,000 to artists to travel abroad to develop their work. As the application would take two months to process, she asked the college to hold her place until January which they were willing to do. The RAB's award was put in a high-interest bank account to make a little more money. To raise the remainder of the funds needed, she undertook summer project work through a local visual arts organisation and also organised a mural project at a school which paid her for two days work a week over a term. In January 1992, she took up her place.

Rates of Pay

AN Publications publishes an annual survey of fees which self-employed artists receive for different types of work. It covers commissions, residencies, workshops, talks, performances, exhibition fees and design rates and is derived from advertisements and telephone surveys to a range of arts organisations.

For 1992, assuming you are self-employed, for a day's work as an artist in residence, you would expect to charge a minimum of £85. A monthly rate would be between £1,500 and £2,250, and an annual rate between £12,000-£18,000. Never budget your fees at below 'going rates' as this undervalues what you do and will cause people to whom you make proposals to doubt your professionalism. Always up-date the figure for fees once a year by at least the rate of inflation.

Approach

A fundraising application, whatever the source, will be helped if you:

- make contact with relevant officers for preliminary discussions – to find out policies and how they relate to your proposal
- spend time getting to know how the potential funder's organisation works
- write a concise application with accurate facts and figures
- budget accurately and realistically
- don't apply over the limit of an organisation's guidelines or it will be automatically rejected
- don't apply for small amounts to organisations who give large grants, or your application may not be taken seriously
- find out who makes the decisions and be sure they understand your project – talk to officers, councillors and others in advance.

When making an initial written approach, send a well-presented, two-page proposal with covering letter and good quality supporting documentation. Avoid using 'art jargon'. Adjust your application to the

Artweek
An artweek in 1992 which included open studios, exhibitions, projects, residencies and a programme of live art events, had an overall budget of £25,000. The person who undertook the fundraising on a voluntary basis, started a year in advance and spent the equivalent of 20 hours a week over a three-month period. Using reference material such as *Making Ways,* **and having spoken to other artweek organisers, he contacted over 1,000 companies with amounts varying from £25 – £3,000 coming from over 30 of them. In all, £11,000 came from businesses, £2,000 from the Business Sponsorship Incentive Scheme, £3,000 from local charitable trusts, £1,500 from the borough council, £500 from the county council and £2,000 from the regional arts board. Funds were sought for specific events or projects, with requests tailored to a sponsor's particular interests. The majority of fundraising requests were made over the telephone, with letters used to follow up a verbal agreement. A mail-shot to potentially interested companies was 'a complete waste of time'. The arts board's input was 'matched' with commercial sponsorship and charitable trusts were the only organisations willing to help fund core costs. In addition to the basic budget, the value of voluntary free help was around £15,000. All sponsors were listed on the artweek's headed paper.**

policies and priorities of each of the organisations to whom you apply, although bear in mind that they may confer!

A fund-raising application, like a project proposal, needs to:

- explain who you are and the project for which you require funding
- the project's aims and objectives
- the project's audience
- how the organisation will benefit from supporting it
- the benefit to the project's audience
- the total cost of the project and amount you are seeking from that organisation.

Make sure that:

- the paperwork lists those 'heading' your organisation – treasurer, chair, secretary, etc
- you address the application to a named person – find out by telephone to whom applications should go
- it gives the time, date and place of event, etc
- it includes the overall budget, showing income from all sources.

A potential sponsor or funder may need additional information, especially if you want a substantial grant. Prepare the necessary back-up material at the same time as writing an application so it is ready when needed.

If you have to meet a potential sponsor or funder you need:

- to feel confident you can present yourself and your project effectively, perhaps to someone without great knowledge of the arts
- to know what the funder's policies and past involvement with funding arts projects are
- to be business-like and follow up the meeting with a letter confirming what has been agreed.

Time-scale

With all applications whether made locally, regionally or nationally, allow at least six months and if possible, up to twelve months to raise the funds. This is because:

Solo Studio

A printmaker in need of space to set up a print studio approached a local school with unoccupied classrooms and said she would provide a day a week teaching in exchange for the space. The school agreed to this and later provided funds for her to run occasional in-service training courses for teachers there. The scheme, now in its seventh year, has been extended to other schools.

- some trusts have fixed cycles for considering applications
- 'popular' sources are generally over-subscribed and an application may have to wait six months to get to a meeting
- local businesses may need to refer to the regional or head office
- local authorities cannot allocate funds until budgets are agreed, and applications generally go to a committee of councillors
- allow time to involve people who can support your project to the decision-makers
- if a funder turns the application down, you need enough time to take it elsewhere
- no-one ever seems to have any funds left between November and March if their financial year ends on March 31!

It is useful to liaise with others working in visual and media arts to ensure that you are not duplicating or competing by applying to the same people at the same time. Better to work cooperatively than competitively!

Follow-through

With any project funded from public or private sources, it is important to:

- follow up a verbal offer with a letter confirming the agreement
- agree the method of acknowledging sponsorship or support for a project with sponsors so they will be happy to sponsor again
- include names of sponsors and grant awarding bodies on publicity and press and media information
- keep sponsors informed about what you are doing
- fulfil conditions of grant aid as outlined in offer letters, otherwise funds may be reclaimed

- document the outcome of the project and send photographs, cuttings and other coverage to sponsors or grant awarding bodies; you can also use it to endorse future proposals
- invite people who have supported the project to a special preview or launch event
- keep an annotated list of the outcome of all applications to save time in the future
- keep a record of income and expenditure for your benefit and to give to funders. Get advice on this if you are unsure about bookkeeping – don't damage your reputation by presenting information in a poor way!

Don't give up if your application isn't successful. Another sponsor may like it, or a different project may interest that sponsor next time.

12 • Strength in numbers

David Butler & Visual artists, in common with writers, work alone. For many artists that
Susan Jones isn't a problem in terms of production, though contact with other artists
is important for critical feedback on their work. Some artists find that
collective action gives them power both to achieve their aims and to
demonstrate to the 'art establishment' that their methods have long-term
benefits.

Associations

The feeling that an area of work is unrecognised or undervalued has
been a forceful motivator for artists, makers and photographers to
organise themselves into pressure groups. The 'Noticeboard' section of
Artists Newsletter points to an ever increasing number of artform
groupings, ranging from felt work to braidmaking and from ceramics to
photography.

The Printmakers' Council, established more than 20 years ago,
has been instrumental in raising the profile of their medium through
exhibitions, demonstrations, marketing schemes and other
consciousness-raising activities. It holds a register of members and
gives general advice. A strength is engenered from working with others.
Printmaker Ian Stephens said *'I like to belong to a society because I need
the contact to be able to measure my own work against others and I need
the approval in what can be an isolated activity'*.

The National Artists' Association, formed in 1985, describes
itself as a *'powerful collective voice for all visual artists'*. Its work ranges
from lobbying and campaigning on issues which affect the cultural and
economic status of artists to holding conferences, undertaking research
into contracts and codes of practice, and working with the Arts &
Entertainment Training Council on establishing the parameters and
assessment criteria for National Vocational Qualifications in the visual
arts. The potential for a national body to establish insurance packages

Confrontation, a painting in oil on canvas by Bhajan Hunjan whose work is registered at Panchayat, the arts and education resource centre based in London which also curated the touring exhibition 'Crossing Black Waters'.

and discounts on materials for its members grows as membership grows. So does its potential to be truly representative. More voices means a louder noise and a greater ability to influence the art establishment and government.

Gender, ethnic origin, disability and other cultural and political issues set another powerful agenda for artists to come together. Autograph, the association for Black photographers, challenges the lack of representation for Black photographers who've historically been denied an audience for their work. It aims to produce and tour exhibitions, run workshops, publish books and the monthly *Autograph Newsletter,* and also set up a photographic agency and a permanent archive of the field of work. The agency takes a 50% cut of the library sales and charges minimum service fee for handling picture requests. It has produced guidelines given to members before they submit material.

The Women Artists Slide Library – a membership organisation open to women artists, art historians and writers – holds a register of over 21,000 images of work by women artists, along with an archive of writing, articles and books on women artists. Publisher of the *Women's Art Magazine*, it organises exhibitions, conferences and seminars. WASL has been instrumental in gaining recognition for the status of women artists, providing a forum (and the research material) for critical debate, and networking with other members.

The African and Asian Artists Archive, although not a membership organisation, has provided an important focus for the work artists of African, Asian and Caribbean origin. Consulted by curators, educationalists, commissioners and others, it has enabled many of the artists represented on it to gain opportunities to show their work to the public.

Collectives

Collectives and co-operatives are still rare in this country, and many fold within three years of starting. The artist-founded and managed Collective Gallery in Edinburgh is a notable exception. Started in 1984, the collective took over four former shop units, reburbishing them as gallery and shop in 1992 with funds from arts and economic development sources. The realisation of this major project demonstrates what an artist-controlled approach can achieve. A councillor for Edinburgh District Council's economic development section commented *'It is good to be opening a gallery instead of closing one, especially as this one is involved with promoting artists rather than the interests of an arts entrepreneur'*.

An artist-led approach often captures the imagination of private sponsors and public officials. When the Whitstable Artists and Musicians Collective instigated a project to create a series of sea benches for a refurbishment of Whitstable seafront using 100 year-old wood salvaged from the beach through renewal of the sea defences, it was able to raise a budget of around £12,000 from a mixture of public and private sources.

Studios

The Norwich-based Warehouse Artists Group began with Trevor Burgess, looking for a larger, affordable studio. Converted to the benefits of setting up a group purely because of the hard realities of the property market, he now sees many practical advantages too.

The Cracker Factory
'The aim of the exhibition is to take art out into the public domain, the accessible to the community at large the innovative art of young artists.' The exhibition, of site-related and installation work by 18 artists from the UK, Europe and USA, was held in an old Victorian sawmill on the edge of central Edinburgh.

He adds *'The group's structure is important to get right from the start. We decided upon a co-operative and received invaluable advice from the local co-operative development agency. Rules and meetings may sometimes be tiresome, but they have helped us work effectively together. All the group agrees the security of affordable studios, and the benefits of working with other artists, are well worth the trouble.'*

Exhibitions

Artists and makers may come together for exhibition purposes. Often frustrated by the lack of opportunity to do so through the gallery system. The 62 Group of textile artists was formed by embroiderers concerned in the '60s at the lack of outlets for their work. Membership grew rapidly and now with 68 members, includes artists working in print, weave and assemblage. It mounts one major and several other exhibitions a year and also produces slide packs with descriptive notes sold to institutions and individuals.

The Cracker Factory project, initiated by a post-graduate student, was a response to lack of suitable exhibition and working space in Edinburgh. Using disused sawmills, they found a way of *'making things happen in an uninspiring and rather negative situation for the arts in general and for art education in particular'.* The 18 artists involved – from Scotland, Europe and the USA – organised the event made site-specific works often using the mill's resources, their aim being to *'Take art out into the public domain, to make accessible to the community at large in innovative work of young artists'.*

Using the focus of Glasgow's 'Mayfest', six artists from the West of Scotland devised and presented 'The Greatest Show on Earth' in their studios.

Artweeks & open studios

see 5 • Exhibiting

The Oxfordshire Visual Arts Week, first organised in 1984 as a programme of open studios, has been an exemplar for artists all over the country, showing it is possible for artists to control how they and their work is represented. Many artweeks are now organised, coinciding with existing arts festivals where artists' groups can use the publicity machines which are already in place to widen audiences for their events. In London, the East End Open Studios week is now linked with the 'Whitechapel Open'. Debbie Duffin, organiser of the open studios event stresses the need for collective responsibility. *'Some people will be unable or unwilling to help and it is important not to expect too much from too few people.'*

Activity-based

Strong ideological links can be the motivating force behind a group's setting up. Artists for the Environment in Rochdale (AFTER), formed in 1987 by Paul Haywood, Karen Lyons, Paul McLaren and Emrys Morgan, sought new strategies for presenting environmental works. Projects include siting permanent and temporary work in outside locations, often working without funding and using found materials, work with festivals, residencies, exhibitions and live art performances. They also offer information and exchange through a network of *'120 associated artists in Britain, Europe and the former USSR, USA, Canada and Iceland'.*

A sizeable community of artists living and working in an area is an important factor in developing an artform and encouraging support and recognition for it. Hull Time-Based Arts began in 1984 when a group of artists began to develop collaborative working. They, like other artist-led live art organisations moved into centre stage when they became major commissioners and promoters of live art and installation work nationally. With Humberside Polytechnic's art department they have been instrumental in making Hull a centre for time-based work and encouraging the Ferens Art Gallery to develop a designated live art space.

Organisation

To be effective, a group needs structure and identity. Daniel Dahl and Magnus Irvin said of Barbican Arts Group's studio move *'Without a strong identity and structure and our previous experience of working together, we would not have been able to make this move'.*

It is not only a question of getting the structure right in the beginning, it is also crucial to assess and adjust it along the way to keep it working effectively. Any group, whether coming together for a specific project or for long-term development needs to define its aims and objectives clearly and map out a structure which will enable them to be realised. This involves an investment of time and commitment.

The bigger the group, the more responsibilities it gathers and the more precise its organisational structures need to be. On the other hand, more people means more skills and a better share-out of workload.

Although you won't want bureaucracy to take over, tasks need to be taken on, and the more experienced acknowledge the need to hand on their experience to incoming members in a constructive way so that continuing in an artists' organisation isn't dependent on 'longevity of service'.

Achievements

As well as side stepping the 'art establishment', collective action can achieve:

- recognition and status for a particular group, area of work or medium
- lobbying for change, resources, power
- ability to raise funds for projects
- sharing of ideas, skills, resources
- the creation of resources like studios, workshops or galleries
- work opportunities
- affordable workspace, materials, equipment
- regular communication with like-minded people.

Group checklist

To operate effectively as a group:

Status
- define your aims and write them down – but be aware of the need to revise them as you develop
- establish a legal status – unincorporated association, limited company, partnership, co-operative which enables you to open a bank account, receive grants, take on leases and be taken seriously

Communication
- give the group an 'identity' by getting a letterhead and leaflet
- every group needs to have a 'contact point and person' so that others can communicate with them
- establish effective ways of seeking opinions amongst a group and making collective decisions.

Operating
- share out jobs and create formal methods for gaining basic skills and passing them on
- if you take on paid staff, make sure you acknowledge their needs and aspirations as well as telling them yours
- keep written records of what has been decided at meetings and who has agreed to do things
- encourage active participation and contribution from all members.

Stefan Szozelkun. *Immigration Ritual,* commissioned by Hull Time-Based Arts in 1989. This event took place over a week at the Orchard Parking Housing Estate and culminated in a ritual journey, using fork-lift trucks to move the 'house', from the Estate to the Fisherman's Memorial on Hessle Road.

Inevitably, groups encounter problems along the way. These range from a strong personality over-powering collective decision-making, to an artist not paying their studio rent.

Although groups shouldn't avoid constructive criticism, praise for good things done should preface critical remarks. Putting over feelings and worries in a tactful and diplomatic way is far more likely to resolve a problem than overtly laying the blame on others.

Successful groups deal with all these issues and, importantly, don't forget to applaud themselves when they've done something well!

13 • Agents

Public art agencies

Susan Jones   There's no doubt the work being done by public art agencies is succeeding in finding a great deal of new opportunities and sources of funding for artists. As well as growth in the number and scope of see 9 • Residencies commissioned projects, the number of placements for art in hospitals and art in schools and other community schemes multiply throughout the country. The agencies 'sell' the ways in which artists and community see 10 • Commissions can work together for mutual benefit.. Many placements result in commissions and sales of the artists' work.

Selection

Consultancy is usually part of the package offered by an artists' agency, a service for which they'll generally charge the client a fee as part of the overall budget. The client may approach the agency with an idea, or the agency may have the idea then go out and sell it. Once a project has been confirmed, the agency will usually be active in the selection process. For many agencies, the method of selecting artists and makers for commissions or purchases usually consists of competition between a short-list of invited artists. Clients view slides of work by regional and national artists to draw this up.

Alternatively projects are advertised as an open competition, although this inevitably increases the costs and extends the timescales for getting projects off the ground. For a large commission this process, plus the final production of the work, its installation and the necessary raising of funds can take in excess of three years. To reduce some of this time factor (a problem noted by many agencies), competitions are used less for selection, and increasing use is made of artists' registers and slide indexes. Agencies have developed their own slide indexes, as well as making use of those held by regional arts boards. Some also make a practice of visiting studios and workshops, sometimes taking clients with them, and may do the rounds of exhibitions and art schools hunting out new artists for their files.

Arts Resource, the Sunderland based artist led organisation, has been working with the Great North Forest project in Tyne & Wear. Artists including Gale Spinks, Chris Sell, Chris Kent and Neil Malloy ran workshops with Sunderland schools to mark the initial creation of the community forest.

see 16 • Publicity & promotion

It is critical for artists to make sure thoy are well represented on registers and slide indexes – these usually require a selection of slides accompanied by a CV and statement about the work. Information should be kept up to date, and agencies will also often require an idea of prices of work. Where interviews are held – eg for a placement – the agency will probably play a key role in interviewing and advising the client as to which artist would be most suitable, particularly if the client hasn't any previous experience in working with artists.

Consultation

Agencies will usually act as consultants on site for commissioned work, and most encourage clients to involve the artist at the very earliest stage of a project. The degree of consultation needed will vary from client to client and on the number of parties involved. Local authorities might want to consult tenants of a local estate; maquettes or mural proposals may be displayed in local libraries or another public site so comments can be collected prior to decision-making. The process can be lengthy and may involve many committee meetings.

Most agents will also give general advice to artists in negotiations with a client, with drawing up contracts and in coping with any problems that may arise.

Differences

Each public art agency has a different policy and emphasis, structure, funding sources and staffing, although all have increased the range of clients and artists they deal with. Several regional arts boards undertake agency work. Sometimes this is handled by the visual arts officer or, where the workload has become significant, they have appointed a special commissions or public art coordinator, or funded a freelance person to work on their behalf. Others have helped establish and fund independent organisations to specialise in this field.

Supporting artists

Most public art agencies claim to be supportive of artists' initiatives but in practice very few find it easy or possible to respond whole-heartedly to artists' proposals. In most situations, artists are involved only after others have thought up the idea.

Although no code of practice to set minimum conditions and fees yet exists for residencies and commissions, there is a greater emphasis on the exchange of information through workshops, conferences and through publications. It is nevertheless the case many residencies and commissions, even those supported by the regional arts boards are inadequately funded and thought out.

What has also not been fully resolved is how to handle the complexity of partnerships involved in public art – artist and community, artist and funders, funders and developers, education and public art – and the communications necessary.

Equally important, what say should the public have about the artwork to be placed in their environment? Should artists confirm or challenge expectations, record experiences or make personal interpretations of them?

Artists' agents

Oliver Bevan   Many artists who do not show regularly with a gallery believe they need an agent to place their work with galleries, negotiate good deals on their behalf, and generally promote them. While there are no end of people describing themselves as artists' agents there are virtually none who fit the above description. The nearest approximation is ironically the successful gallery which represents the artist, helps organise studio space, arranges exhibitions abroad, etc.

Books and illustrations are destined for a mass market, so the money involved can make it well worth an agent's efforts. But when the art market is saturated as it is here, there is little need for that sort of agent. Galleries receive very few approaches from agents seeking to place artists, they prefer to accept recommendations from their own stable and from critics. The graduation shows of the more prestigious post-graduate courses offer a wealth of preselected talent which can be drawn on by new and established galleries alike. Looking for an agent as a means of getting a gallery seems to be a virtual non-starter. But as a means of making some sales and getting work seen it has plenty going for it.

Which type?

The simplest definition of an agent is someone who acts on someone else's behalf. Broadly speaking they break down into two main types, 'embryo galleries' and 'active portfolios'. The former carries relatively few artists, less than twenty, and may well turn into a gallery with a clientele for your work. This kind of agency will tend to operate by putting on exhibitions and will try to keep some examples of its artists' work to show clients. The advantages over a conventional gallery are obvious: low overheads and flexibility. Disadvantages are that venues are constantly changing and lack of basic space makes it difficult to offer clients a selection of actual works to choose from. It is probably not in this kind of agency's interest to try to place its artists with other galleries.

The active portfolio concept with a hundred or more artists may have some areas of overlap with this approach. They may both put on exhibitions and be looking for the same kinds of client. One advantage to the client is the much greater selection of artists offered without any loss of personal service. The artist may make some sales and get some exposure in galleries. It is hard to discriminate between agents and other related businesses such as corporate art consultants who keep a large stock of artists' work on file. The main distinction is that their first loyalty is to their corporate clients, however interested they may be in a particular artist's work.

What kind of agent is best? It depends on your temperament. If you find it hard to promote yourself the more personal approach of the embryo gallery would probably serve you well. If you are good at promoting yourself and have several other irons in the fire, an active portfolio could be a useful additional outlet for your work. Finding agents is not easy. *Yellow Pages* is useless as the compilers have combined 'artists' and 'artistes'; there may be a few illustrators agents. The classified sections of art magazines may yield one or two but phoning some of the rentable gallery spaces is the most likely way. Placing advertising in magazines such as *Artists Newsletter* or *Arts Review* could also yield results. If you wish to undertake illustration, then consult *Artists*

see 25 • Contacts and 16 • Publicity & promotion

and Writers Year Book or the *Freelance Ilustrators Handbook*. There is at present no list of fine artists' agents.

Precautions

You should clear your mind on a number of points before consigning your work to an agent:

- **What is their track record?** A direct enquiry can cause offence but ask to see the portfolio and contact one of the artists already represented. If you loathe all the work you are probably unwise to get involved. Find out about the agent's understanding and awareness of contemporary art and its history, in which fields the agent has contacts, the length of time he/she has been trading and the success rate. There is no professional association of artists agents, anyone can set themselves up.

see 23 • Contracts

- **What is the financial agreement?** 'Tell me what you want for it and I will add my percentage' is not adequate as you need to control the price the work sells for and the price you receive. Expect to pay between 30% and 50% commission depending on how much promotion is being done. If the agent is VAT registered, VAT will be added to the selling price but will the price be quoted to buyers inclusive or exclusive of VAT? If you are not VAT registered the agent will still need to charge you VAT on their commission.

- **Will you be included in a brochure, card or catalogue?** You may be asked for money up front to do this so assess the benefits carefully.

- **Are you required to be exclusive to this agent?** My advice is to avoid exclusivity if possible because it limits your freedom. From the agents' point of view to spend energy, time and money promoting an artist only to have him/her head-hunted by a smarter outfit is very galling. A good compromise is to limit the exclusivity geographically and the period of time. Eighteen months I would regard as a maximum after which it should be reviewed annually, think ahead – if your career takes off you might need to move to a more prestigious agent or gallery and a contract restricting you could prove frustrating. Agree to some advantage for your agent if you are head-hunted, for instance 10% of proceeds from your first show with a new gallery.

- **Will you be told who has bought your work?** It is very tempting for the artist or the client to cut out the agent and deal direct. Agents quite reasonably wish to prevent this. If they go out of business taking the lists of buyers with them this can be disastrous for the artist. A compromise: the agent agrees to divulge the buyers' names and the artist agrees not to contact the buyers directly as long as the agent is representing the artist.

see 16 • Publicity & promotion To get the most out of an agent you must be prepared to put something in. Provide what is asked for, updated CV, slides of new work, delivery of work. Keep in regular contact, especially in the 'active portfolio' type of agency, where your work will spring to the agent's mind more readily because he/she is better informed about the developments in it. Many agencies are working close to the limit for a one-person business so the offer of help to hang a show or move work can be invaluable. The spin-off is likely to be an increased effort to sell your work. Unlike a gallery, with an agent you are in competition with the rest of the portfolio.

Approaching an agent

If you have located an agent whom you want to approach, the first stage is to make contact by either writing or phoning to find out whether he/she wants to take on new artists and what you should send. It is never a good idea to mail out slides without first making enquiries. If the agent wants to see slides and CV it is essential to supply an SAE. Art fairs and private views are bad occasions for flashing your slides around.

Agreement appointing an agent:

- name and Address of Agent
- detail extent of Agent's Duties: arrange and handle sales, arrange exhibitions; arrange commissions for new work, arrange documentation; arrange publicity material, press coverage; arrange residencies, workshops, lectures; licence reproduction rights
- is the Agency exclusive or can the artist appoint other agents? Is it to operate only in the UK, Europe, USA, worldwide? Can the artist make independent arrangements? Does the artist have the right to veto arrangements made by Agent?
- how is the Agent to be paid? When and on what basis?
- how is the artist to be paid? When and on what basis?
- how long is Agreement to last and is it renewable?
- how can the Agreement be terminated and what notice is required?
- how can the Agreement be altered in future?
- signed by Artist and Agent
- date.

14 • Skill sharing

Part-time teaching

Cameron Scott   For artists/designers, part-time teaching is a handy income supplement, you do not normally need a teaching certificate and it is relatively well paid. It usually only provides 36 weeks work a year, and most establishments will only employ you for twelve or less hours a week. It is risky, in that you are normally working to a week's notice, with no guarantee of employment the following year.

Employment can be for complete days, but unfortunately it is common to be offered two hours Monday, four hours Tuesday, and so forth. This, including travelling time, can drastically shorten the time left to do your own work, so try to find your own balance.

Part-time teaching at polytechnic level is now severely limited, but there is a great range and variety of teaching jobs available. Two important points to remember are that most jobs go to those who go out to find them, and it is your work being seen which normally gets you your first job.

Finding teaching

Posts are advertised in the *Times Educational* and *Higher Educational Supplements,* the Tuesday *Guardian, Artists Newsletter*, local daily, evening or weekly papers. Advertised positions are the tip of the iceberg, the majority of jobs are waiting for you to ask for them.

They occur in BA Hons, BTEC Higher Diplomas, BEds, BTEC National Diplomas in all areas of specialisation, General Art and Design, Foundation, Pre-foundation, Regional and College Diplomas, GCSE, Training and Enterprise Council, part-time day and evening classes. They mostly take place in colleges of Further Education, Schools of Art, Polytechnics, Colleges of Higher Education, Universities and Technical Colleges.

There are more possibilities. Day and evening classes for the general public covering every conceivable art area are found in colleges of further education, arts centres, community centres or schools. Other classes exist in prisons, borstals, youth clubs, WIs, community centres, hospitals, mental institutions, armed forces and galleries, in addition to weekend and holiday courses. For supply teaching in schools, you have to be teacher-trained. On the lowest pay scale is demonstrator/technician which, if you are encouraged to use your aesthetic judgement as well as your technical skills, is a good entry into teaching.

Gaining an interview

see 16 • Publicity &
publicity

This should be done by a combination of formal and informal approaches. Start with the curriculum vitae and letter of application, then follow this up with more direct methods.

The CV is to gain you an interview, so take care over it. You can send the same CV with all applications, but the letter of application needs to be slanted to the job you are applying for. Don't just repeat the CV, use it to bring out other qualities which aren't listed. For a job teaching drawing/illustration to graphic students, show you are aware of the restrictions, but excited by the creative aspects; applying to teach general drawing on a foundation course, show a willingness to work with students in all areas of specialisation. Make it short and succinct.

Interviews for part-timers are normally held towards the end of the summer term, so mail your CV and letter during May. If you are still at college, see if you can send them out through the college. Formally, your application should be sent to the Principal, who gives it to the Head of Department, who photocopies it for any interested section. Applications are pieces of paper, and pieces of paper are lost in all establishments, so mail it to the Head of Department. For complete saturation mail one to each section who might employ you. If you can find out the name of the head of section, all the better. In your mailing, include art advisors, as they often run classes, in-service training, etc.

Keep a note of who you've sent information to, and when. If you've heard nothing in a month, telephone the head of section, to whom you've applied (checking with the college telephonist for their name). This helps you pinpoint them in the future. Remind them of your application, check on developments, and keep the conversation going. Don't take no for an answer. The purpose of the phone call is to gain an interview. Browbeat the person until you gain satisfaction. Go on long enough, and they'll agree to something just to get you off the phone.

If you are told there are no jobs, ask if your folder can be looked through for future reference. If again no, ask if you can look round the department. From my own experience, it's difficult to refuse such a request. When you turn up, take your folder and, with an innocent face, say you misunderstood and usually someone will look through your folder. Use any lever you can think of to get yourself into that college.

Always ask when the college will next be looking for part-timers and if given a date make sure you follow it up. When courses start in September, there are often panics due to increased student numbers, etc so ring around again. If the college puts on exhibitions, ask to be put on the mailing list, and always turn up for private views. Be persistent.

The interview

Have your work well organised. I've been presented with a brown paper bag, out of which tumbled a dozen slides. That just lost the job. Have a good folder, and well-mounted/presented work. If you are bringing slides, telephone beforehand, ask for a projector to be set up and arrive in plenty of time to get yourself organised before the interview. Read all the college publicity, so you know what they offer. Phone up, pretending to be a potential student, and obtain details. Having done your homework, make sure you drop it into the conversation, eg 'I believe you run a two-year fashion course with a marketing option'. You are trying to impress, so impress. But not with heavy art language. Teachers are communicators, keep your answers succinct, don't ramble. Have questions prepared, eg 'What happens to your students after the course?' 'How much time do students have for drawing each week?'

If you are offered a job, accept (unless you've plenty other work), and worry about problems afterwards. Most colleges can re-arrange times, but ask about that the day you start. Accept even if it's low level work, it's another line on your CV. Accept, it may lead to other, better work. Accept, it pays your bills.

Other possibilities

If you have something particular to offer, perhaps a one-off lecture or a particular technical demonstration, which is out of the normal order of things, circulate this information. Not as part of your letter of application, but by a separate mailing. Funding in colleges, for special lectures, is often separate from the part-time budget, so a department unable to offer part-time teaching may be able to offer you the odd lecture.

Starting

If you have gained a part-time teaching position, it's probably because you were one of the better students when you were at college, and it's easy to think all students will be much like you – wanting to work and willing to work. But it doesn't always work out that way. Remember back to your own training, the lazy ones, the poor ones, the ones thrown off the course. You have to deal with all types and levels of ability and dedication.

This will be particularly true of part-time day and evening classes, where you may have to teach a 50-year old who last did art at secondary school, to the person who has attended classes for years and can teach you more about watercolours than you can teach them; and you may not have other staff around to discuss the problems with.

It takes more than an ability and an enthusiasm for your subject to be able to teach it well. You have to be willing to work hard with your students, accept all you try will not work, be frustrated by the talented student who won't work for you, and be annoyed by the pair who never stop gossiping.

One of the problems you will encounter is discipline. Whether to be friendly or strict. It's nice to be liked, but you are there to teach and often it's necessary to impose strict discipline to achieve results, and students at all levels will attempt to take advantage of you.

There is also stage fright when facing a group for the first time, and having to make yourself understood. You will have to adjust your teaching to the level you are teaching, which can be difficult, when you are teaching more than one level. There is also the problem of continuity, resulting from only seeing a group once a week, and not being able to keep contact with what else the students have been doing.

However, when you pin the group's work on the wall for the crit, and you see the students have learned from you, and are willing and able to talk about their work, teaching is great. I wish that always happened, but it doesn't, so be prepared for elation but also disillusionment.

Running your own classes

Oliver Bevan Traditionally part-time teaching used to support struggling artists, but as cuts in art education have removed all hope of steady part-time teaching in art schools numbers of artists have initiated their own teaching programmes either in their studios or in rented classrooms. The main problem is getting started, or to be more precise finding students prepared to pay an unsubsidised fee, especially if they are used to local authority rates.

Advertising

see 16 • Publicity & promotion It only works if you stick at it which can prove rather expensive. I had a few shots at different advertising, in *The Guardian, Harpers/Queen, The Artist, The RA Magazine,* and local papers. Repeated ads in *The Artist* produced replies and an occasional take-up. One-offs produced virtually no reaction. This can be a major drain on resources unless you have a very unusual skill which is in demand or a visually stunning location for

**Workshop in progress at Oliver
Bevan's London studio.**

the course. It is worth emphasising the technical aspect of your teaching as this is what most people believe they need.

Poaching

Some classes are built on a nucleus of students from a local authority class or a summer school. If you can teach on a summer school or residential course, students with whom you relate well may come to your own sessions. You can pay back the school by recommending it to your class.

Leap frogging

This worked best for me. I contacted 'friends' organisations and offered to raise money by doing workshops in my studio for their membership, a percentage of the takings going back to the organisation. Modern art history courses are often interested in providing some practical experience for students. Some local authority galleries have friends organisations and may be glad of a new activity to offer.

Premises

see 17 • A place
to work
If you have a large studio in which you can house the class they will appreciate your willingness to share and it will become one of the attractions of your teaching. If your studio is small you may be able to rent a room on an hourly basis from a local school, something they are keen to do now with the change over to self-management. The best way to locate an empty art room is through your local adult education centre. Many schools are used for adult education in the evenings and some let rooms over weekends to adult groups. Check its suitability carefully, particularly if you are going to work with messy or dangerous substances. Art rooms and labs are the most suitable. Without running water it is useless.

Students

Teaching paying students in your own studio is very different from school or art college. They can simply get up and go leaving a hole in your wallet. Another danger is someone who drives you mad or fails to get on with the rest, which does not matter for a one-day workshop but can be quite destructive over a whole term. Students of this kind usually select themselves out, but occasionally this does not happen and you find a bad atmosphere developing. Prevention is better than cure. Make sure all new students are aware the first six weeks or so is probationary. This can be included in a studio code of practice.

You will need plenty of tact when criticising work to avoid deflating and damaging egos. People do not do their best work as a result of being cut down to size; rather the reverse, they thrive on a blend of encouragement and frankness. If you can identify the positive qualities first and then indicate what factors are undermining those positives, then constructive criticism has taken place. Although this is the obvious way to proceed as a teacher, it seems to have escaped the notice of many lecturers in art colleges.

Studio code of practice

Everyone should read and agree to abide by this list of requirements which should cover:

- payment – including deposits, refunds and cancellations
- materials – stating what if any are included in the fee and whether others are available to purchase at the studio
- safety – where to put bags and other luggage, maintaining unobstructed gangways, dealing with used white spirit and other chemicals
- clearing up procedure – what you expect of each student
- emergency – location of First Aid Box, fire extinguisher, getting out in case of fire, nearest telephone.

Monitor

When you have established the class to some degree you may need a helper, to set up, clear up, even collect fees. The trustee principle is excellent. Offer a student a special rate, eg half fees, to take on the role.

Mailshots

There will be occasions when you wish to contact all current and ex-students. A visitors book signed by all students coming to one-day workshops and short courses is invaluable. Mailshots are cheaper than advertising and much better targeted. I send out a newsletter at intervals with brief information on forthcoming workshops, exhibitions by members and myself, changes to the premises, fees, etc. With this go detailed sheets about projects and if possible a postcard. These written texts need careful editing; they are selling documents and must be succinct, lively and positive.

Insurance

see 22 • Insurance Public liability insurance is essential and can be tacked onto an existing studio policy for relatively little extra. It cannot generally be taken out as a separate policy.

Safety

see 18 • Health & safety and 26 • Further reading It is your responsibility to run a studio which complies with the Health and Safety Legislation. To do this you must produce a COSHH assessment. This is a major subject in its own right and I suggest you refer to *Artists Handbooks: Health & Safety* by Tim Challis and Gary Roberts published by AN Publications.

Fees

see 11 • Project planning & fundraising An economic level for you must take into account lean periods, hire of models, insurance premiums, and quarterly bills and advertising. It will probably fall between three and five pounds per hour. Deposits in order to reserve a place on a course, and full payment in advance are recommended to discourage late cancellations.

In conclusion

I am recommending something like the traditional atelier approach to teaching, and if you are able to work alongside your students, the atmosphere is unrivalled. I would not worry about over-influence because you will either have this effect by being charismatic or you may enjoy and promote diversity. The early years will be hard going; it took me four years to generate anything like a living wage from my classes. Word of mouth at that point takes over as the main method of recruitment. I have found teaching my own classes very rewarding and much preferable to the power plays and anxieties about the future that have to be endured in art college, or the constant battle to maintain discipline in school.

Running holiday courses

Sharon McKee Some artists are now setting up and running their own painting holidays to subsidise their practice.

It is an option to consider if you have the knowledge and ability to teach others, feel able to arrange a holiday people would enjoy and even want to come back to another year, and have access to suitable facilities. People who take up the offer of a holiday with painting tuition included are more likely to be amateur than professional artists and traditional picturesque landscapes could be a prerequisite.

see 16 • Publicity & promotion

When you first set up the most important consideration will be to advertise. Make sure you budget for the cost of publicity. You can advertise in a number of publications, it's best to start off with artist-aimed ones such as *Artists Newsletter, The Artist* or *Arts Review,* before taking it a step further and trying the nationals, such as *The Guardian* on a Monday.

It is usually a matter of trial and error more than anything else to determine which publications get the most response from your advertisements. It is worthwhile scattering half a dozen ads in different types of publications before deciding which ones to use regularly – ask the people who enquire about your course where they saw your advert.

To be able to cope with teaching perhaps a different group of people every week you have to enjoy other people's company. You will have to plan exactly what you are able to offer: accommodation, meals, materials, studio space, gallery visits, specialist tutoring, etc. Not all of these will be expected to be included, it depends what sort of service you want to give. Painters could be expected to take their own materials, but have a small stock of materials available to buy if they need to. This is the most practical choice if you are just setting up holidays for the first time – if you invest in a large stock of materials to have available 'just in case' you could find yourself stuck with them, and out of pocket at the end of the season.

If you don't want to start to start running a hotel type of business, try arranging accommodation nearby with the price included in the package.

Pricing

Check around already established painting holidays to see what they are charging and what the price includes. The average in this country is between £150-£250 per person per week, depending on what sort of deal it actually is.

If you are renting out holiday accommodation prices should be based on local bed and breakfast houses or small hotels, with extra charges for such things as evening meals, studio space, tutorial sessions, etc.

You may want to just offer your teaching services and leave the decision of finding accommodation up to the visitor, in which case you should work out an hourly rate based on private tutoring fees. In this case you could try advertising at local tourist facilities, such as information and advice centres, local hotels, B&Bs, and in tourist information packs.

If you are going to offer to arrange the accommodation and include the price in the package, you may be able to strike up some kind of deal with local hoteliers, with a discount on charges for supplying them with custom, or you may know someone local who would be willing and has the room to take on small groups of people throughout the summer.

Whatever type of activity you decide to arrange, always work out a realistic price based on the extra costs you will incur and remember to consider your profit margin.

Before you decide that summer holidays are the ideal money making scheme for you, talk to someone who has already done it, then you can learn by their mistakes.

Sessional work

Lee Corner Extra-mural teaching, running classes with the WEA, working on projects in hospitals or with the probation service, involvement with any educational activity not linked to a recognised course is 'sessional work'.

All this and undervalued too

A number of reasons are given for the growth in sessional work opportunities over the past few years. Some put it down to the demise of teaching opportunities for visual artists – the traditional 'earner' allowing time to pursue private studio practice; some suggest changes in the nature of arts funding resulting in fewer direct grants and bursaries and more demands to prove arts organisations' commitment to accessibility; others might cite a growing political awareness and a desire amongst artists to join the struggle for cultural democracy through collective or collaborative creativity.

Whether the work takes place with the youth service, the regional arts board, community groups, or local colleges, the pitfalls are potentially enormous. Unless the worker has a clear understanding of the work to be undertaken – both in planning and execution – and a negotiated contract, at the very least they could be asking for trouble.

At worst, sessional art workers have no entitlement to employment protection rights and no job security. They are vulnerable, open to exploitation, and undervalued. The work can result from someone else's administrative accountability ('But we've got to have something in the rural areas'); a needy public relations exercise; or free publicity for the host organisation. Above all the arts worker will probably be someone's way of expressing an accessibility policy.

At best, being a sessional worker can create new challenges; give opportunities to explore new methods of working; be freedom from

Children with photograms from a workshop run by Debbie Humphry at a community centre.
Photo: Debbie Humphry
© Photofusion

isolation. It can allow the development of personal skills and the possibility of engaging with others. It can create opportunity for contact with isolated communities – people with mental disabilities, those in prison, elderly people. Above all, sessional workers are paid as artists – not teachers or therapists, but artists.

'I was waiting for the bus after the first session in the hospital and I suddenly thought 'God I'm an artist' and for the last two years I'd just been unemployed or on the dole and suddenly I was getting money for being an artist. It gave me self-respect.' Bryn Jayes

Many of the problems are a result not only of the spasmodic nature of the work, but also the range of employment/employers.

Therapy?
There are often misunderstandings about the nature of work with people with special needs, and one of these is due directly to the looseness with which the word 'therapy' is bandied about.

Most people involved with this area would reject the notion of providing therapy for clear reasons: art therapy is a professional specialisation, though the art therapist may have initially pursued a fine art training s/he has chosen to pursue a career as a therapist, attained appropriate academic qualifications, found full or part-time employment in an institution, become part of a treatment team, and is concerned with 'the totality of the patient – the history, family, immediate problems, goals of treatment, etc.'

The encouragement of personal creativity, which results from a belief that everyone has a creative potential, is a prime factor in much sessional work. The aim is often to facilitate creative and artistic activity with a view to redressing the imbalances of power, influence and decision-making, which tend to be present in many establishments. The arts are thus contributing to more developed self-awareness and self-confidence, and a voice for those who are generally disenfranchised.

While there may be overlaps in the practice of art therapists and sessional arts workers the distinctions will probably lie in the perceived goals, the approach and the relationship which is developed.

Approaches

Throughout the areas available to sessional workers there is an enormous potential for artists to initiate their own projects. Such initiatives might range from an artist noticing the local elderly persons' home, going in for a chat, coming away with an idea for a project, and contacting the local social services, healthcare organisation or even RAB, to put forward the idea. Over the last ten years much of this sessional work has taken place through the Shape/Art Link network. It is not helpful to make generalisations about Shape/Art Link services and the best advice is to make contact with the local coordinator.

It is important to note most arts organisations positively welcome such approaches as they are always looking for ways of developing work and new initiatives are crucial to this. While, in the case of some RABs particularly, the red-tape and paperwork might appear off-putting, it must be remembered these organisations have a specific brief based on the accessibility of the arts and an idea from a potential sessional worker will, generally, be listened to.

see 11 • Project planning & fundraising Alternatively, artists might group together, advertise their skills and undertake sessional contracts suited to particular skills but coordinated through the group. While this might be the ideal, most sessional arts workers are isolated individuals.

Feedback

It is important to emphasise a particularly positive aspect of sessional arts workers. The nature of the relationship between the worker and the group is frequently supposed to be one-way, you feed them. Experience would forcefully prove the contrary. The relationship is two-way at the very least. Artists find that their own practice, ideas, methods and perceptions are equally influenced by the group and this cannot be denied. This may be temporary and technical, *'Seeing the success of the members of the group using the monoprint method, I have for the present postponed my work concerned with etching to produce a selection of images by this process'*, Les Hickinbottom. Or to do with changed perceptions, *'I was already tackling the problems of making work which is accountable beyond the inward criteria of the studio or gallery but the naïvity in which the patients approach their painting has refreshed my attitude to my own work. Whether this shows in my pictures as much as I would like, I do not know, but it is important for me,'* Bryn Jayes.

'On the face of it there is no reason why any arts project should work in an institution, a hospital, prison, probation centre, or whatever.

The participants come together in a strange environment to share in an activity that, while being the project's raison d'être, has very different definitions and associations for all involved. For the artists it is a total activity evolving out of time spent at college and further years developing the private studio practice necessary to secure a firm basis for their continued involvement in that activity. For the others it is often an activity that carries with it dim recollections of childhood and of being at school. An activity that as they get older they feel less qualified to take part in or even voice an opinion on.

But these projects are successful and each time success is different and unique to that particular project and group of people. Why? I don't think I know. But in the project at St Matthews we found ourselves in a position to strip the Art out of art and recognise we were not making 'works of art'. What we were making instead were evidences of shared activity where the stamping individuality on inert materials was more important than gilt frames and pedestals.

For me there has been the opportunity to learn from the easy, inventive responses people make when faced with new materials and processes, and my present work is as it is because I have been privileged to see those responses.

For the other participants their success is that in a setting that is inherently anonymous they have found a means of expression, a voice, that is both individual and collective.' David Patten

15 • Abroad

Brian Baker Opportunities for makers and artists to work internationally are varied but all require considerable self-motivation and perseverance. For the more established there are possibilities of public commissions or major exhibitions leading to sales. With dubious economic sense of working outside the UK, a difficult balance of enterprise and caution is called for.

Barbara Taylor's tale of craftspeople losing more than they could afford when taking part in the Californian British Art Fair in Orange County in 1990 (*Artists Newsletter,* May 91) is salutary. Lots of people do travel and exchange, however, though often long-running personal contacts within a city or country are probably essential.

Oxford-based Helen Ganly had been travelling to the old Czecho-Slovakia and contacting dissident artists for years when this led to a chance to lecture in Poland, at an independent symposium at Przemysl, near the Czech border. This led to a workshop symposium in the last months of communist rule with free board and lodging along with charitable support for travel. By 1990 independent artists used former communist-controlled facilities for the autumn symposium. Visiting artists stayed in a small hotel and worked in a 16th century castle.

Ganly found selling work in Poland is uneconomic. Also the down side of the changes has been the closure of small galleries and loss of studios as rents rise. Whilst working in Poland Ganly makes work which she exhibits there and later sells elsewhere. It is difficult to achieve viability. Recently, some resources obtained from the Government enabled the symposium to be held with living costs and studio space for visiting artists provided but again they had to pay their own fares.

Glasgow-based sculptor Jim Buckley was one of 17 artists who travelled at the end of the 1990 Year of Culture on officially-organised exchanges in which the base costs were met out of the Festival budget. Buckley went to Odense in Denmark for three months at the beginning of 1991. The scheme, which continues, is reciprocal. It was better funded than most. Buckley had accommodation and studio costs covered and also £150 a week income for living costs. He says he made a lot of work

Exodus, Helen Ganly,
installation, Krasiczyn Castle,
Poland, 1991

and spent much time in the library doing research. 'Basically the exchange was for the benefit of the artist. I was fairly reclusive and enjoyed the freedom of having time to work'.

The 1990 exchanges were arranged at short notice by administrator Amanda Brown, of Glasgow DC, who is attempting to establish longer lead-up times on future reciprocal arrangements. She points out that great care is needed on delineating what is required so the necessary facilities are ready for the arriving artist.

Brown has set up a system by which selection of artists for the exchanges is normally made by the receiving town or organisation from slides and written statements. She points out Glasgow is unusual in its network of artists' organisations and with many countries she needs to work through the official galleries to unlock resources and facilities.

Margaret Tietze and Christine Kinsey visited Philadelphia in 1991 as a result of an exchange exhibition set up between the Muse

Lorna Green, *The Doors Are Open...*, 1991 Doors/bricks. "Das andere Gedächtnis". Kampnagel, Hambrug, Germany

Cooperative there and the Wales 75 group. Tietze was influenced by the work she saw and the artists she met, Kinsey more so.

Chris Kinsey's work features images drawn from her South Wales roots. Her confidence in this approach was enhanced by her time in Philadelphia where she found the themes she explored were universal and connected with the work of other women artists.

The work of ten artists based in Wales was shipped to Philadelphia for a mixed media exhibition in the summer. In September the show went to a small gallery in Bethlehem. Tietze and Kinsey went over twice and conducted workshops and delivered lectures. Funding was obtained from the Welsh Arts Council and charities but the exchange could only go ahead after Tietze secured support for shipping the work. Grislex, a local company, exports to Pennsylvania and agreed to ship out the work with one of their consignments as a public relations gesture. Getting the work back was the final piece in the jigsaw, resolved when the British American Arts Association persuaded the US section of the British Council to provide the necessary £600. As with most ventures, full costs were not covered. Kinsey used accommodation provided by the Muse Cooperative, Tietze has family in Philadelphia.

In retrospect, Tietze believes more should have been done from Wales to promote the show. It's a mistake to assume hosts and contacts will organise this. Sales of work might have been greater with more advance publicity.

Sculptor Lorna Green has realised several large-scale site specific works around the world. In 1990 she made a piece 'The Doors are Open' associated with a conference in Hamburg. About women artists, the piece also reflected the political changes in Germany. Manchester-based Green went twice to the city at the University of Hamburg's expense, once for a week to make the installation, and then for the conference, at which she gave a talk based on her research into women sculptors in the UK.

Green's rule of thumb on such international ventures is that the package available must at least fully cover all outgoings. She has found new work often follows on. Her Hamburg work led to a commission for Leeds University in association with a conference there on artists and art historians. Again, she spoke at the conference.

In 1988 her work at an International Sculpture conference in Ireland led to an invitation to a month's residency at Perth Institute of Contemporary Art. Whilst in Australia Green gave lectures and made work. Subsequently, her experience there has informed the span of her lecturing to students here on visiting fellowships.

Lorna Green emphasises the importance of language in working across boundaries. '*I speak French and some German and my school Latin helps too. It is crucial artists get their act together with languages.*'

International trips can generate momentum for major follow-up. Tacita Dean won a student exchange to Greece in 1987 which led on to a scholarship the following year, an opportunity to take studio space and exhibit the work she made there at a small Athens gallery. She sold most of the work, important since her permit did not allow her to take paid work in Greece. Her friend, painter Sarah Wicks, established contacts with several Greek artists through visits in the late 1980s.

This led to the two initiating an ambitious project to set up a UK/Greece exhibition exchange. The shows will take place in 1993 if the final elements of the package, which has already attracted sponsorship – including free travel for all the artists from Thompsons Holidays – are put in place. Mainly younger contemporary artists reflecting most disciplines, the exhibition of Greek artists in Britain, which may tour, will also include work specially made by Lizzie Calligas and George Lepass.

Deborah Gardner spent 12 months in Australia. A British Council scholarship and grants from Northern Arts and Newcastle University got her there with enough money for three months. Tyne & Wear-based Gardner says she took it 'step by step' after her April 1990 arrival. '*I was mainly in Victoria. I got paid for working in art colleges and obtained some residencies, mainly in schools*'. She had organised some in advance. Contacts in local artists associations led to an invitation to use studio space near Melbourne and she also made some commissioned work for an education authority.

Heather Eastes **and** Jenny Fell**,**
Jug – Rites of Passage
Libations
Photo: Stephen Reader

Aberystwyth-based Jenny Fell and Heather Eastes participation in Dusseldorf's year-long 'art in unexpected places' was made possible by Eastes' repute and contacts in Germany. Fell made three clay vessels which Eastes decorated in sgraffito. They were placed for a month in the main Hofgarten Park.

Dusseldorf municipality contributed resources to all artists and the Welsh Arts Council paid £500 for Eastes and Fell's travel. Eastes, who used to live in Dusseldorf, had a solo exhibition there in 1992.

For printmaker and ceramicist Fell it was a first public work. During the month the pieces were in Hofgarten Park the artists had to act as security to make sure they weren't stolen. They transported the work by car. For Fell 'the whole experience was good because it opened my eyes to public art being accepted and to seeing people's reactions. In the park they picked the pieces up, in a gallery the public are intimidated'.

Delphine Barraclough was commissioned to photograph the Vietnamese community in Paris. She applied for Prince's Trust support after working with the Vietnamese community in London and having had the idea of a project in mind for several months.

She was in Paris for a month spending most of her time tracking people down, following up leads, and talking with people to win their confidence. She reflects she actually spent little time behind the lens. The £1000 award covered her travel and day to day living expenses. Her accommodation was free as she stayed with friends and she did all her processing and printing back in London. There was a small amount left over which she treated as her 'wages' though this would not have been so had she been paying for a room.

Workshop by Karen Rann **with students from the Academy of Applied Arts, Budapest, May 1991**
Photo: Karen Rann

As the work was done specifically for the communities there is no sales income from it. Barraclough says, *'It improved my profile. After I came back I was pleased that new contacts got in touch with me as a result.'* Her work was exhibited in London subsequently.

Another 1991 beneficiary of the Prince's Trust's Richard Mills Travel Fellowships was installation/performance artist Karen Rann. Utilising the £1000 from the Trust and a second award, £250 from the Henrietta Bowder Fellowship, Rann was in Budapest for eight weeks.

She was fortunate to be able to secure free studio space over the Tolgyfa Gallery. This was used by the art college for teaching and was available since none takes place during the weeks before exams or, of course, during holidays. Rann reports that in future such spaces may have to be rented out to bring in much-needed income to the College.

Rann held workshops with students during her stay, which culminated in a performance piece on her last day. Her connections with Hungarian artists were established when she gave workshops a few years ago at a European Architectural Students Assembly in Turin.

During her summer's work, Rann, whose work is all time-based, secured an exhibition which took place in January at the Dorottya Street Gallery in Budapest. The invitation to have her own show arose from meeting the gallery director who liked her approach.

Karen Rann is able to avoid transport costs as her installations are small enough for her to take as hand luggage. During her time back in Budapest in January she had a free flat which is at the Gallery's disposal. The exhibition led to her receiving a commission from the German government for a piece for their embassy in Budapest.

She says that in many East European countries it is easier for institutions to pay in kind with flats, materials and studios than in currency. She, however, on both trips, was able to earn enough in cash from running workshops to cover her living costs. Hull-based Rann is due to return to Budapest later in 1992 on a British Council studentship for nine months. With flat and studio provided she will support herself through commissions and workshops. She points out that the lengthy delays in finalising these arrangements pose problems to artists in negotiations for other work here.

16 • Publicity & promotion

Susan Jones with additional material by **David Butler**

If you want your work to get the recognition it deserves, promotion and publicity need to become as important as making the work itself. Promoting yourself and producing publicity needs to be done on a regular basis, rather than left until the last minute. It is a good idea to take advice from other artists or organisations. Perhaps you can share their mailing lists and contacts and collaborate.

Of the overall budget of £25,000 for an artweek in 1992, around £9,000 went on publicity. This included a one-colour A1 folded programme describing all events and activities, with 20,000 printed costing £2,000. It was circulated through existing arts mail-shots, libraries, tourist information centres and through their own direct mail shot from compiling a mailing list on database to use for that and future events. General and specific press releases produced on a word processor plus an information pack for press and media cost in the region of £2,000, and a 40-page illustrated catalogue with a full-colour cover was sponsored to the value of £5,000. A public relations firm's in-kind sponsorship was to organise the opening preview and party, which gained the event coverage on TV and local newspapers.

The most important points to decide when setting out to promote or publicise are:
• who are you trying to attract?
• what is the most effective way to do so?

Although there may seem to be a standard format for publicity which can be applied every time, each situation really needs individual attention. You need to:

• plan in advance
• decide which groups you want to attract – business people, schools, private collectors, tourists, etc – and direct the majority of your publicity at those 'target groups'
• decide on your budget for publicity and examine each item you propose for cost-effectiveness
• don't under-estimate the value of free publicity – which comes from sending press releases and good photographs to local, regional and national press and media, or to the specialist visual arts, crafts and media magazines.

Pre-planning and awareness of the time-scales of those who can help is the cornerstone to success. If your role is to raise money for the project as well as to publicise it once set up, you may need to allow as long as a year to promote a small to medium-scale project properly.

To coincide with taking her work with other British makers to the Frankfurt Trade Fair, textile artist Erica Just produced an attractive information pack to give to prospective buyers and commissioners over there and at home. Her slightly larger than A5 size wallet-type folder was printed in one colour, with her name and artform on the front with a line drawing demonstrating the types of images she weaves. The inside folded over face contained a statement about the processes she uses in her work and the relationship between her paintings and woven works. The back face gave a CV detailing her qualifications, exhibitions, awards, where her work had been published plus a list of forthcoming exhibitions. The separate leaflet inside, with colour image on the front and a picture of herself and statement on the back, was printed in three languages to make it suitable for the trade fair. The folder is a container for a selection of colour postcards and the contents can be varied according to circumstances.

Make a schedule of who you need to contact and when, so you don't miss an important deadline.

- If you are using publicity to raise awareness and funds for a project, make sure you know who to approach and how long each organisation will take to reach decisions about giving money.
- To gain national publicity, you'll need to circulate colour and black and white images and information at least six months in advance for glossy magazines, quarterly journals and specialist periodicals or if you are seeking a 'feature' on a TV arts programme.
- For regional publicity, allow at least three months in advance to gain coverage in monthly publications and What's On guides.
- For local newspapers and radio, make an initial contact around a month in advance to get an editorial feature or interview; listings can be left until ten days in advance.
- If you pay for advertising, you are more likely to get editorial coverage in the art press.
- It may be fruitful to go out and meet some of your 'target' audience 'face-to-face' to encourage involvement and support for your project; this could include visits to schools, business clubs, etc.

Where, when?

Once you have a clear 'picture' of who you want to attract, the words and images you choose should acknowledge their interests and needs. Make sure, therefore, that your publicity tells the recipient WHO, WHAT, WHERE, WHEN?.

There is a 'rule', the AIDA rule, for making sure your copy covers everything needed:

- it should ATTRACT – so that it will get noticed
- it should INFORM – so the audience knows who, what, when and where
- it should create DESIRE – should be persuasive
- it should induce ACTION – tell them what you want them to do and when.

Spend time writing the words. Get specialist help, especially if you plan to produce an expensive colour brochure. 'Art jargon' is very off-putting. Phrases like 'issue-based site-specific work' mean very little to most people. Try reading the words out to someone in your family or to friends who don't have an art background.

- keep the text short and clear
- send different press releases over a period of time, to gather momentum for a project or to emphasise different aspects of it
- don't send too much material – try opening the envelope to see how it feels to receive the publicity material. Paper-clipping the covering letter to the other items so they are read in the right order is more likely to get the recipient's attention
- with a group event or exhibition, rather than sending out a CV for each person, write a summary with a few sentences about everyone
- end your press release with *'Please contact... if you need more information.'* Give a day-time telephone number and say when you can be contacted – eg Monday-Thursday, 10-4.

Follow-up

Because people who are interested invariably follow up by telephone, all publicity items should include:

- telephone number
- contact name
- any restrictions on contact.

Anticipate the following:

- if the press arranges to call: is there something or someone to photograph, and someone to talk about the work or project?
- if you are only available at specific times or days do you need to borrow or invest in an answering machine to receive messages?
- if you have been writing to sponsors and some are interested to discuss a project further, do you feel happy about having a meeting with people who may know little about art and who will want you to 'sell' them the idea?

Building contacts

If you regularly deal with publicity and promotion for visual arts projects, try to build up and keep up-to-date an annotated 'contacts' list on index cards. Having a 'named person' on a mailing list can save considerable time and energy when you start to follow up press releases, etc.

If possible, put your mailing list on to a word processor to give you sticky address labels and personalised letters for other promotions. If you store only names and addresses on a computer for your own personal use, you don't need to register under the Data Protection Act.

Your events are more likely to be successful if they don't coincide with others aimed at the audience you wish to attract. If you cooperate with other organisers or groups in your area this will help to ensure that:

- you are not overlapping on dates
- you save money by sharing mail out and/or print costs, eg complementary programmes or events can be linked for press purposes, ie three solo exhibitions could be described as a mini 'visual arts and crafts festival'
- you aren't trying to raise funds for projects from the same firms or sponsors at the same time, or anticipating using the same facilities at the same time as other groups.

Documentation

It is essential to document your work throughout the year as the visual description of your work forms the basis of all your publicity and promotion.

- **Slides** – are essential for applications to regional arts boards, agencies, to put into specialist indexes and to send to glossy magazines. They need to be good-quality and to do your work justice. Alternatively, use a photographer experienced in documenting visual arts work who has been recommended by other artists or galleries. When sending slides off, rather than sending them in boxes, put them into plastic slide pages in your presentation folder – see next section. Colour photocopiers can take slides, and enlarged colour copies can also be added to your folder.
- **Black and white photographs** – are invaluable to send to the art press and local newspapers. If you take your own, combine it with the colour slide taking, by borrowing another camera!

- **Colour prints** – can be presented in folders and colour photo-copied for display purposes. Laminated colour prints or photo-copies are a relatively inexpensive way of putting information on a gallery wall.
- **Media documentation** – it can be useful to document participatory projects on video or film, where images and sound track can be used to put over a complete picture of what happened. A video can be shown at future exhibitions or other events.

Publicity items

A visual arts partnership, in response to an increasing demand for information about their work, produced a full-colour A3 folded to A5 leaflet/poster describing their overall philosophy and approach to art in public as well as illustrations of completed performances and sculpture. The cost of £2,000 for 3,000 brochures was 50% funded by a regional arts board grant for publicity to assist arts businesses. It has been distributed through a paid-for mail-shot in a book related to their field of work, at conferences and seminars and is also used to send to general enquirers. They see the brochure as a way of raising their 'credibility rating' and gaining new work from public and private sector clients.

Publicity items can be employed under two broad headings:

Promoting you, your work, your services

- brochure or leaflet – ideally with colour or good black and white examples of work, outline of experience and background, price lists, charges for services, etc
- covering letter – publicity material is more likely to be read if accompanied by a letter, to personalise the approach and give you a chance to say something of particular interest to the person receiving it
- presentation folder – photographs of your work need to be well-presented and self-explanatory. A plastic-sleeved A4 folder is ideal for presenting photographs, press cuttings, statements and other relevant information for an interview or meeting
- press release to mark a specific occasion – the launch of a business, the making of new work or offer to run workshops

Promoting an event

- poster – the size, image and text will depend on whom you wish to attract
- press release – be aware of the difference in emphasis and language between specialist magazines and local press
- invitation card or letter to specific number of identified people to come to the launch of an exhibition, commission, première of a media production or residency

IOU Theatre produced a single-colour folded leaflet for 'Boundary', a series of performances in Bradford. The front, containing their logo, the title of the performance, an interesting descriptive paragraph and the venue's logo and address contained two intriguing head images related to the 'disembodied heads' mentioned in the text. Inside was additional information with a border of provoking images of faces, bodies and hands. The back had a brief history of the company, a further invitation to come to the performances, and an excellent quote on their work from *City Limits.* It also contained contact address and telephone number along with five sponsors logos.

The leaflet was also designed to be folded down (instructions printed on it) into a 'game' in which the inside images would appear from under flaps!

- information sheet to accompany an event – catalogue/sheet with prices or background material for an exhibition; information on techniques, materials, sources for a commission, background to a residency, etc
- leaflet to publicise a specific event, either sent out through the post or picked up in libraries, galleries, information centres, etc
- photographs – black and white and colour, of current and previous pieces to promote your work to potential clients, exhibition organisers, press and media, funders or sponsors.

Note, however, that personal contact and word-of-mouth are often the most effective ways to attract local interest and to gain press coverage of arts events.

Curriculum vitae

A curriculum vitae (CV) is a basic tool for promotion and is usually varied according to the circumstances in which it is used. You may need to accentuate some aspects of your experience or play down others. A CV, which must be typed, generally contains:

- name
- address – including postcode
- telephone number – day and evening and, if you haven't a telephone, give a contact number for urgent messages
- date of birth – only if you want to give it
- nationality
- education – show qualifications and awards
- other professional qualifications
- experience – past projects and activities; this section can be adjusted to emphasise your eligibility for the job, commission or other opportunity
- awards
- personal statement about your work and enthusiasms – only write this if you feel you can do it well!

If you can arrange it, get your CV put onto a word processor so it can be easily updated and altered for different applications. Although a CV tends to be presented as a typed sheet with headings for name, address, age, qualifications, exhibitions, awards, commissions and other related work, some artists prefer to turn the material into two or three paragraphs which can be used on the back of a postcard, on a press release or on an introductory panel on a gallery wall. For example:

Lesley Hicks was born in Cleveland in 1964 and studied painting at Newcastle University and the Royal Academy Schools, graduating in 1989. She has shown work in a number of group shows including at the Hatton Gallery Newcastle University, Robinson College Cambridge University and the 'Art for Schools' exhibition in Leicestershire in 1989.

Prizes include the John Christie Prize for Painting 1983, the David Murray Landscape Scholarship in 1989, the Richard Ford Travel Award to Madrid in 1989 and a Northern Arts Travel Award to Bulgaria in 1991.

Recent commissions have been for Ocean & Transport and Trading plc and several temporary and permanent murals in schools and community settings in Sunderland where she now has a studio with Sunderland Artists Group.

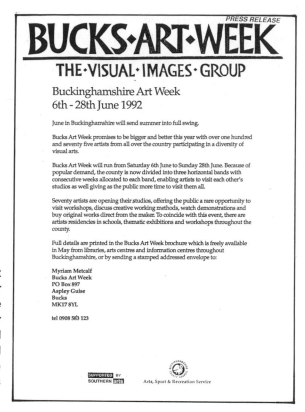

This press release was sent out in a Bucks Art Week folder and with black and white photographs. Organiser Myriam Metcalf sent additional information on request, and had an anwering machine to take messages whilst she was out.

Press release

The wording of a press release should be composed according to the interests and priorities of local, regional, national and specialist press. Journalists make considerable use of press releases, and the free coverage they can give you is definitely worth getting! To find out what interests a newspaper or magazine, read it. Basic research at the library or WH Smith should tell you who covers visual arts and where their interest lies; the average length of an article or news story; what sort of photos they use; whether they interview or just reprint press releases. When writing a press release:

- keep it short – no more than one side of an A4 page
- choose your paper type and colour, type face and layout to reflect the standards and quality of your own art work
- choose an 'angle' to attract the press – human interest for local press, or techniques and materials for the specialists, perhaps your international links, etc for the nationals

- follow the AIDA rule
- send photographs where possible as visual art and craft work is poorly represented in words alone
- make sure it tells the press WHO, WHAT, WHERE, WHEN with contact name and telephone number, as most journalists follow up by telephone.

Photographs

When sending out photographs choose the most appropriate images for each audience. The local press like 'human interest' images and may wish to send their own photographer. (If they do, don't be manipulated into allowing images to be made which you are not happy with.) The art press prefers photos of the work itself. Colour magazines like photographs of the work and of the artist.

- Send images in the right format: black and white glossy prints to the press, colour slides for glossy magazines and supplements. Check the size required – 35mm, 2"x2", 5"x4", etc. If you haven't got what they want send what you have, try to get their interest and then see what you can work out. It is pointless commissioning large format transparencies if they are not going to be used.
- Photos should be of good quality and in focus. Slide images can be improved. If a slide of a 2D work shows a lot of background around the edges, block out unwanted areas by sticking opaque tape on the back of the slide. The difference can be striking.
- Slide indexes require 35mm colour slides. Some may also keep photographs, so ask about sending these too. If applying for an award, residency, commission, exhibition, etc you will usually be responding to specific instructions – eg 'send ten 35mm colour slides of recent work, include two details'. Do what it asks. If you send slides when they want photographs they may not look at your work. If you only have slides don't rush out and commission someone to photograph your work again.
  Colour and black & white photographs can be made from slides and vice versa, though quality can vary enormously.
- Photos should be clearly labelled with 'this way up', the name of the artist, title of work, medium, size, date made and any credit for photographer and a return address. Indicate if it is a detail of a work. Don't write on the photo itself, use a sticky label on the back. Have labels printed up with standard information and add what is pertinent to each photo. It is very important that this information is

Full-colour printed postcards are often used as general publicity material. To print 1,000 costs around £120. The back should contain a caption and the maker's name, address and telephone number. Postcards can be sold through galleries and art bookshops, given out as an alternative 'business card', and also included with other material in an 'information pack' tailored to suit specific purposes. The backs can be overprinted to announce exhibitions, events, open studios or performances. Illustrated is Paddy Killer's *Il Rinascimento*, printed to coincide with an exhibition but used as general publicity and to sell with other exhibitions afterwards.

stuck on the back of the photo and not sent with it. Separate sheets of paper are easily lost – then your photo will be wrongly credited and not returned. Label slides on the front (show the word 'front' and indicate the top) You may have to put your address on the back.

- Indicate if they are part of a set or are needed back by a particular date.

- Keep a record of which images you send to whom in case they ask for more!

- Always put slides in a transparent wallet. You can then paperclip the wallet to other information (CV, press release). Photos can be attached direct but be careful not to damage them with the paper clip. Always send slides and photos in a stiffened envelope. Give them a week to arrive then ring up and see if they are there. Not all recipients will automatically return photographs. If you want them back, send a stamped addressed envelope. And remember – make sure you always keep one complete set of slides or photos for yourself!

Copyright

The 1988 Copyright Act introduced a new set of rights – moral rights. These require that an artist be properly credited as the creator of an artwork, provided s/he has asserted that right – this is known as the right of authorship. In simple terms this means attaching a statement saying you want to be credited as the artist under a particular name. Proper labelling of your photographs would do this. Another right is the right of integrity which prevents your work being distorted or mutilated – eg cropping a photograph.

Unfortunately, rights of authorship and integrity do not apply to newspapers, magazines or similar periodicals, so you have no protection in statute law to have your photographs credited. You could, however, have it built into a contract, which is probably the best way to deal with any copyright question. This can be a simple letter saying that conditions of publication include being identified as the artist and that photographs are not to be cropped without consent.

With most magazines, being credited as the artist will not be a problem though cropping might be. Your problem is more likely to be feeling that the caption properly reflects your work. One way of ensuring this is to send a list of captions with your photographs.

For example...

The following examples outline strategies involved in promoting and publicising visual arts and media activities and projects.

Residency

These are the stages which involve publicity and promotion:

- with artist-initiated projects, telling potential hosts what you have to offer
- publicising a residency for fundraising purposes
- once it's running, using publicity to make contact with interested people – workforce, children and staff, management, the local community
- alerting press and media – locally, regionally nationally
- publicising highlights or new developments as the residency runs

MANCHESTER POLYTECHNIC FACULTY OF ART AND DESIGN

DEGREE SHOWS 1992

Private View Invitation for Friday 19th June 6pm to 9pm
see reverse of card for list of venues and locations

DEGREE SHOWS 1992

Holden Gallery (14) Grosvenor Building
Cavendish Street Manchester M15 6BR
061-247 1705 Saturday 20 June to
Wednesday 24 June inclusive 10am to
6pm Weekdays 10am to 4pm Weekends.
Fine Art (18) Medlock Fine Art Centre
Chester Street · Manchester.
Foundation (14) Grosvenor Studios
Grosvenor Building · Cavendish Street
Manchester.
Textiles/Fashion (6) Cavendish Studios
Cavendish Building · Cavendish Street
Manchester.
Communication Media (23) Righton
Building Cavendish Street · Manchester.
Three Dimensional Design (14) Holden
Gallery · Grosvenor Building · Cavendish
Street · Manchester.

Architecture and Landscape (14) from
Monday 6 July to Wednesday 8 July
10am to 6pm Holden Gallery
Grosvenor Building Cavendish Street
Manchester.

MANCHESTER POLYTECHNIC

The front, with a striking full-colour image, credits the artist, sets out the basic information and asks readers to turn over for more information. The back provides details of the exhibitions and venues and contains a map with numbered references of how to find them.

- publicising the conclusion of the residency – the exhibition, the completed commission, the advantages for participants, value to the community, etc.

Commission

This list of stages in a commission which require publicity includes some points which only apply to large-scale projects:

- promoting yourself and your work to potential commissioners and clients
- publicising the project to raise funds
- publicising the project during the consultation processes. For a public art commission, this includes through the local authority planning and committee processes
- alerting press and media – locally, regionally, nationally
- publicising major stages of completion and subsidiary events or related work
- publicising the unveiling of a large outdoor piece or the first showing of a film or video, the public's and commissioner's response and any events arising
- promoting the completed commission to the specialist press or media for reviews and articles to help your career.

Studios

If you need local council support to locate affordable studio space and grants for refurbishment or running costs, use publicity in the local press to put your needs into the public eye, so that councillors and others will be supporting you prior to applications going in. You could:

• publicise the search for studio or workshop space – locally and regionally
• establish the credibility of the artists involved to potential landlords, sponsors, etc
• publicise the studios as part of a campaign to raise funds for renovations, improvements, reduction in rent or rates, etc
• announce a group's establishment in premises, to acknowledge the support of funders or sponsors
• publicise what the building has to offer to the public, to specialists, to potential users, other artists, purchasers, gallery directors, etc
• publicise events or activities there – open days, workshops, demonstrations, exhibitions
• promote future projects which need support
• publicise vacant studio space.

Business set up

This is a way of focusing on the aspects of your work which you want to develop in the future and, of developing new contacts. Publicity can be used for:

• launching your business – the products and services you offer
• publicising past successful projects or activities
• publicising a move to larger premises, collaborations with others
• holding a specific event for the press/media or other relevant people to remind them about your products or services
• publicising the receipt of an award, grant, sponsorship or other noteworthy accolade.

Exhibition

Whether in a public gallery or an 'alternative' space, an exhibition always needs publicity and promotion, either to supplement what exists or to pin-point a specific aspect. The stages when promotion is needed are:

• promotion to get an exhibition – applying to a gallery or selling the idea of an exhibition to the owner of a disused supermarket
• pre-publicity – announcing in advance that the exhibition is planned, to fund-raisers or to link with other activities

- advance publicity – to get coverage in magazines or on TV arts programmes with deadlines months in advance.

When the exhibition is up:

- launch publicity – preview, press releases locally/regionally and nationally
- creating a special event to encourage publicists – a press preview, performance, etc
- publicity to announce any fruitful or newsworthy outcome of the exhibition – sales, commissions other exhibitions and opportunities, etc.

17 • A place to work

Home or away?

David Briers Artists suddenly stepping outside the environment of full-time art education quite commonly find themselves on the horns of a dilemma. On the one hand they may be sharing cramped and unseemly rented accommodation, or even the unfixed abode of a squat, or may be forced to return for a while to the parental nest – none of these being a good place to start work.

On the other hand, an artist who has found it possible to arrange a suitable working space at home may be reluctant to consider the possibility that the very proximity of their activity as an artist to the kitchen or television set may be the root of a number of problems.

A real artist!

Alongside the practical restraints which affect the decision of whether to work at home or in an outside studio may lurk the influences of professional expectations and peer group pressures. As collective group studios and studio-based artists' associations flourish in cities, securing one of these studios seems sometimes to have been undertaken by the graduate as if it were the 'done thing'. If there is one maxim those leaving college need to keep reminding themselves, it might be: you don't *have* to do anything. It may take a while – years – to find out what work environment suits you best, and it may not necessarily be what everyone else seems to be chasing. Having a 'real studio' does not make you a 'real artist'.

If you don't have a studio, it doesn't mean you can't be an artist. The chicken and egg sequence of the studio producing the artwork is not necessarily the one-way sequence generally supposed. Joseph Beuys supposedly said his best drawings were done on his mother's kitchen table, RB Kitaj and John Hoyland started off making paintings in their front rooms, Morris Louis' best canvases were painted in his basement.

Jane Smith in her front room workshop in an ordinary terrace house in a popular tourist area. *'The day I left college in 1982, I converted my front room into a workshop. It was a fairly large, light and sunny room and made a good space with the inclusion of equipment and shelving. Beyond the kitchen there was a small back extension in which I housed the kiln and glazes. My living space was contained within the kitchen and two bedrooms, one for my daughter, the other my bed-sitting room. Fortunately I had marvellous and very supportive neighbours who did not seem to feel my front room workshop was a let-down. All the other houses had dining rooms in the front with neatly laid breakfast tables but my scruffy busy-looking room caused interest and approval rather than disapproval.'*

Living with work

Beyond the unavoidable constraints of physical, financial and legal limitations, another major factor determining whether you work at home or elsewhere will be whether you live with someone else, particularly if 'someone else' includes a baby or small

see 18 • Health & safety

children. Here again, although the set of circumstances presented by having children is impossible to ignore, the ways of fitting it into the jigsaw of your activities as an artist are manifold, and dependent entirely on what works best for you.

Such decisions are commonly seen to relate to privacy and self-discipline. Total privacy is of course impossible, even at home, and a studio elsewhere may paradoxically offer more privacy. Anyone who has worked at home for any length of time will tell you of the innumerable interruptions from those trying to sell you insurance, double-glazing, stone-cladding, and assorted forms of religious belief. Sometimes such interruptions can provide useful excuses not to work, just as a TV set can become like opium, and you may find yourself watching Australian soap operas in the afternoon instead of facing up to a problematic canvas.

Ethics at work

Because of the way most of us have been brought up, working at home can easily produce feelings of guilt, and self-accusations of laziness from which even the most industrious and prolific artists have admitted suffering. It is easy to work longer than is good for you at home, and proper breaks and a bit of exercise should be built into your work pattern.

see 18 • Health & safety There is no need to become a health freak (heaven forbid), but conscious attention is needed to avoid slipping into a vicious spiral of seediness and negative introversion without realising it. Therein lie the seeds of agoraphobia.

Unfortunately the dictum persists that good art can only come out of mortifying working conditions. The catalogue for a group studio exhibition a few years ago included the following statement '... *by definition an artist who is willing to rent and maintain a studio which is all too often physically uncomfortable, cannot but take his work seriously and expect to be taken seriously*'. The implicit supposition that more suitable conditions would produce work which is not serious is just one of the nonsenses which might divert the inexperienced artist from devising a set of conditions which works for them. Being able to decide where, how and when you work is one of the privileges (and there are few enough) accorded to a self-employed person. Do not waste it.

Working at home

Adrian Barr-Smith with additional material by **David Butler** Problems in working at home may arise for one or more of the following reasons:

Illegality

An owner/occupier with a mortgage is usually bound by a term of the deed to use the premises only as a residential dwelling. If the mortgagees (building society, bank, etc) discover the artist is working at home, they may terminate the mortgage facility or, more commonly, require them to cease working there.

A tenant is similarly placed if his/her lease or tenancy agreement contains a clause (most do) requiring them to use the premises only for residential purposes. A tenant with protection under the Rent Acts, loses it if s/he is 'carrying on a business' (ie any trade or professional activity) at home.

A solution to the problems of both is to insist, if confronted, that their artistic activity is merely a 'hobby' interest, ie a 'Sunday' painter.

An alternative solution, which is preferable, may not be appropriate in all cases. A simple letter can be written to the mortgagees or landlord explaining the artist intends to work from home in the foreseeable future due to extenuating circumstances, etc. Many building societies are happy to accept this provided certain safeguard measures are taken.

Artists who are wary of informing mortgagees or landlord that they work at home, should take care to restrict the use of any business letterhead showing their home address.

Building & public liability insurance

see 22 • Insurance An owner/occupier with a mortgage usually pays insurance premiums on the policy which the mortgagees take out against the structure collapsing, or against death or injury caused to members of the public at the premises. Such a policy will, like the mortgage deed, prohibit any use of the premises other than residential. If the insurers discover the artist is working at home, they may cancel the policy, or worse avoid liability in the event of any claim.

A tenant with a lease will often pay premiums on a building insurance policy taken out by the landlords. If the tenant is an artist, by working at home s/he runs the same risk as the owner/occupier. For preference, notify the insurers. Provided the risks are not increased, eg by the use of volatile chemicals, this should not materially affect the premiums.

Contents insurance

Any artist working at home may have a policy covering household contents. Insurance policies require disclosure of every 'material fact'. Whether or not the policy is intended to cover work, equipment, etc, the insurers should be informed of any artistic activity or storage of work.

Planning regulations

For the purposes of the planning regulations, crafts, painting and sculpture are classed as 'light industry' and you should check with the local authority that your studio has the necessary planning permission. If not you will have to apply for change of use. This can take some time though the planning office should be able to give an informal opinion fairly quickly. If you do structural alterations you will probably need to comply with building regulations and may need planning permission.

A building in a residential area can be used for any activities 'incidental to the enjoyment of the dwelling house as such'. The artist working at home should always argue that his/her artistic activity is a 'hobby', ie merely incidental to his/her residence at the premises. Planning permission is required where an artist:

- intensifies his/her operation, eg by employing assistants or actively selling work at home
- changes the use to light industrial purposes
- alters the external appearance of the house (except by painting it)
- improves/alters the construction, eg by building a shed or an extension (unless the size of the building is **not** increased by a tenth or 50 cubic metres)
- constructs a driveway.

The planning officer at the Local Authority will give a preliminary view as to whether permission is required and the chances of succeeding.

Breach of the regulations is not a criminal offence. Officers will allow time for compliance with the regulations. If dissatisfied they will serve an Enforcement Notice which compels you to comply within a reasonable period (usually 28 days). If aggrieved you should appeal.

Unless there is excessive traffic or noise, problems will probably arise due to over zealous officials or poor relations with neighbours.

Health & safety and fire regulations

If you are employing people or opening your premises to the public you will have to comply with fire regulations. You should check on this even if the above doesn't apply.

Consult the local fire officer for requirements for fire exits, corridor widths, fire fighting equipment, emergency procedures and safety regulation, at an early stage to find out how expensive taking on the building is going to be.

Artists' and makers' materials and equipment – paint, resin, wood, rubbish, solvent, kilns, welding and electrical tools, etc – are all potential fire and health hazards, more so when stored in shared spaces. Consider also the implications of potential pollutants, or noise, as it may affect studio holders and neighbours.

Community Charge & Business Rates

Since the introduction of the Unified Business Rate premises have been classed as domestic or commercial. There is no mixed-use category. If you are working at home and want to reclassify a part of your house you will first need to apply to the planning office for change of use. They will notify the rates department who in turn will notify the valuation officer at the Inland Revenue. The valuation officer will decide whether it is worthwhile reclassifying part of the premises or not. If you are going to convert the whole ground floor of your home to a workshop and store then most likely it will be reclassified and you will end up paying UBR and community charge. If it is one room in the attic then possibly UBR won't be levied and you will just pay community charge.

UBR can be exorbitently high (for instance one studio group pays £37,000 UBR per annum compared to £7,000 rent). An advantage of UBR is that, unlike community charge, it is tax deductible.

Tax

see 20 • Employment status & tax The self-employed artist usually deducts a proportion of household expenses when calculating income tax liability.

Capital Gains Tax (CGT) complications can arise when an owner/occupier sells his/her house. Any profit on the sale of an artist's home is usually exempt from CGT if it is his/her principal private residence. But the Inland Revenue may not exempt part of the profit if the artist has been claiming tax deduction in respect of that proportion.

For example, an artist buys a house for £36,000. They paint at home and claim 25% of household overheads – including mortgage repayments – as deductible business expenses. After five years, they sell the house for £60,000 – net profit £24,000. If they had not painted at home, that profit would be exempt. But their tax inspector will probably insist they pay CGT on 25% of the profit, ie £6,000.

The rationale for this is simply the part of the dwelling claimed as a business expense cannot also have been used for residential purposes.

Social Security

see 19 • Benefits An artist 'signing on' as unemployed is entitled to income support in respect of his/her accommodation needs and living expenses. The Department of Social Security (DSS) will usually pay the claimant's rent if a tenant, or mortgage interest payments if an owner/occupier. But where the artist works at home, the DSS will not pay the proportion of the cost attributable to the work space.

Neighbours

Artists who work at home will frequently encounter problems if they do not enjoy a friendly relationship with their neighbours. Problems can be avoided by paying conscious attention to:

* noise (particularly late-night)
* traffic (generally coming and going)
* parking (obstructing driveways)
* refuse and rubbish
* external appearance of the property.

Neighbours who create trouble are usually motivated not by malevolence, but by fear that the value of their property, or their enjoyment of it, is threatened.

Finding a studio

Adrian Barr-Smith

Assess needs

The first task is to decide what is required. Correctly assessing individual needs at the outset avoids wasting time viewing unsuitable premises.

When determining needs, artists should consider:

- is living accommodation also required?
- will space be self-contained or shared?
- what geographical location?
- what size (in square feet)?
- daylight or artificial light?
- ease of access (eg bulky objects)
- right of access (limited or 24 hours)
- facilities: power supply, heating, water supply, WC/washing
- special requirements (eg soundproofing)
- security risk (eg valuable equipment)
- how many artists involved, who will handle lease, accounts, etc?

What can I afford?

Before setting out, it is advisable to make an objective assessment of your means. Taking on a studio can involve a heavy 'capital' (ie one-off) commitment, as well as the 'revenue' (ie running) costs.

An artist who cannot afford the expense is well advised not to waste time looking for a bargain offer. Dream studios (ie inexpensive ones) no longer exist, if they ever did! An artist who can afford the commitment should consider whether they can borrow money and buy a freehold/long leasehold space.

How do I search?

Searching is the hardest and most soul-destroying task. Avoid being persuaded to spend time viewing unsuitable or over-expensive buildings. The following are suggested methods, in order of probable effectiveness:

- approach a helpful organisation (Acme, SPACE, WASPS, RAB or Arts Council)
- talk to other artists, lecturers, friends
- advertise, on notice boards, in *Artists Newsletter,* etc

- cycle round streets, armed with notebook, camera
- drive/bus round streets, you'll see more than by underground, but less than on two wheels
- walk (you'll cover a smaller area)
- visit suitable estate agents, ie who handle suitable property, not luxury penthouses, specify requirements, ask to be sent particulars of potential spaces
- telephone/write to suitable estate agents
- write to local authority (estates department)
- write to landlords of other artists' studios
- scan advertisements in local papers.

Where do I look?
Obvious possibilities may be in the run-down inner-city locality, for example:

- above shops in the high street
- tops of warehouses
- disused shops, factories, churches, warehouses, schools
- areas blighted by redevelopment proposals (ask the local authority planning department, the tell-tale sign is boarded-up buildings)
- locations keen to attract occupants – industrial estates, enterprise zones, etc.

Once an artist has found a building they must assess, as objectively as possible, whether the space is suitable.

How do I trace the owner?
If the space has been located through the landlord/agent etc, no problem. An artist who spots an unoccupied building should be able to trace the owner by one of the following means:

- estate agent's board on building
- neighbours
- shop/pub on corner of street
- local authority planning department
- local rates office

A Scottish artist once suggested that a sure-fire way to contact the owner of unoccupied premises was to move in straightaway. Unfortunately, many landlords are reluctant to come to an agreement with a squatter in these circumstances and may instead eject them.

What will the space cost?

An intending tenant must estimate as accurately as possible what will be the capital and revenue costs of the space.

Capital costs

These one-off expenses may include:

- alterations/repairs to roof, floor, walls (must comply with local building regulations and have approval of district surveyor)
- installation of fire-doors/fire-proofing/means of escape (must have approval of local fire officer)
- installation of power supply, re-wiring, etc
- installation of water supply, plumbing, wastepipe, drains, etc (responsibility of borough engineer)
- purchasing fixtures from landlord/outgoing tenant
- miscellaneous DIY supplies and restoration jobs
- survey or legal fees.

These can be crippling expenses and must be met before the space becomes workable. Artists should be wary of committing such money in a studio with a short life expectancy. Most local authorities will under-estimate the period of time available for occupation. But grants towards conversion and establishment costs will not be available unless the occupancy is likely to continue for a reasonable length of time.

Revenue costs

These ongoing expenses may include:

- rent
- general rates
- water rates and sewerage charges
- building insurance premiums (get a quotation)
- third party insurance premiums (to cover members of the public)
- contents insurance premiums (equipment, work, etc)
- service charges (caretaker, rubbish collection, etc)
- minor repairs
- heat and light
- telephone
- transport from home to studio.

Negotiations with landlord

Having added up the potential expenses, the prospective tenant should not proceed further unless they can make a better-than-derisory offer. Negotiating methods vary but the following should serve as a guide:

- never offer the asking price, it's usually inflated
- if it is unoccupied the landlord may accept a very low offer
- don't make a derisory offer without good reason (this may prove counter-productive and abort the negotiations before they start)
- glamorise the offer, especially if it's low (when making a proposal, particularly to a local authority, explain who you are, what you want to do in the space, and point out how your occupancy can benefit the landlord – caretaking role, prevention of vandalism/squatting, preservation of fabric, cultural benefit to the community, etc)
- rents are expressed in square feet per year, eg 'Studio 20 x 13ft: £3 per sq ft', ie the total rent is £780 per annum or £15 per week
- rent-free periods can often be arranged where a tenant has to carry out repairs before occupying the space. A typical example: an artist agrees with their landlord a rent-free period of three months if they carry out, at their own expense, agreed repairs. The artist pays the first quarter's rent in advance in December and moves in. They carry out the repairs by March and the landlord inspects the work. The landlord is happy with it and the rent-free period operates from April to June, when the next quarter's rent is due

see 23 • Contracts

- all written or verbal negotiations should be conducted on a 'without prejudice' or, more commonly, 'subject to contract' basis. These words, which should appear at the top of all offer letters etc, indicate the agreement will be later recorded in a formal contract and either party can withdraw at any time before then
- an artist should be aware of weakening security by accepting a lease which requires them to use the premises other than for the purposes which they intend, eg if the lease specifies 'use: storage', the artist is not legally entitled to use it for working or living.

Formalities

It is important any agreement is recorded in writing before any money is handed over or irrevocable commitment undertaken. It may be as simple as an exchange of letters, or as complicated as a lease with 50 clauses. The documents are normally drawn up by the landlord's solicitor/agent. In all such cases, artists should seek legal advice from a solicitor.

The formal arrangement made is usually one of four types:

'Legalised' squat

The artist's presence is tolerated by the owners, who can revoke their tacit permission at any time. This tends to be attractive at the outset because it is easy. It is not a worthwhile proposition in the long term because it is precarious and insecure (artists have no right to have services – gas, electricity – connected).

Licence

Written or verbal agreement for occupation by artist ('licensee') which is not a tenancy – usually because the artist shares the space and does not have exclusive possession. Upon termination the licensee is entitled to be given specified notice, eg if paying weekly, one week's notice. Studio licences are increasingly common because the rights of the artist occupier are limited and the arrangement is attractive to property owners.

Tenancy

Written or verbal agreement for occupation by artist ('tenant') usually weekly or monthly. Upon termination the tenant is entitled to be given specified notice.

If it is a 'studio' tenancy lasting over six months, the Landlord and Tenant Act 1954 (Part II) ensures it continues automatically after expiry, unless terminated by notice given by the landlord. The tenant should immediately give counter-notice s/he is unwilling to give up the tenancy. If s/he had a tenancy exceeding twelve months, the tenant can only be removed if:

- the tenant has breached his/her obligations ('covenants')
- s/he has persistently delayed paying rent
- the landlord offers reasonable alternative accommodation
- the landlord intends to demolish or renovate the building
- the landlord intends to occupy the premises for business or residential purposes.

Many tenancies and leases are granted only on condition that the tenant waives their rights under this Act. The Act, which covers 'business' (ie non-residential) premises, applies unless specifically excluded with the sanction of the County Court.

Lease

Contract between landlord ('lessor') and tenant ('lessee') must be written and contains all the covenants binding each side. If a lease (or tenancy) is for a term of several years, the tenant is under an implied obligation to carry out timely repairs. A lease terminates upon expiry of the fixed term unless continued automatically by the Landlord and Tenant Act as above.

In all four instances, the occupant(s) cannot be evicted from the premises, even after expiry of proper notice, without a court order.

Checklist

Most documents, whether leases, tenancy agreements or licences, will contain terms dealing with the following points:

- name and address of landlord
- name and address of tenant (all names if more than one artist)
- date of commencement of agreement
- rent, paid weekly/monthly, etc (artists are advised to pay by bankers order where possible)
- is surety required to guarantee payment of rent?
- whether rent will be 'reviewed', ie increased (if so, how often?)
- is a deposit required? If so, what will it be credited against, eg unpaid rent, damage, etc?
- building insurance premium, usually paid by tenant
- rates, payable by the 'occupier' and usually paid by tenant
- is service charge payable? If so what services are offered, eg caretaker, heating, etc?
- interior repairs and decoration – landlord usually responsible
- exterior decoration – tenant often responsible
- purpose for which premises may be used (ie studio)
- duration of agreement, ie length of occupancy
- option to renew or extend agreement (on what terms?)
- option to terminate agreement before expiry
- whether agreement can be 'assigned' (and studio handed over) to another artist with/without landlord's consent
- whether subletting allowed – of whole/part of premises
- legal fees – usually paid by tenant
- references required (previous landlord, bank, accountant, etc)
- date of agreement
- signatures of both parties.

Use this as a checklist to ensure that all points have been discussed with the landlord, before the lawyers are called in.

Joining a group studio

David Briers Renting a studio unit within a disused warehouse, school or factory run by an association or collective of artists is certainly cheaper, but has its

Exterior of Mile End Chapel where Art Space Portsmouth established new studios in 1992
Photo: John McPherson

pros and cons. You cannot, usually, locate such a studio space and move straight in. There is likely to be a waiting list, there may also be a selection procedure and even some form of interview. If you are involved in actually setting up a group of studios you may have to contribute a great deal of your own unpaid time, energy and materials to making good a studio space which would not otherwise exist. The building itself is likely to have been secured as a low-cost group tenancy on a short-term basis, either because it or the area it is in are due for eventual demolition or re-development. You will have no real security of tenure, and may only be granted a licence to work there by the association, revocable on a monthly or even weekly basis. Some artists find it difficult to work with the spectre of possible eviction hanging over their heads.

Some studio spaces in such complexes are magnificently solidly built, but often large areas are sub-divided by chipboard partitions with

Interior of Red Herring Studios Brighton. These are typical of the converted old buildings converted by artists for studios. The introduction of the Unified Business Rate was potentially disastrous for studio groups with rates set to rise astronomically. Only charitable status giving statutory central government relief of 80%, or discretionary relief by the local council (the cost being borne by the community charge payer), has staved off potential closures for some groups. Issues like this need addressing by government, arts bodies and artists. Secure, good studio space at affordable rents is essential not only for artists but also for the area where those artists live and work. A thriving indigenous arts community produces work for its locality and provides a network for cultural exchange into and out of the locality.

no sound-proofing. Privacy is only summarily maintained, and a continual commentary from the transistor radio with its battery running out next door can soon pall. Indeed, the very aspects of such a community of art practice which are attractive to some artists, may alienate others.

And remember you will have to take some part, however small, in the management, be it as an unpaid administrator, contributor to members' meetings, or just being on the rota to clean the lavatory. If you want to shut the door to your studio and pretend the rest of the world – and other artists – doesn't exist, don't join a studio organisation.

There are compensations to working in group studios, of course, not least that of feeling part of an evident artistic community – of having something immediately adjacent to measure up to, in terms of practice as well as end result. In practical terms, group studios tend to have a higher profile than individual studios. They are places local arts administrators know about, and they may drop in on you when visiting someone else. Some group studios seek to build towards providing greater professional security for the artist, while others are exploring alternative ways of working from a studio. Some seek and secure exhibitions as a group, and even have their own gallery. Shared equipment or tools, however, is a facility more often spoken of than put into practice.

Many artists are involved in sharing studio space with others, usually to reduce costs. There are other benefits. For example, when searching for space or carrying out conversion work the tasks can be divided up. The presence of other artists can lend stability; the ability to pay bills is not dependent solely upon the cash-flow of one individual.

Whenever artists collaborate for this purpose they should be careful to decide the following and record decisions in an appropriate fashion, eg minutes of a meeting:

- who members of the group are
- what the aims of the group are
- which members will undertake: chair, spokesperson; secretary, convening meetings, writing letters; Treasurer, finances
- to keep a separate bank account for group business
- what the rights and obligations of members are to each other, eg in the event of the group becoming Insolvent
- whether a formal constitution is required
- whether any tenancy/lease should be in the name of the group, or of one or more individual members.

Groups can be established quite informally, as above. If a more formal structure is necessary, members can legally constitute themselves as an unincorporated association, cooperative, housing association, company limited by guarantee, or trust.

18 • Health & safety

Tim Challis
& Gary Roberts

There is no purpose in exaggerating and pretending art involves risks as shattering as industry can. Even so, the materials and processes of the arts and crafts are often the same as those used in industry and involve the same hazards, albeit on a less dramatic scale.

If the process you are using involves the same hazards as a similar one in industry, it is wise to adopt the same safety precautions. This is supported by law. Many artists may not realise it, but those earning a living from their work fall under the jurisdiction of the Health and Safety at Work Act 1974, and associated legislation.

see 26 • Further reading

However, there are problems facing artists wishing to comply fully with the law. Art and craft processes can present their own peculiar demands, perhaps not always sympathetically answered by the guidelines of industry. In *Artists Handbooks: Health & Safety* we translated the rules and regulations of industry into a form easily usable by the working artist. This is a synopsis of that, but the onus must be on the individual to research areas more fully where necessary.

The law

The Health and Safety at Work Act 1974 is quite unequivocal in its application to everybody at a place of work, whether employer, employee or member of the public. Part 1, section 3 demands self-employed people, irrespective of whether they employ others, must ensure their own safety as well as that of people around them. The law also applies to both self-employed artists and students in an art college.

Paradoxically, official provision for health and safety in the small workshop or studio is almost non-existent. The Health and Safety Executive produces the occasional leaflet aimed at such businesses, but otherwise expects people to consult the information for large industries. Even this was unlikely to be enforced. As well as the

Executive's inability to carry out frequent inspections, it was not aware of small workshops and studios.

The new COSHH regulations

Towards the end of 1989, the 'Control of Substances Hazardous to Health Regulations 1988' (COSHH) came into force. Under this act all employers must carry out a COSHH assessment, including self-employed artists and craftspeople. Only those who do not earn income from their work escape this but they would be wise to carry out a COSHH-style assessment. After all, you face the same hazards whether your being paid for it or not! If you're employed by someone else, it's their responsibility to see an assessment is carried out. Remember, colleges and schools are workplaces and the employer (education authority, trust, etc) must ensure that an assessment is done. If you're worried a COSHH assessment has not been done, refer to the HSE booklet *'COSHH assessments: a step-by-step guide to assessment and the skills needed for it'*. These regulations also increase the likelihood of small studio and workshops receiving a visit from the HSE. The legal duty to carry out an assesment is absolute, and artists could face prosecution if they don't comply.

COSHH in brief

The COSHH regulations stipulate that every employer who uses (or whose employees use) hazardous substances must assess their dangers, the precautions that are being taken and areas where control needs to be improved.

'Hazardous substances' even include typing correction fluid, aerosols and glues containing solvents, so nearly every workplace will need to do at least a brief assessment.

The results of this assessment must be recorded in such a way they can be examined by a factory inspector.

Good housekeeping

Good housekeeping is essential for a safe working environment. Generally, it is just common sense – the advantages of cleanliness and tidiness are self-evident. Dirt and spills of chemicals or liquids should be vacuumed or wet-mopped, but never swept with a dry brush. Where dangerous dusts (eg silica) are concerned, it is important to use a commercial rather than domestic vacuum cleaner. Many domestic vacuum cleaners are incapable of filtering out hazardous, microscopic particles of dust, and simply spray them back into the breathing zone. The floor should be non-slip, preferably one level, and free of obstructions. Smoking, eating or drinking must be forbidden in a dusty atmosphere – they increase the chance of ingesting hazardous chemicals or dust. People working with chemicals or materials at home should avoid contaminating the living area, and never use the kitchen as a workroom. Where chemicals must be disposed of, do it thoughtfully. It is illegal to pour toxic hazardous chemicals down a sink. If in doubt consult the Disposal of Poisonous Wastes Act 1972.

One rule of thumb should be remembered. If the process is hazardous, substitute it with one less dangerous. If this is not possible isolate the process, eg screening off and ventilating part of the studio. If this is impractical, protect everybody in contact with the process with suitable protective clothing. Remember: substitute, isolate or protect.

Safety consciousness

Prevention is always better than cure. To minimise risk the following general precautions should be observed.

Inhalation

Adequate general ventilation as well as extraction equipment at localised work areas is vital to keep dust and fume problems to a minimum. Suitable face masks or respirators should be worn for any process likely to produce excessive dust or fumes. Wherever possible, confine dust-producing work to extraction cubicles. Tools and workshops should be wet-mopped, not brushed, immediately after work is finished, and overalls and work clothes should be cleaned regularly.

Check the exact nature of materials being used before work commences. The ability of solvents to vaporise at very low temperatures is a particular cause for concern. The exact effect depends upon which particular solvent is encountered. However, in general, short-term exposure produces a narcotic effect, whilst liver and kidney damage and nervous disorders are common long-term hazards.

Ingestion

Accidental ingestion of hazardous materials may occur through eating, drinking or smoking in the work area. These should therefore be banned. Hands should be thoroughly washed after contact with toxic substances.

Skin contact

Adequate protective clothing and goggles should be worn to protect against hot, corrosive or dermatitic materials. Some substances, eg phenol, benzene and carbon tetrachloride, are capable of penetrating the skin without direct contact, entering the circulatory system and causing extensive damage. Obviously, adequate ventilation is essential.

Skin contact with solvents is particularly hazardous due to their ability to dissolve body fats and become absorbed into the skin and circulatory system. This initially causes dermatitis, but eventually all parts of the body can be affected, especially the liver and kidneys. Adequate protective clothing should be worn. Uncovered cuts and abrasions on the skin facilitate and encourage contamination.

Protective clothing

Face & eye protection

Work involving acids or solvents should never be carried out without goggles or a plastic face shield. Eyes must also be protected during grinding, chipping and drilling processes. Visible, infra-red and ultra-violot light are the main hazards to be guarded against during heat processes, such as welding or foundry work. The face and eyes should be protected by a helmet and goggles, or hand-shield fitted with the correct filter lenses. If there is a risk of spatter of hot slag, a full head-helmet should be worn. The three main types of eye protection available are: spectacles with impact-resistant lenses and side shields, flexible or cushioned goggles and chipping- or eyecup-goggles.

Hand protection

The hands are most commonly exposed to hazards. It is essential they are adequately protected. Barrier cream should be used in conjunction with gloves as it may not provide protection in its own right.

Body protection

Overall protection is especially necessary for work involving high temperatures. A flameproof overall and leather apron should be worn for welding. As foundry work involves the pouring of molten metal, the following protective clothing should be worn: spats or gaiters, high-impact visors, heat-resistant gloves and a leather or similar heat-resistant apron. When working with toxic or corrosive chemicals, flame-resistant or cloth aprons should be worn over the body.

Respirators

Respirators are not a substitute for adequate ventilation. Any respirator has limited effectiveness over long periods, especially if it does not comfortably fit the face. Check for a proper fit by covering the air outlet and breathing in. You should not notice any air leaking around the nose or chin. Try the same exercise breathing out with the exhaust closed. The straps should not have to be tightened excessively to maintain a close fit. Respirators should be regularly checked and cleaned.

Air-purifying respirators consist of two parts, the face mask and the filter which removes contaminants from the air being breathed. The correct filter must be selected for the particular hazardous material encountered. Change filters regularly. Air-supplying respirators should be used when more obviously harmful materials are encountered. An uncontaminated air supply is provided either from a self-contained breathing apparatus, a compressed gas cylinder or a compressor. Inexpensive paper or cloth masks are not an effective protection against toxic materials and should only be worn as a barrier against non-toxic nuisance dusts.

Lighting

Minimum requirements, as stated in paragraph 52 of the Standards for School Premises Regulations 1972, should be observed. Most colleges and professionals usually adhere to levels of lighting recommended in the *Illuminated Engineering Society Code for Interior Lighting*.

Certain areas may require different levels of lighting. For instance, forge and brazing hearth areas should have subdued lighting, but individual machines may require supplementary lighting. This must only be of a very low voltage, preferably 12 or 24 volts. Light intensity should increase according to the fineness and skill factor of the work. Whereas 200 lux may be adequate for rough sawing and coarse bench work, 500 lux may be required for fine detail work and around 1000 lux for very fine engraving or measuring work. Some examples of recommended lighting levels are: sheet metal work = 400 lux; painting and spraying = up to 500 lux; retouching and colour matching = at least 1,000 lux.

Extreme changes of light intensity between different areas of the studio are dangerous and should be avoided. If possible, try to achieve recommended levels of light by natural means and only use artificial light as a supplement.

Noise

Studio noise may cause potentially dangerous distractions of concentration. If machinery noise causes discomfort, wear ear muffs. If possible, work in short spells, taking frequent breaks.

Habitual exposure to excessive levels of noise may cause tiredness, nausea and eventually temporary or even permanent deafness.

Ventilation

Adequate ventilation should be the first means of controlling air contaminated with toxic substances. This can be achieved by diluting the contaminant to a level below that hazardous to health (general ventilation), or removing the contaminant at the point of generation (local ventilation). General ventilation is less efficient than local and may even prevent fine dust from settling, prolonging its presence in the breathing zone. An individual working with a particular substance, eg a solvent, may be at risk from a harmful level of exposure even though the general level is safe. In such situations, local exhaust is obviously an advantage. The following should be noted when using a local ventilation system:

• enclose the source as effectively as possible

• capture the contaminant with moving air of adequate velocity

• keep contaminants out of the breathing zone by not working between the vapour source and the exhaust fan

• ensure exhausted air is replaced by clean air, ie adequate general ventilation

• discharge contaminated air in such a manner as to prevent it from re-entering the work place.

Safety in creative processes

Machinery

Many of the general precautions concerning electrical machinery are again a matter of common sense. It is important to remember almost all machines are covered by one or more of the regulations which must be adhered to for compliance with the Health and Safety at Work Act. Your local Health and Safety Executive office will be able to advise you which regulations apply to which machine, (eg woodworking machinery must comply with Woodworking Machinery Regulations 1974, which provide requirements for the safeguarding of machines, and safe ventilation, illumination and noise levels in areas where they are operated.)

Machines must be vibration-free, and securely fixed. The Health and Safety Executive recommends a space of at least three feet should be kept on three sides of the machine. Machines of all types should be stopped when not in use, and be fitted with the correct guard. Emphasis should be placed on ways of cutting out electricity supplies in an emergency. A main circuit breaker should be in every room where electrical equipment is used, and each machine fitted with an isolating switch. Minor precautions, eg ensuring correct fusing values and professional servicing, considerably reduce the risk of accidents.

Power tools

- select the proper tool for the work. Never try to force a tool to do one thing when it is specifically designed to do something else
- ensure all tools are double-earthed or fully insulated. Extension leads should be avoided as they increase the risk of earthing faults
- ensure all blades and bits are sharp, clean and regularly maintained
- remove adjusting keys and wrenches before turning on the tool
- never make adjustments to a tool while the power is switched on
- never leave a tool running unattended
- only use power tools when it is essential and traffic minimal.

Highly flammable liquids & sprays

The Electricity at Work Regulations under the Health and Safety at Work Act apply to art and craft studios.

There are three statutory classifications of flammability:

- **highly flammable:** liquids with a flashpoint of 32°C (90°F) or below
- **flammable:** materials with a flashpoint above 32°C
- **petroleum mixtures:** those with a flashpoint of 23°C (73°F) or below are by definition highly flammable.

A flashpoint is a method of rating the relative flammability of liquids. The lowest temperature at which a liquid gives off a flammable vapour/air mixture which can be ignited by sparks or static electricity is known as its flashpoint. If a substance is cooled below its flashpoint the danger of ignition is much reduced.

Only use highly flammable liquids at a temperature lower than the liquid's flashpoint. Consider the liquid's properties and conditions of usage when assessing whether or not a dangerous concentration is likely to occur. For instance, a vaporised liquid used as a spray may still be ignited at low temperature by an ignition source of sufficient energy.

Cleanliness is the most effective precaution against fire or explosion where highly flammable liquids are concerned. Places where highly flammable deposits accumulate should be thoroughly cleaned at least once a week. Use plastic, wood or phosphor-bronze scrapers, rather than metal, to remove nitro-cellulose residue. Spray booths can be cleaned more efficiently if preparatory coatings of sheet material or hardening liquid are applied to the booth surfaces before use and peeled off afterwards. When spraying highly flammable materials, clear dry filters should be used for each different material to eliminate the risk of spontaneous combustion of interacting residue.

Ceramics

One of the chief hazards in a ceramics studio is the inhalation of silica dust from clay. Clay is composed of various mineral silicates. Of these, flint, quartz and calcinated sand (crystobalite) all have an equally high content of free crystalline silica. If inhaled in the form of dust, silica destroys the body's natural defences in the lungs, causing irreversible damage. The first sign of possible poisoning is increased breathlessness. After years, exposure can lead to silicosis, a form of pneumoconiosis which can prove fatal. Scrap clay presents a considerable dust hazard once dried. All scraps should be deposited in covered containers.

Dust production may also be a problem when handling powdered glaze. Glazes contain silica and a flux or frit which usually contains lead. Lead compounds are highly soluble and can easily be dissolved into the bloodstream if inhaled in a powder or dust form. The permissible soluble lead content in a glaze is outlined in the Low Solubility Regulations. Any glaze which does not conform to these should obviously not be used. If unsure, contact your local Health and Safety Executive office for advice.

For preparing your own glaze use a low-solubility lead frit such as lead bisilicate and bear in mind when grinding down that the solubility of the lead frit increases as the fineness of the particle size decreases. Leadless frits are available. These substitute borax for lead. However, borax is also toxic in its raw state.

Colouring pigments which may be included in the glaze contain a multitude of chemicals many of which, such as cadmium and chromium, are hazardous in powdered form. Beware of toxic vapours which may be released when glazes are fired. Vapour-glazing techniques require special care. Kilns used for vapour-glazing techniques should be fitted with extraction equipment. Solvents present in decorating inks may present an inhalation hazard.

Accidental ingestion of toxic materials is a potential hazard associated with ceramic products designed for use as eating and drinking utensils. Leakage of lead, cadmium and other chemicals from incorrectly formulated or improperly fired glazes and colours may be caused by the action of organic acids present in food or drink. Acetic acid in vinegar, citric acid in fruits and acids in coffee are amongst those organic acids capable of producing such a reaction. Remembering forthcoming changes in UK product liability laws to bring them more into line with the United States, artists should be especially careful to guard against this possibility.

Incorrect formulation of glazes can occur quite easily. The use of lead frits does not guarantee a safe glaze. The relatively low temperatures involved in raku firing may affect the solubility of lead frits, and this process is therefore not recommended for food ware.

The ratio of glaze ingredients, thickness of application, duration and temperature of firing and the condition of the kiln atmosphere are all factors which affect the amount of lead extractable from the glaze. Therefore, glazes should not be combined with other components without retesting the amount of soluble lead present. For example, a commercially produced, clear glaze may be perfectly safe until a colourant is added, which causes a massive increase in lead-release. Copper oxide is especially dangerous in this respect and as such its use should be avoided. It has in fact been abandoned in industry.

Skin contact with solvents present in decorative inks must be avoided. Prolonged skin contact with clay slips and glaze suspensions may cause dermatitis. Gloves should be worn when handling dermatitic materials. Barrier creams alone are not satisfactory, and should only be used in conjunction with gloves as an extra safeguard.

Glasswork

Flint is the most hazardous source of dust in a glass studio as it has a high content of free crystalline silica (see silica in ceramics, above). Inhalation of toxic dusts can occur during batch mixing. Batch mixtures may contain lead oxide and a variety of sulphates and nitrates. The cutting, grinding or polishing of glass can present further dust hazards. A supply of water should be readily available to minimise dust production. Ensure electrical motors and switches are completely protected where water is used.

Lead and other toxic substances are contained in stain pigments. These can become airborne if the stain is applied by an air-spray gun or if pigment is brushed or blown away from the glaze to achieve various contrasts before firing. Painted or stained glass produces noxious fumes when fired. An extraction hood should be fitted above any area where this is done. Lead fumes may be produced from solders, especially if they are overheated. The copper foil technique involves more solder than the lead came technique, and so involves more risk.

When etching with acid, a container of sodium bicarbonate solution should be readily available for rapid immersion of any part of the body. It is useful to dye the acid a colour to ensure easy identification.

Painting

Dry pigments are a dust hazard. A variety of hazardous chemicals may be present. Aerosol sprays can produce a mist of pigment dust and solvent, as can airbrushes and compressed air guns. Epoxy- and polyurethane-based paints are particularly hazardous.

Artists who indulge in the foolhardy but common practice of 'pointing' the paintbrush with the lips and tongue would do well to note the presence, albeit in comparatively small quantities, of such poisons as arsenic, cadmium and lead in widely-used art paints.

Photography

A variety of photographic materials may prove hazardous over a prolonged period of inhalation. Adequate darkroom ventilation is essential. The mixing of stock solutions poses the most serious hazard as the chemicals are in their concentrated form. Skin should be well-protected to prevent irritation or dermatitis; there may be a delayed reaction effect whereby this occurs some time after initial contact. Colour developers are more likely to cause skin irritation than black and white.

Printing

- **Etching** – Concentrated acids release toxic fumes. The preparation of home-made grounds should not be attempted. Any contact of zinc with hydrochloric or sulphuric acid will produce highly toxic arsene gas.
- **Aquatinting** – Rosin dust is highly toxic. Spray lacquers used for aquatinting plates may produce highly concentrated solvent and propellent mist. Ammonium hydroxide vapour is a severe irritant.
- **Silkscreening** – The main hazard is the presence of solvents in inks, bases, thinners, retarders and silkscreen wash fluids. All possible ventilating and good-housekeeping measures should be taken to avoid over-exposure to solvents released from such materials.
- **Lithography** – Some talcs (french chalk) or talc/resin mixtures contain asbestos, and should be avoided.

• **Photoprinting** – If the carbon arc is used as a light source, toxic fumes are produced. Dangerous amounts of these can be inhaled without noticeable initial discomfort. Carbon arcs should therefore be directly vented to the outside atmosphere.

Many printing processes involve chemicals which are dangerous when in contact with the skin. When etching, protective clothing should be worn to guard against burns from acid. It is especially important to wear goggles. In aquatinting, ammonium hydroxide liquid and vapour causes severe burns, and contact with rosin dust and spray should be avoided. All the silkscreen solvents mentioned above can be dermatitic to varying degrees. Avoid hand contact with process camera lamps, even when cold, as this could lead to shattering when they are in use. Exposure to mercury vapour lamps in printing-down tables can cause skin burns and conjunctivitis in the eyes. With lithography, desensitising etches, especially those which contain potassium dichromate, nitric acid and phosphoric acid, should be handled with extreme care. Lithographic crayons and tusche contain lamp black which is a mild irritant to the eyes and possibly skin and is a suspected carcinogen; avoid skin contact.

Sculpture & modelling
Fumes from forging and casting metals are toxic. All metal fumes, especially zinc oxide, can cause metal fume fever, the symptoms of which are similar to influenza. Oxyacetylene and electric-arc welding create a variety of toxic by-products, the exact nature of which depends upon what is being welded. The welding of galvanised or coated metal is extremely risky in this respect. When soldering, care should be taken with tin, lead and silver solders, all of which release toxic fumes. Silver is especially dangerous when used with fluoride fluxes. Silica (see ceramics) may be released as dust from sand used in the shell-moulding process. In this process it is also preferable to use a micro-crystalline moulding compound such as 'Gell-Flex' rather than vinamould resin binders which may release toxic vapours on decomposition. When finishing metals by grinding or abrading, take adequate precautions against airborne dust.

• **Plastics** – Many plastics release toxic fumes on combustion. Resin dust is toxic, as are the fumes from accelerator solutions and fumes and dusts from the various forms of catalysts. Only certain plastics are suitable for welding. Check beforehand on any likely fume release.

• **Stone** – Stone dust is potentially dangerous due to the presence of silica. Certain stones such as granite and quartz, have a higher silica content than others, such as limestone and marble.

- **Wood** – Respiratory ailments arise due to sustained exposure to wood dust. Certain dusts can produce a reaction after only a few hours, some are carcinogenic. South American boxwood, beech and Western red cedar are a few of the most dangerous types of wood dusts. Measures should be taken to avoid inhalation.

As with other processes, the sculptor must take particular care to avoid skin contact whilst working. With metal, eye and body protection should always be worn to guard against heat and splashes when forging and casting. Infra-red and visible radiation created by welding causes burns, headaches, fatigue and eye damage if adequate protective clothing is not worn. When finishing metals, dust produced from grinding and abrading may cause dermatitic and eye problems. With plastics, dusts and fumes should be treated as potentially dermatitic. Wood dusts, as well as wood treatments and additives, are potentially dermatitic. Dust, oil, sap and extracts from many species of wood can cause skin irritation in prone individuals. Some woods are primary irritants capable of affecting anyone if proper protective clothing measures are not taken.

Textile crafts

Solvents in textile dyes present a major inhalation hazard which should be guarded against. Dust from direct dyes is a suspected carcinogen. All steps should be taken to minimise dust problems created by spinning. Sustained exposure to cotton, flax and hemp dust can cause byssinosis (brown lung). Some animal fibres, such as wool, yarn or hair, can cause anthrax. Care should be taken against inhalation of materials associated with photoprinting textiles. Batik wax should only be heated in a double pan as it releases toxic acrolein fumes if overheated. Avoid skin contact with dyes. All direct dyes, disperse dyes, fibre-reactive dyes and mordant dyes are highly dermatitic and possibly carcinogenic.

First aid

Whilst the philosophy of safety is prevention rather than cure, it is prudent and often a legal requirement for people to be properly prepared for accidents to occur. First aid cabinets are a must, and the contents should follow the guidelines of the First Aid Regulations 1981. Keen first aiders could join an organisation such as the National Register of First Aiders in London, or take special training courses for a small cost. In either case, it is important to study a recognised manual (such as that of the St John's Ambulance Brigade), and try to learn the basics of treating an injured person – it could be yourself that benefits from such precautions one day!

Feeling good –
working well

This all refers specifically to safety but remember your general health and well-being is as important to your work as anything else. Giving yourself some general rules about working conditions, even if you can not always keep them, is a good idea.

Try not to overcrowd the studio with people or things. That does not mean renting a huge studio on your own. A bit of thought about storage and allocation of working spaces can improve the use even if it does not make it perfect. Heat the studio to a comfortable temperature. This not only makes working more pleasant, it also avoids the risk of accidents. If the studio is large and costly to heat try screening off part of it, particularly in winter, as a warm area. Be careful when doing this of fire risks from gas heaters. Keep a fire extinguisher if possible, check it regularly and make sure you know what it will and won't do (eg never use a water extinguisher on electrical fires, burning oil or solvents).

Do not allow your work to force you to eat irregularly or badly. Food like rest, keeps you going. Do not let physical exertion destroy your creative energy. Be careful when lifting or carrying, working in a fixed or awkward position, straining your eyes, etc. Don't heave your sculpture around yourself. Get help, it is better than a bad back.

Try not to work too long hours. Give yourself a maximum to work in any one day. Have a proper break at lunch and tea time. Stop for short rests, particularly if you are working a long day or feel over-tired. Have time off, even if it is only a half-day holiday and remember even artists are entitled to take to their beds when ill. Arrange your time to suit yourself but not to punish yourself.

19 • Benefits

Sharon McKee Many artists qualify for state benefits because they are in a category of people who on average have quite low earnings or have periods where, because they are working on a long term project, they have no money coming in.

It may be that you find it difficult to get any benefit because the Department of Employment will not recognise that you are unemployed because you are an artist. But you do not have to be unemployed to qualify for all Social Security benefits, some you can claim if you are self-employed, working part-time, or are on a low wage.

This chapter does not purport to be a comprehensive guide to all benefits which you may claim. Two very useful guides are leaflets *FB2 Which Benefit?* and *NI196 Social Security Benefit Rates,* which give up-to-date guidance and rates of a wide range of benefits, which may alter in April each year. Further details can be obtained from the offices of the Department of Social Security, your Citizens Advice Bureau or Unemployment Benefit Office, the addresses of which can be found in your local telephone directory.

see 20 • Employment status & tax The majority of National Insurance contributions is paid into the National Insurance Fund, out of which contributory benefits are paid. The remainder is paid into the Redundancy Fund and the National Health Service. The class of National Insurance you pay will depend upon your status of employment. When you are not working, for instance if you are sick or unemployed, you can sometimes apply for credits instead of having to pay contributions, these credits can help you qualify for some benefits.

Contributory benefits include:

• Unemployment benefit
• Sickness benefit
• Invalidity benefit, including pension and allowance
• Retirement pension

- State maternity allowance
- Widow's benefit.

Eligibility for contributory benefits:

Benefit	Employed	Self-employed
Sickness benefit	Yes	Yes
Statutory sickpay	Yes	No
Invalidity benefit	Yes	No
Statutory maternity pay	Yes	No
Maternity allowance	Yes	Yes
Retirement pension	Yes	Yes
Widow's benefit	Yes	Yes
Unemployment benefit	Yes	No

Non contributory benefits:

- Child benefit
- One-parent benefit

Means tested, non-contributory benefits

- Income support
- Family credit

The main benefits you are likely to claim include:

Unemployment benefit

This is a weekly flat rate, which increases for any adult dependant the claimant may have. Eligibility depends on the claimant's contribution record. Other conditions include:

- the claimant must be fit for work and available for work
- show s/he is actively seeking work
- must not place unreasonable restrictions on the type of work they will accept.

It is paid for the first year only of any spell of unemployment and will not be paid for the first three days of unemployment.

You may be disqualified from receiving the benefit for up to 26 weeks in certain cases, eg if you left a job voluntarily or were dismissed due to misconduct.

You must register your claim immediately as benefit will not normally be paid for days prior to the claim.

Income support

May be claimed in conjunction with unemployment benefit or if you are on a low wage. Income support is supposed to pay the difference between an individual or family's weekly net income and the amount required to meet their assessed needs (this includes basic living expenses, some special additional costs and certain housing costs).

You will not be eligible for income support if you have £8,000 or more capital, ie savings; if you have over £3,000 the amount of income support will be reduced. If you are married or living with someone, only one partner may make a claim, as a family will be addressed as a unit. You will also not be eligible if you or your partner work for 24 hours a week or more.

Housing benefit

Can be claimed whether you are unemployed or not. It is claimed from the local authority. A tenant must occupy the dwelling as a home and be liable to make rent payments. There will be a reduction if a house is shared with anyone other than a spouse. If you have more than £3,000 capital (savings and investments) this will affect housing benefit. If you have more than £16,000 capital you are not eligible.

Family credit

This is a weekly payment to a family with at least one child, with additional payments for each child. It is a non-contributory benefit, it is dependent on the claimant's net weekly income and capital.

At least one adult of the family must be in full-time (24 hours a week or more) remunerative work, this includes self-employment. A claimant together with their partner must have less than £8,000 capital between them. S/he will be assessed for a 26 week period after which you can seek a further award.

One parent benefit

This is single flat rate payment, not affected by the number of children. The claimant does not have to be the child's parent but they must live alone and not be cohabiting.

Disability living allowance

This is a new tax free benefit introduced in February 1992. It is not income related and the amount depends on how much care a person needs and the difficulty they have in getting around. This replaces the attendance and mobility allowances, and claims to help more people who were not eligible for those benefits.

Disability working allowance

This was introduced in April 1992 as an income related benefit. Claimants must be over 16 and working at least 16 hours a week, a temporary job must last a minimum of five weeks, have been receiving invalidity benefit, severe disablement allowance, a disability premium with income support, housing benefit, or community charge benefit for at least one of the 56 days before the claim.

When on Enterprise Allowance

Enterprise Allowance, or 'Business Boost' as it is called in Sunderland, is designed to encourage and enable unemployed to set up as a self-employed or small businesses. It is now run by the Training and Enterprise Councils which have brought regional variations to the way in which it is operated.

It pays a subsidy of £40 a week and gives business counselling, but apart from that someone on Enterprise Allowance is treated as any other self-employed person. Applicants will need to prepare a business plan and show that they have sufficient financing, which in some TECs is simply defined as £1000 being available (loan, etc) at the commencent of the business.

For details of how Enterprise Allowance operates in your area contact your local Training and Enterprise Council which can be found in *Yellow Pages* under 'Training'.

When self-employed

Income support, family credit and housing benefit can all be claimed even if you are self-employed, providing you fulfil the standard prerequisites. Assessment as to whether you qualify for these benefits are similar for all three. Your income will be taken into account when judging if it needs to be supplemented by benefits: earnings, benefits, maintenance and any 'other' will be calculated into a weekly basis, any capital over £3,000 is regarded as 'income'. Income support is taxable under Schedule E, while Family Credit is tax free.

see 20 • Employment status & tax When you are self-employed you normally pay Class 2 and Class 4 contributions unless there are certain exemptions. Class 3 is a voluntary contribution, which anyone can pay. It is worth considering this if your contribution record is not sufficient to qualify you for benefits which you feel you may need to claim in the future.

Your local Social Security Officer can find out the level of your contribution record, and give advice on what benefits this entitles you to and whether it would be worth paying Class 3 to make yourself eligible for others.

Class 2 count towards entitlement to certain contributory benefits, but not unemployment benefit.

Pensions

The basic pension is a flat rate, part of the contributory state Retirement Pension. This is paid to anyone whose contribution record satisfies certain contribution conditions. Self-employed and voluntary contributions can be counted for this purpose. State pensions are not high and it may be worthwhile joining a private pension scheme.

Sickness

If you are self-employed you cannot qualify for statutory sick pay unless you are also employed and earnings are above the lower earnings level for National Insurance contribution purposes. But you may be entitled to sickness benefit, for up to 28 weeks, if you have paid enough Class 1 or Class 2 contributions.

Maternity

If you are not actually employed, you cannot qualify for statutory maternity pay, but you will probably be able to claim maternity allowance, which can be paid for 18 weeks, starting from the 11th week before your baby is due, or later if you are still working. To be eligible for maternity allowance, you will have had to pay enough Class 1 or Class 2 contributions.

Unemployment

A self-employed person may be able to claim unemployment benefit if:

* you have paid sufficient Class 1 contributions in the past, while an employee, to at least receive the reduced rate of unemployment benefit. This rules out a person who was wholly self-employed during the tax year to which the second contribution condition (below) relates
* you must be prepared to work as an employee
* must have paid Class 1 contributions in either of the last two tax years, prior to the calendar year of claim
* must have paid or been credited with Class 1 contributions in both of the last two tax years, ending in the calendar year before the unemployment began.

Normally to qualify for unemployment benefit you have to be capable of work, unemployed and available for work and 'actively seeking work' but it can also be claimed for a 'period of interruption of employment'.

This period of interruption has its own definition. Any two days of unemployment separated by no more than five clear days (not including Sundays) can be linked to form a period of interruption of employment. Any number of days can be linked together in this way, provided they are not isolated by more than five days. These days may be linked together with other such days, providing that two periods are no more than eight weeks apart. You may be able to claim while working part-time, eg part-time teaching. Ask at your local Unemployment Benefit Office or advice centre.

Lower earnings limit

If earnings are below this level, neither employer nor employee is liable to pay Class 1 contributions.

The LEL for 1990/1 is £46 per week. If a person has more than one job, each earnings are usually treated separately for contribution purposes. Occasionally the law will determine that they be aggregated, eg if a person has more than one contract with the same employer.

Other help

As well as the other benefits listed at the beginning, help can also be gained to pay for such things as dental treatment, sight tests, prescriptions, milk, vitamins and clothing for children. Legal aid is available and you may, through Social Security, have access to a social fund loan, although money from this is often difficult to obtain and inadequate.

Medical and Social Security abroad

The UK has medical care and Social Security agreements with some other countries which may help you to get treatment and benefits while you are abroad.

Your Social Security benefits can be affected if you leave the UK for more than a few weeks, for example if you or your child leave for more than eight weeks, you usually won't get child benefit or one-parent benefit.

Appeals

If you feel you have been unfairly treated and have been turned down for a benefit you believe you are entitled to, or think you are entitled to more money than you have been awarded, you are well within your rights to make an appeal.

Notice must be given in writing, within three months of the decision, to your local social security office (preferably the one which made the decision you are appealing against). You can get a form from them. Citizens Advice Bureaux, local authority Social Security Departments and claimants unions can all offer advice.

20 • Employment status & tax

Stewart Young
(of Dodd & Co
Chartered
Accountants) The definition of being employed or self-employed is in practice not always clear-cut. Many artists find themselves employed, self-employed and even unemployed all at the same time, others who thought they were self-employed are told by the tax office they are only carrying on a hobby. What is the significance of these different types of status?

Unemployed

see 19 • Benefits Provided you have paid sufficient National Insurance contributions and you are not undertaking any other paid work, you should be entitled to unemployment benefit and possibly income support. The tax position is that these benefits are taxable but in most cases will not actually be taxed because they will be covered by your personal allowance, ie the amount of income you can earn in a year without paying tax. If you are still unemployed the following April 5, the tax office will do a calculation to see if you are entitled to a tax refund. This arises because of the way the PAYE (Pay As You Earn) system works. An assumption is made that you will be in work for the whole tax year, and, if you are paid monthly, one-twelfth of your personal allowance is set against your pay each month. If you leave work half-way through the tax year then you have only had half of your allowance. So the tax office waits until the end of the tax year to see if you can get another job, then calculates your position.

Example

Debbie, a single woman, worked as a teacher until October 5, 1991 when she was made redundant. During the six months from April 5, 1991 she earned £5,000 and paid £838 in tax. She then claimed taxable benefits of £975 in the period up to April 5, 1992. Her personal allowance for the year as a single woman was £3,295 and her tax position is as follows:

	£	tax
Earnings	5000	838
Taxable benefits	975	
	5975	
Less personal allowance	3295	
Taxable at 25%	2680 =	670
Repayment due to Debbie		£168

Debbie will receive a cheque from the Inland Revenue for £168.

For most artists, a period of unemployment occurs between leaving employment and becoming self-employed.

The question arises as to how long you can continue to claim unemployment benefit, once you have started practising your art. The answer is determined by two conditions imposed on claimants.

• There is an earnings restriction of £2 per day.

• You must be available for work if a suitable vacancy arises.

So you can continue to claim, as long as you are prepared to take a job if it is offered to you or until your earnings exceed the limit of £2 per day.

Employed

In the example above, Debbie worked as a teacher in a comprehensive school and there was no doubt about her tax status. She was an employee of the local education authority and was taxed under the PAYE system. She had a 'contract of service' with her employer who exerted a high degree of control over the terms and conditions of her employment. For tax purposes, Debbie was therefore 'employed' as opposed to being 'self-employed' and she would have been taxed under Schedule E.

The tax schedules are simply a means of categorising an individual's income from all sources, and they range from Schedule A to Schedule F with some of the schedules being subdivided into cases.

The schedules we are interested in are Schedule D Case I or II, Schedule D Case VI and Schedule E. Income falling under each schedule is taxed in a different way, and that is where the importance lies.

Let us return to Debbie. The vast majority of people in work are taxed, like Debbie, under the PAYE scheme. Tax and National Insurance contributions are deducted from earnings at source. The amount of expenses which they can claim against their tax is restricted to those expenses incurred 'wholly exclusively and necessarily' in the performance of their duties, a condition which is interpreted very narrowly by the courts.

Self-employed

see 21 • Trading
status

The category most artists will fall into is being self-employed which comes under Schedule D Case I or II.

The key to being treated as self-employed is being able to convince the tax office that you are carrying out your trade or profession 'on a commercial basis with a view to the realisation of profits'. If you can do that there are advantages to be had, mainly in the amount of expenses you can claim and also in what you can do if you make a loss. With regard to expenses, Debbie on Schedule E you will recall had to follow the 'wholly exclusively and necessarily' rule, but a self-employed person, because of the tax laws, only has to incur expenses 'wholly and exclusively' for them to be allowed. This may not seem much of a distinction but it can make quite a considerable difference to your tax bill.

Hobby

If you fail to convince the tax office that you are practising your art 'on a commercial basis with a view to the realisation of profits' then the result will be that they will claim you are merely indulging in a hobby, and any profits you make will be taxed under Schedule D Case VI. The importance of this is not so much when you make a profit, as when you make a loss. Losses from a hobby can only be carried forward and set against any profits which may arise in the future. Losses from a trade or profession however could be carried forward, but could also be set-off against any other income you might have, thus resulting in a tax repayment. No wonder the tax office try to convince you it is only a hobby!

A mixture

Frequently an artist will be self-employed but also have part-time employment. For tax purposes this income will be assessed under Schedule D Case I or II and Schedule E but three important points are:

- The earnings from teaching should not be included as income in the self-employed accounts, otherwise it may be taxed twice. Instead the net amount received, after deduction of tax and national insurance, should be shown as cash introduced into the business and should be entered separately on the Income Tax Return.

- I mentioned earlier everyone is entitled to a personal allowance of tax-free income each year. It is your right as a tax payer to have this allowance allocated against whichever of your income you want, and it can even be split up. This will be achieved by adjusting your Notice of Coding, which is the instructions from the tax office to your employers telling them how much tax to deduct from your earnings under PAYE. Generally speaking, it is preferable to have your allowance set against your earnings from employment rather than self-employment because this defers payment of the tax. For example, if you are running an evening class at the local art college and expect to earn £500 in the year, write to your tax office and tell them to instruct the college to give you £500 of allowance against that income. That way you should receive the income gross without tax deducted. It is far better to do it that way than to have to claim a refund at the end of the year, which can be very time-consuming.

The Inland Revenue has recently been taking a hard line on course expenses received by a person with a mixture of employment and self-employment. As the expenses are not incurred 'exclusively' for either tax schedule the Revenue is attempting to deny any relief.

One final comment – going back to the example of Debbie claiming a tax repayment. If you leave your employment to become self-employed don't wait until the end of the tax year before claiming a refund. You have your full personal allowance for the year to set against your earnings from employment which will usually result in a repayment. If you do this you should remember any self-employed earnings that year will then all be taxable, but the cash-flow advantages certainly make it worthwhile.

The preparation of accounts

If you have decided to go self-employed, either on a full-time or part-time basis, the first thing to consider on the financial side is the type of accounting records you will require. If this could be summarised in one rule, it would be – keep it simple. Book-keeping is just common sense and a methodical approach. Debits, credits and the mysteries of double-entry can safely be ignored. All that is needed is a record of your income and expenditure together with any supporting documentation. Even if you already have a personal bank account, open either a separate business account or a second personal account and try to use it for all your business transactions. Try and get a receipt for all of your expenses and issue copy invoices for your sales. Your bank statements provide a record of all your cheque transactions so all you need to do is to keep a note of cash received and spent. Sometimes you might meet a business expense using a cheque from your personal bank account or using cash from another source. A record should be kept of such expenses as they can still be claimed for. Remember, you are basically going to have to pay tax on the difference between your income and expenditure, and the lower this is (legitimately!), the less tax you will have to pay.

Not all expenditure reduces your tax bill directly. Accountants like to distinguish between what they call 'Revenue' and 'Capital' expenditure. Revenue expenditure consists of such things as:

- studio (rent, rates, insurance) or proportion of domestic expenses
- studio light and heat
- repairs to studio and studio equipment
- telephone or proportion of domestic bill
- cleaning or replacement of working clothes
- materials
- small tools and items of equipment (£50 maximum per item, above this items would be classed as capital costs – note this is a rule of thumb only)
- framing expenses
- commission paid to agents/galleries
- exhibition charges and expenses
- photography, publicity, advertising
- newspapers, magazines, subscriptions
- books (£50 rule of thumb)
- printing and photocopying
- postage and stationery
- catalogues and admission to exhibitions
- travelling expenses (UK) – from work place to business only
- motor vehicle running expenses or proportion of private vehicle
- foreign travel expenses related directly to the business
- fees for assistants
- bank charges and interest on bank loan-overdraft
- accountancy and legal fees
- miscellaneous expenses.

These expenses are set against your income in full in the accounting period in which they are incurred. Capital expenditure on the other hand is expenditure on the purchase of assets for use in your business, eg a camera, an easel or a car. This is not claimed in full in the accounting period in which it is incurred, but the cost of the asset is spread out over its useful life as estimated by the Inland Revenue, and a proportion of the cost is given against your profits for each year in the period. It is done in such a way that more relief is given in earlier years than later, a system known as the reducing-balance basis. The deductions themselves are referred to as capital allowances.

Example

Tony has been a photographer for several years. In the year ended December 31, 1991 he had income from commissions of £9,000 and incurred revenue expenditure of £4,000. He also bought a camera in the autumn sales for £300. His taxable profit for 1992/93 would be as follows:

	£
Income from commissions	9,000
Less revenue expenditure	4,000
Profit per accounts	5,000
Less capital allowance	(75)
Taxable Profit	£4925

Capital Allowances on the camera have been claimed on 25% of the expenditure, leaving £225 unclaimed. In the next tax year 1993/94, Tony would be able to claim 25% of the unclaimed balance, or £56 leaving £169 unclaimed. This process would continue until either all the expenditure was claimed or the camera was sold or scrapped.

Before leaving the subject of accounts, I want to highlight two areas which often cause problems:

Use of house

Some artists are fortunate enough to have their own studio which may be rented or leased or perhaps shared with others. If so, all the running expenses such as rent, heating, lighting, rates, etc, can be claimed in the accounts as revenue expenses. Frequently, however, many start off using part of their house as a studio, either setting aside a room or just working where they can whenever a room is free. In that case, they should still claim for a proportion of the running costs of the house, which could be said to be attributable to the business usage.

The exact proportion is a matter for negotiation with the tax office but they will accept any reasonable basis of apportionment. In the example above, let us suppose Tony lives in a six-room house including a cellar and he uses one room as his photography studio and the cellar as a darkroom. He should claim in his accounts one-third of his expenditure on water rates, insurance, repairs, heating and lighting. Community charge/council tax is a tax on an individual and cannot be claimed as a business expense, though Unified Business Rate can be.

Motor expenses

Many artists have a car or a motorbike which they use partly on business and part privately. It is difficult deciding just how much should be claimed as a business expense. One way would be to keep a note of all mileage incurred in the year distinguishing private from business and apportioning total motor expenses, including petrol, road tax, insurance and repairs, in that ratio. This is often inconvenient, however, and the best thing is to keep a record of all expenses and then estimate a percentage for business use. The basis of apportionment should be clearly shown in the accounts and you should be prepared to justify it to the tax office.

How your tax is calculated

In the example in the last section, Tony had been a photographer for several years and his accounts for the year ended December 31, 1991 formed the basis for his tax assessment for the tax year 1992/93, which is the year ending April 5, 1993. This basis of assessment is known as the PY (Previous Year) basis and is used for all self-employed people once they have been trading for a few years. The reason is to give you time to prepare accounts and have them agreed with the tax office before your tax becomes due for payment. When a person starts up in business, however, some fancy footwork is required to get them onto the PY basis. Without going into too much detail, if the year to December 31, 1990 had been Tony's first year of trading, and he had made a taxable profit of £1,200, then his tax assessments would have been as follows:

- **1989/90** – profits for the period January 1, 1990 to April 5, 1990: 3/12 x £1,200 = £300

- **1990/91** – profits for the first 12 months of trading: £1,200

- **1991/92** – profits of the previous year, being the year ended December 31, 1990: £1,200

- **1992/93** – as before, based on the accounts for the year ended December 31, 1991: £5,000 before capital allowances

Note that it takes Tony three years to get onto the PY basis, and most importantly, the tax assessments for each of those three years are based on the same set of accounts for the year of trading up to December 31, 1990. It is therefore vital to keep your profits down in the first year to as little as possible. If you can make a loss in your first year, then you will not have to pay any tax for the first three years of assessment.

Let me now look at these two possibilities in more detail:

Scenario 1 – you make a profit

Tony's tax assessment for 1992/93 was to be based on his profits after capital allowances of £4,925 in the year to December 31, 1991. Suppose, as described above in 'A Mixture', Tony is single with a personal allowance of £3,455 for the year and two part-time lecturing posts at local colleges, So that no tax should be deducted from his earnings from these employments, he has instructed his tax office to apportion his personal allowance as follows:

To University	£1,500
To Polytechnic	£500
	£2,000
Balance available against profits from self-employment	£1,445
Total personal allowance	£3,445

His tax assessment for his self-employment will then look like this:

Profits as a photographer	£4,925
Less balance of allowances	£1,445
Taxable profits	£3,480

Tony's income tax liability for the year will then be £3,480 at 25% = £870. This will be payable in two equal instalments of £435 on January 1, 1993 and July 1, 1993. Tony is not liable for Class 4 national insurance contributions, about which more later.

Scenario 2 – you make a loss

Whilst making a loss in your first year might not please your bank manager, it can be good news from a tax point of view. Firstly, as mentioned earlier, you will pay no tax for at least the first three years. Secondly, provided you have convinced the tax office you were certainly trying to make a profit, and so are being assessed under Schedule D Case I or II, there are three things you can do with the loss:

- you can carry it forward against future profits, reducing one of your future tax bills. This is all you can do with a loss under Schedule D Case VI if you are deemed to be only indulging in a hobby.
- you can set it off against any other income you may have had in the year, which has suffered tax. This changed with effect from April 6, 1991. tax can now be reversed.
- in the first four years of trading you can carry the loss back to three years earlier and set it off against your income of that year. For example, a loss arising in 1992/3 could be relieved against income arising in 1989/90.

As a generalisation, in the first four years of trading it is more advantageous to carry a loss back rather than use it in the same year, if only because the Inland Revenue pays interest on tax repayments relating to fiscal years ending more than twelve months before the date of repayments. A word of warning – there is a complicated interaction between loss relief and personal allowance, and if you want to be sure of getting the maximum relief possible you should consult an accountant.

Other taxation

The above deals only with personal taxation which is what will directly affect most artists. Anyone who has established themselves as a limited company, partnership, association, charity or whatever, either to operate a business or for the purposes of a studio group or the like, may become liable to such things as corporation tax, audited accounts, etc. If you are operating in this way you should seek professional advice both from an accountant and from other groups operating in a similar way to yourself.

National Insurance

see 19 • Benefits In addition to income tax, another liability is National Insurance contributions. These come in four varieties:

- **Class 1** – These are deducted from earnings as an employee, which as previously stated are taxed under Schedule E. In addition to the employee's contribution there is also an employer's contribution which is a further payment by the employer on top of what has been deducted from your earnings. Class 1 contributions start as soon as your earnings from a particular employment reach a certain level. Employees often deliberately pay their workers below this level to avoid paying the contribution.

- **Class 2** – This used to be known as the 'stamp' because you kept a record of your contributions by buying special stamps and sticking them on a card. Above a certain earnings level, all self-employed people have to pay Class 2 contributions which are a flat rate each week. They can now be paid by direct debit if required.

- **Class 3** – These are voluntary contributions, again at a flat weekly rate, which can be paid by those not otherwise liable to pay contributions, in order to maintain their entitlement to benefit.

- **Class 4** – This is in the form of an additional tax on profits for self-employed people. It is calculated as a percentage of profits between a lower and upper limit.

The self-employed are liable to two types of contribution, Class 2 and Class 4. An important point concerns the small earnings exemption for Class 2 contributions. If your earnings are, or you anticipate they will be, less than a certain level (the small earnings exemption) you can claim exemption from Class 2 contributions. or a refund if you have already paid them. Leaflet N1 27A from your local DSS office explains the procedure, but you should be aware that by not paying you may be affecting your entitlement to future benefits.

Class 4 contributions are calculated on the profits of your business above a certain threshold and are paid in two instalments at the same time as your income tax (normally on January 1 in the year of assessment, and July 1 following the year of assessment). A deduction equivalent to one half of your total Class 4 contribution is allowed against your profits for income tax purposes.

VAT

This stands for Value Added Tax and is usually best avoided. However, if your taxable turnover exceeds certain maximum levels (£36,600 per annum, excluding grants, from March 11, 1992), then registration is compulsory. You will then be required to charge VAT on your output, and every three months you will have to add up the VAT you have charged, deduct from it VAT you have paid in running the business, and pay the difference to the VAT authorities. If on the other hand you have paid out more VAT than you have taken in, you will get a refund. VAT is a very complicated area. If you think you should be registered, and particularly if you are involved in importing or exporting, you should seek professional advice.

21 • Trading status

Nick Sharp Deciding what legal form is best for your particular circumstances is not always simple. It depends on, eg tax, costs of formation and on-going administrative costs, the risk of failure and personal liability for debts incurred, public disclosure, the need to raise finance, employment of staff, ownership of property, the relationship you have with your trading partners and whether the principal aim of your enterprise is to make profits or not. There are few hard and fast rules; it is a good idea to talk to others to see what solutions they have had. If you can, speak to a solicitor or accountant. This is only an outline of the various possibilities.

Sole trader

If you are on your own, this is what you will automatically be. You do not have to register your business with any authority. If you use a trade name you must show your name and address as proprietor on all business stationery, on a notice in the premises and anywhere you are working where the public have access. You do not have to submit accounts to Companies House, neither are you subject to the laws affecting directors under the Companies Acts. You will have to pay National Insurance contributions and submit annual accounts to HM Inspector of Taxes.

You will be responsible for paying any tax due on your business, and if your turnover (not profits) exceeds the VAT threshold (in 1992, £36,600 in any year) you need to add VAT to invoices and sales and complete quarterly VAT returns.

You will be personally liable for any debts you incur in your business. Since there is no distinction between your personal assets and those you use for your business, if you do incur debts that cannot be repaid, your personal assets (eg your home) may have to be sold.

Partnership

Up to 20 people carrying on a business 'with a view to profit' can be a partnership. You can form one without any written agreement, but because the Partnership Act 1890 implies agreement between you on certain issues unless you have agreed otherwise, to ensure you don't certain issues unless you have agreed otherwise, to ensure you don't have inappropriate rules imposed on you, always have a clear written agreement on matters such as sharing profits and losses, and provision of capital.

Use the following as a checklist for partnership agreements:

- name and nature of business and commencing date
- amount of capital provided by each partner; provisions for withdrawal
- clear definition of the role and authority of each partner
- arrangements and authorities for operating bank account(s)
- preparation of annual accounts
- apportioning of profits and losses (equal or unequal shares)
- voting rights (equal or one or more partners having control)
- insurance and amounts to be covered
- duration of the partnership (reviews or renewals)
- arrangements for arbitration if partners disagree
- provisions for prolonged sickness of a partner
- provision for holidays and other time off
- provision and use of cars
- pension benefits
- arrangements for admitting new partners
- provisions preventing partners from competing with the partnership (if appropriate)
- provisions for the death of a partner
- provision for the retirement or leaving of a partner
- arrangements for dissolving the partnership.
- ownership of work and ownership of copyright in the work jointly produced by the partnership.

To the outside world, every partner can commit all the partners to any agreement and each is liable (to the extent of his/her personal assets) for all the debts of the business. For these reasons, partnerships are not very popular in the visual arts, used only where there is trust between the individuals concerned.

Each partner pays tax at his or her individual rates on any income from the partnership. Partnership accounts will need to be prepared for submission to the Inland Revenue, but these need not be audited. There is no need to register a partnership or file returns at Companies House.

Unincorporated association

Most artists groups tend to be these, as are others whose primary aim is not profit, eg members' clubs, community associations, trade unions.

Unincorporated associations can exist without a formal constitution, but it is always wise to have one to ensure everyone knows where they stand and procedures for voting, decision-making etc. A constitution can be quite simple and the process of setting up an unincorporated association can be cheap and quick. You should have a Committee or Council of Management who will take responsibility for most decisions and for overseeing the group's finances.

Because it has no legal identity of its own and in legal terms is only a collection of individuals, an unincorporated association cannot start legal action, borrow money or enter into contracts in its own name, and cannot hold property without appointing trustees (usually members) to do so on its behalf. Officers of unincorporated associations can be personally liable for the debts of the group, as can individual members if they have signed a contract in their own name.

Trusts

A trust is a legal structure where land, money or other property is held in the names of trustees for certain defined purposes, and is usually constituted by a formal trust deed drawn up by a solicitor. For technical legal reasons, a trust will not normally be suitable unless the body concerned is capable of being registered as a charity.

Confusion arises with references to 'trustees' where, for instance, an art group holds the lease of the group's premises. This occurs because a group (not having its own separate legal identity) can only hold property in the name of up to four of its members, who (the law says) will automatically hold the property 'on trust for', or on behalf of, the group. This arises informally, without need for a written trust deed.

Limited companies

All companies are legal entities quite separate from their members, unlike all the above. They can sue, hold property and enter into contracts in their own names. The owners will not be liable for debts and liabilities but if the company needs to borrow money, they are often asked to give personal guarantees to the bank. Directors can also be personally liable for debts incurred while the company is, or is near, insolvent.

There are two types of limited companies: those limited by shares (eg commercial companies); those limited by guarantee (usually charities or non-profit distributing companies). Companies limited by shares are owned by shareholders (a minimum of two) and run by boards of directors; guarantee companies have members and are usually run by a council or committee of management. The directors or council of management are elected by the shareholders or members. In either case, the liability of the members or shareholder to pay if the company owes money is limited to a purely nominal amount, usually £1.

At least two people are required to set up a company. Formation and running costs tend to be high, annual returns have to be submitted to Companies House and accounts have to be audited and filed each year. The constitution, annual accounts and other documents filed at Companies House are all open to public inspection. A company structure is suitable for any size of organisation and a ready-made constitution is provided in the Companies Act 1985.

Before opting to form a company, consider whether the expense and administartive requirements are justified by the benefits of corporate status and limited liability. You should also take advice from an accountant regarding tax and NI contributions. Companies pay tax at special corporation tax rates on their profits.

Disadvantages include:

- company must operate PAYE system on all salaries and wages
- company pays employer's N.I. contributions on all salaries and wages
- it costs up to £200 to incorporate using an agent
- annual professional auditing of accounts is a statutory requirement
- professional tax and accounting advice is almost essential
- annual accounts and returns must be submitted to Companies House
- company details are open to public examination
- directors are subject to company law, insolvency acts, etc
- changes of directors and other matters to be filed at Companies House (including changes to constitution) – there are fines and penalties for late filing
- voluntary dissolution is complex.

Cooperatives

Groups of more than seven people can form a registered cooperative under the Industrial and Provident Society Acts 1965-78. You must be carrying on a business industry or trade and be 'a bona-fide cooperative society', ie established on sound cooperative principles, including open and voluntary membership, equal voting rights and distribution of profits on basis of participation, not, for instance capital invested.

If you qualify, you can register with the Registrar of Friendly Societies. Model rules are provided by ICOM and others. The current formation fee is slightly higher than for forming a company, but the formalities are less rigid. As with a limited company, individual members are not liable for the debts and liabilities beyond a nominal amount.

You do not need to form an Industrial and Provident Society registered co-operative if you want an organisation run on cooperative principles. Less than seven people can form a coop and register with the Registrar of Companies. Partnerships, unincorporated associations and limited companies can all operate on cooperative lines.

Charities

Registered charities are non profit-distributing bodies which fulfil the complex legal definition of 'charity'. This must always involve a sufficient element of benefit to the public; in the view of the Charity Commissioners, this is often incompatible with benefiting the members, so most artists groups are excluded. If you think you may be eligible, talk to a solicitor or the NCVO, which offers advice service to the voluntary sector.

Charities can exist in the form of unincorporated associations, trusts or companies limited by guarantee; the choice can be important if you are applying for registration. Substantial trading activity may stop a group obtaining charitable status, but If the trading is only secondary, a separate non-charitable body (eg a limited company) can he set up to conduct the trading, which will pay its profit to the charity, so preserving charitable status.

Main benefits are reduced rates/poll tax, relief from income tax on profits and tax relief for donors. Under the Charities Act 1992, charities will be subjected to increasing supervision and scrutiny.

22 • Insurance

Chris McCready
with additional
material from
*Artists Handbooks:
Money Matters*

Artists, as small business people, need adequate and appropriate insurance cover. It may be complex, requiring individual, sometimes specialist advice. But whether you work from home (three million do), a studio, or business premises, your needs can be fairly easily assessed.

You need to be properly insured for two main reasons: firstly, your statutory or legal responsibilities need to be addressed; secondly, you need to assess the effect on you, your livelihood and the livelihood of others dependent upon you, that a number of eventualities might bring.

The cover
Statutory responsibilities: if at any time you enter into what may be construed as an employer/employee relationship with anyone (including freelance assistants, models, even your own children) you must have employers liability insurance by law. It is, in any event, essential cover in the light of ever-increasing amounts awarded by courts for injury compensation claims. Fortunately, this cover is usually cheap to acquire.

The second aspect of insurance needs is more complicated and you will be presented with a fairly long list of eventualities that you could insure against. You must decide what you definitely need, what you would like and what you can afford.

The experts
You will need expert advice. Before contacting an insurance broker (simply an agent, acting on your behalf, to place your insurance with an insurer and being financially reimbursed via commission calculated on the cost, or premium, of that insurance) or the actual insurers themselves, it is important to understand how insurance works.

Essentially, by taking out an insurance policy, you have asked someone to accept the risk to you of financial loss caused by whatever it is you are insuring against. Whether you take out this policy through a broker or direct with insurers (or underwriters), makes no difference. But, in the event of a claim, having a broker to act as an intermediary between you and the compensation payer can be an advantage.

The skill of the broker lies in grasping the intricacies of your business. Whilst many operate in niche or specialist areas such as small businesses, never assume knowledge on their part. Spell it out.

Having briefed your broker and filled in a 'menu' (proposal form) of cover required, they take it to the insurer/underwriter. The skill of the underwriter lies in assessing the risk and the 'odds' or likelihood of their having to pay you in the event of a claim. When they apply this data against the sum insured (their liability) and by a formula derived from many sources, including experience, they will arrive at a sum (the premium) you must pay, in exchange for their accepting the risk.

The market place

Many insurance companies have made advances in meeting the needs of small business, by designing flexible policies. They have taken the refreshing view that we do not really want to be faced with over-complicated proposal forms and a plethora of legal jargon. Eagle Star's Tradestar policy has even won a Plain English Campaign Award. Others offer such attractions as a Legal Help Line. Some add easy to manage monthly payment schemes or even no claims discounts.

Needs and desires

Treat insurance as much a part of what you do as the cost of the raw materials you work with; don't stint (but don't overdo it) and remember, insurance is only an unnecessary evil until you need it. At that point it becomes absolutely essential.

Break down your requirements before approaching brokers or insurance companies. The better organised and aware you are the better the understanding and, therefore, advice you will receive.

Decide what it is you're insuring and the effect the occurrence of this risk will have on you. What may be a definite need for some may not be important for others. That's why most insurers work on a 'Menu Basis', giving you the option to 'bolt-on' different aspects and risks.

To determine your needs and desires, approach the subject under three main insurance areas:

• your work and work place

• yourself and your income

• your home and contents.

First familiarise yourself with the types of insurance available. Below are the main types of cover, what they mean and (*very* approximately) what they are likely to cost. In all cases, *the Proposer* is you. *Cover* means items and circumstances (or risk) being insured.

Work & work place

Contents

Cover: All risks of physical loss or damage whilst at the proposer's premises.

Consisting of: Stock, fixtures, fittings, showcases, machinery, plant, tools, equipment, reference books, decorations and improvements, grilles, burglar alarms, computers and accessories.

Extensions: Other locations: Stock, fixtures and fittings at fairs, exhibitions, repairers' and restorers' premises, private and/or commercial clients' premises, auction rooms, galleries and own residence and anywhere else in the world.
Transit : As above and whilst in transit to other locations.

NB: If the proposer's premises form part of a cooperative workshop or similar, it is possible cover of theft may be limited to theft involving forcible and/or violent entry to or exit from the premises.

Cost guide: £5 premium per £1000 insured.

Legal liability to the public

Cover: Indemnity for accidental personal injury and accidental damage to property of the public.

NB: Every self-employed person should really have this insurance. This is particularly true if the artist has a studio or undertakes residencies or works in public places. It insures against any risk of an accident arising as a result of their work, eg someone attending their studio falling over and injuring themselves, or the artist dropping a tool whilst installing a work out of doors and injuring someone.

Cost guide: £75-£100 premium for £1,000,000 indemnity limit.

Products liability

Cover: Indemnity (as above) caused by what you make. Usually subject to UK jurisdiction clause.

Cost guide: Invariably covered by premium for Public Liability. Check to ensure it is included.

Liability to employees

Cover: Provides unlimited indemnity in respect of your legal liability for accidents to employees arising in the course of their employment. Premium can vary according to the nature of your activities.

NB: Statutory requirement under law if at any time you enter into an employer/employee relationship with anyone. For instance, freelance assistants, models, etc. Premium usually calculated on your annual 'wages' bill.

Cost guide: £20 premium (assuming wages bill to be less than £10,000 a year)

Personal accident

Cover: i) Death, loss of eyes, limbs, permanent total disablement; ii) Temporary total disablement.

NB: Most insurers will limit this cover to persons aged between 16 and 70. There will also usually be a time period limitation on payments under ii) above (around 104 weeks, say).

Cost guide: Single annual premium of £75 per person to include the following indemnity: £10,000 capital sum payment (under i), £100 per week (under ii).

If you own your building

Cover: All risks of physical loss or damage.

NB: You will need to demonstrate that the buildings are of proper material construction and in good repair. Nearby rivers, underground workings, signs of subsidence and settlement are of particular interest to insurers. It is particularly important to add to the sum insured a percentage to cover such items as architects' and surveyors' fees and debris removal costs. An addition of approximately 15% of the rebuilding costs is usually recommended. The sum insured should represent the rebuilding cost of the property, not its market value.

Cost guide: £2 premium per £1000 insured.

Sample premiums

	Sum insured £	Premium £
Contents		
at place of business, inc stocks	1,000	65
Contents in transit	1,000	10
Contents whilst at other location	3,000	8
Public/Products Liability	1 million	75
Employer's liability	No limit	20
Personal accident		75
Capital sum insured	10,000	
Weekly Disablement Payment	100	
Total sample premium		**£253**

Household: contents and all risks

see 17 • A place to work If you carry on your business from home or lodge stock, tools or materials, etc used in your business, it is *essential* to declare this. Failure to do so will mean, in the event of a claim, you risk not being compensated for your loss. Even more importantly, it is entirely possible that *all* your cover could be negated. You'd lose everything, home included.

Motor

If you are using your car for business and have to make a claim, you will almost certainly not be covered unless you are insured for Class I (business use). Don't try to obtain a lower premium by restricting your policy to social, domestic cover only. It does not make sense. Nor does not having 'in transit' cover for your equipment, stock, etc

Many insurers treat small business cover as a 'loss leader' in order to cross-sell other insurance (such as Household and Motor). You could have considerable leverage in placing your business if you also offer up these two categories. You are under no obligation, and in any event, both these types of policies are subject to (often) wide fluctuations in premiums. Get another quote before automatically renewing with your current insurers. Don't forget to compare not just the price quoted but the extent of the cover.

In the event of a claim

Notify your insurance broker/company *immediately* by telephone. The broker/insurer will forward you a claims form. If all is straightforward the claim will go through and, sooner or later, you will receive a cheque in compensation.

The insurers may ask that a loss adjuster visit you. They ensure that all is as it should be and that they are able to declare, in their professional capacity, that their client's (the insurer/underwriter) interests are protected and that any payment is fair compensation for the loss. Such a visit is usually routine.

If the loss adjuster decides, however, that the terms of the insurance have been breached (eg burglar alarm or locks defective) or the sum claimed is inflated (eg total loss of an item claimed, when the item is repairable at a lesser sum), he can recommend a lesser offer of compensation. In extreme cases, the loss adjuster can recommend no compensation at all, particularly if 'foul play' is suspected.

If you disagree with the assessment and recommendation on compensation, you are free to negotiate to try and get a better 'deal'. Here a broker can assist in acting as a conduit between you and your insurer. If all else fails there is an Ombudsman available to arbitrate.

Your art, its value and the basis for claim

To compensate fairly for the loss of your art (through burglary or damage, say), the insurer has to arrive at a price on which to base your financial loss.

If you are David Hockney this presents no problem. If you are working on a fixed value commission or contract, or if you have established a market for your work and a market 'value' is attached to it, there is no problem.

If you have not, the basis for settlement of claims is significant. Generally, insurers arrive at a compensation offer for loss or damage to your 'stock' (both completed articles and work in progress) by applying commercial criteria, viz: raw materials plus costs of manufacture = cost.

But if you are part way through a 'speculative' piece of work (ie non-commissioned), materials may account for little. Costs of manufacture could mean your time plus limited overheads, such as lighting. Worse still, you may have been working for months accumulating a 'portfolio' of work, hoping for a showing at a gallery. The loss would be catastrophic. The whole point about art is the impossibility of defining (or valuing) the creative thought and technical skill that allowed you to 'produce' it in the first place. If you do not have a defined marketable value, how can you be compensated? There is no easy answer.

Personal insurance

There are three other types of insurance you may wish to consider: life assurance, permanent health insurance and pensions.

Life assurance

Comes in two forms. The first is self-explanatory, ie a regular premium paid to an insurance company, which will, if the person who is insured dies, pay back a set sum. The bigger the sum required, the bigger the premium. This is often taken out in connection with mortgages, or other big loans, to ensure that if the borrower dies the lender will be repaid. It is also appropriate if the person whose life is insured will leave dependants, such as spouse and children. It ensures they will have a lump sum to replace the income of the person who died.

Permanent health insurance

This provides an income for people unable to work because of ill health. Normally policies do not pay out until the insured person has been unable to work for at least three months. Policies that pay out more quickly are usually very expensive. Policies usually pay out for the remainder of a person's expected working life if incapacity is permanent.

A policy can therefore be an effective 'top up' on state benefits. Taking out such a policy is a matter of choice. The risk may be one you are not interested in protecting yourself against.

Pensions

A pension policy is money put aside now in a favourable saving scheme so you have an additional income to the state retirement pension when you cease work. In practice, retirement is allowed at any age from 50. This form of savings has favourable tax treatment as, subject to age limits, a percentage of a person's income may be paid into a pension policy and these payments considered a trading expense, so reducing tax liability. For a person aged under 35 the limit of income payable into a policy is 17.5% of earnings. For a person aged over 60 it is 40%. The maximum earnings that may be taken into consideration are £60,000.

Warnings

Take particular care with these three types of insurance policy. Life assurance policies, often sold as savings schemes, are not truly life assurance policies but an odd form of saving where you only get a real return if you keep the money in for ten years. Few artists are able to put money aside for such a long period. Be wary.

There are many companies selling these, and most people selling policies earn good commissions. So there is inevitably a high degree of selling taking place. All life assurance and pension sales are now regulated by law but this does not eliminate misleading advice.

Take advice from an independent advisor. Make sure the broker is properly registered to FIMBRA or by the Law Society or an Institute of Chartered Accountants, and insist on their recommendations in writing. Do not sign anything unless you are sure you can afford the policies and understand the costs and potential benefits. If possible, obtain advice from an insurance broker and check it with an accountant, even if you have to pay a small fee to do so.

23 • Contracts

Juliet Burgess
with additional
material by
Nicholas Sharp

A contract is an agreement between two or more people which is legally binding. There are three essential ingredients:

- agreement – one person has made a firm offer which the other has accepted
- an intention to create a legal relationship – this is automatically presumed in a commercial agreement
- consideration – this is the price or something of value in the eyes of the law, such as a promise in return for a counter-promise.

Verbal agreements

A contract need not be in writing to be legally valid, apart from exceptions such as house purchase and credit agreements, provided it contains the three elements above. A verbal agreement will be legally enforceable but the advantages of committing the terms to paper are manifold. Almost all transactions in the business, theatrical and musical worlds are conducted using written contracts. They give:

- a checklist and points of reference
- a professional framework to a business relationship
- proof as to what was agreed should a dispute arise
- an opportunity for the parties to concentrate on the nature of the transaction and their mutual obligations.

What form should a contract take?

A written contract need not be a formal document to be valid. The contractual terms may well be contained in a letter detailing what was agreed. During a telephone conversation take a note of the points covered and at the end read them back to the other person to ensure there is a mutual understanding of what has been agreed. Then confirm those points in a letter as soon as possible afterwards.

Use of a standard contract (the same basic form with details relating to venue, dates, fee, etc changing) will save time re-negotiating all the basic conditions. It also ensures no important point is omitted as it serves as a memorandum of terms to be covered and provides the artist with maximum protection.

Artist's position

In theory it is easy to advocate the use of the artist's own contract but in reality it may prove to be very difficult, especially for the young and inexperienced. The problems are apparent: inequality of bargaining power, lack of confidence, and fear of being considered difficult to work with. You have something valuable to offer and by adopting a professional basis to working relationships in the form of a contract you are not undermining the value or quality of what you do. Insisting on working only with a contract is not being difficult but business-like. This is not at variance with creative integrity. Taking the initiative with a contract will in the short term provide you with more room to manoeuvre and in the long term generally improve working conditions and expectations of the artist.

Negotiating successful contracts

- Successful negotiation ensures the needs of both parties, not just one, are satisfied. It does not involve defeating the other party.
- Know as much as possible about the other party – eg what advances, royalties, fees have they given to others?
- Know as much as possible about what others have achieved in similar deals, and get a copy of their contract for comparison.
- See if you can borrow a sample contract or checklist.
- Before negotiations write down the most important points you need to agree.
- Put all offers in writing.
- Be prepared, on occasions, to lose a deal rather than put up with one you will regret.
- Never leave it open to doubt whether you have agreed to a proposal or not – eg if a publisher writes to you setting out proposed terms and you do not reply, a contract may well be implied even if you didn't want to conclude one.
- Never agree to something, in writing or verbally, when you know you still have points to discuss and agree.
- When all important issues are discussed and agreed, make sure these are embodied in a contract or exchange of letters, which is signed by both parties.

- Keep copies of all correspondence.
- Keep written notes of meetings and important phone conversations.
- Insist on signing a contract or exchanging letters before permitting any work (eg reproductions) to go ahead – it is much more difficult to negotiate from a position of weakness.
- Beware signing something which may later turn out to be a contract.

Ways out

The only way out of a contract is by its own terms – either by those stated or by those implied by law.

By performance
Where each party has completed his or her side of the bargain and nothing more remains to be done.

By agreement
The parties may decide to cancel and mutually abandon their obligations.

By breach
Failure to complete through fault: in this situation the 'injured' party is entitled to claim damages or compensation for the loss caused by the breach. The object is to put the person not at fault in the same financial position had the contract been performed in its entirety. The contract may expressly provide what should be paid in the event of a breach through fault or, if litigation is necessary, the court will decide.

If there is a breach of a vital term the innocent person may treat the contract as at an end and sue; eg a promoter engages an artist for two separate performances and agrees to pay a fee after each. The promoter fails to pay after the first night in breach of the agreement. The artist is entitled to refuse to perform again and sue for damages.

Failure to complete contract but through no fault: the contract may make provision for this and state a person will not be in breach provided they have done all reasonably possible to complete their side of the contract. This might arise if, due to traffic delays or extreme weather conditions, the artist is unable to reach the venue in time.

By frustration
This occurs where, through no fault of either party, it becomes impossible to carry out the contract which automatically ends. The contract would be frustrated if the venue was burnt down or the artist dies or is too ill to

carry it out. It is sensible to include in a contract terms covering cancellation and breach with details such as:

- time scales in respect of the date of cancellation in relation to the exhibition/performance date and percentage of fees payable on cancellation
- which matters will allow the parties to be discharged from the contract, eg sickness, travel difficulties
- insurance to cover cancellation
- clauses linking payment to work done since the contract was agreed and before cancellation.

Contractual disputes

Often disputes are resolved by solutions significantly different from the strict legal position. Insistence on legal rights might be disruptive to a continuing relationship and have a tendency to provide one or other with the reputation of being difficult to work with. Sometimes it is not possible to overcome the problem with the other person involved.

Legal advice

Professional advice from a solicitor should always be taken in situations likely to involve a court action. A solicitor's letter is useful and advice can prevent a case having to come to court. Remember legal proceedings in a court can be very expensive. Free legal advice is available from Citizens Advice Bureaux (CAB) and other advice centres. Law Centres may be able to help. Contact the Law Centres Federation for a list of centres in your area. They may refer you to a solicitor operating Legal Aid schemes. To get Legal Aid you must see a solicitor. If you do not already have one ask your local CAB or Law Centre or someone for a recommendation. You can also refer to *Yellow Pages*. The *Solicitors' Regional Directory* from libraries and Law Centres gives details of the kind of work firms undertake. Eligibility for Legal Aid depends on savings and income and you may be required to contribute to legal costs.

In addition to the Legal Aid Scheme many solicitors are prepared to give up to half an hour's legal advice for £5. (The Green Form scheme can give up to two hours free advice from a solicitor.) This is called a 'fixed fee interview' and is available regardless of your financial status. Solicitors who provide this are listed in the *Solicitors' Regional Directory.*

Questions to ask a solicitor

Although not many solicitors are familiar with artists' problems, you will not always require specialist advice. To help find a solicitor who is competent, interested in your case and affordable:

- ask for a short initial meeting or phone conversation free of charge to explain the problem and find out how the solicitor thinks he or she can help – you should not expect free advice at this meeting
- before seeing the solicitor assemble any correspondence and notes in date order and leave a copy with the solicitor
- establish at the first meeting if you are eligible for Legal Aid or the Green Form scheme – this will depend on your financial situation
- ask for an overall estimate of fees and an hourly rate
- make your own financial position clear
- ask who in the office you will deal with – you may find it is someone straight out of law school and this may be fine in some cases
- in a case where specialist advice is needed ask what kind of work the solicitor usually does and the kind of clients they act for
- do not hesitate to make a decision based on personal impressions. Having a solicitor you like and can work with is important
- discuss the alternatives with your solicitor – expediency, time and cost can sometimes be more important than principle
- keep in regular contact with the solicitor to keep up to date with progress but do not encourage them to write long letters of advice which cost money and may leave you none the wiser – telephone calls or short meetings are better
- respond promptly to telephone calls and letters and tell your solicitor if you are unclear about advice or your case generally.

Court proceedings

Contractual claims are heard in the County Court where less than £1000 is involved and for sums in excess, the High Court has jurisdiction unless it refers the matter to the County Court (increasingly the case for under £50,000). Magistrates and Crown Courts deal only with criminal matters.

Court procedure has been greatly simplified so it is possible to bring a 'small claim' (for sums under £1000) before the court without any knowledge of the law or legal representation. A useful booklet *Small Claims in the County Court,* issued by the Lord Chancellor's Department, is freely available from CAB.

Where more than £1000 is in dispute or if complicated issues need to be resolved take legal advice and get a solicitor to represent you. Litigation should be a last resort. It is expensive in terms of time, hassle and money and you should consider very carefully whether it is worthwhile. There is no point if your opponent isn't in a position to pay up.

24 • Copyright & moral rights

Copyright is a complex issue. This chapter is an overview. If you need more detail look at *Artists Handbooks: Copyright* by Roland Miller (AN Publications). As a general rule don't rely on the law to protect your copyright. Think about it before it becomes a problem and write it into all contractual agreements.

On August 1, 1989 the new copyright law (the Copyright, Designs and Patents Act 1988) came into effect. It replaced the old law 1956, removing anomalies, strengthening artists' rights, bringing UK legislation in line with the Berne Convention on moral rights and making it easier to bring legal action against those who infringe copyright.

Copyright

The new act only affects works produced after the change took place. Work produced before remains protected under the 1956 act. So it is important to be are aware of the provisions of both laws.

What is copyright?

It is the legal right not to suffer any reproduction of an 'artistic work' without the consent of the copyright owner – seeking to ensure any economic benefits from reproductions, etc are under the control of the copyright owner.

What is protected?

Both old and new acts give protection to work which passes three tests:

- It must be produced by a citizen, domicile or resident (or in the case of companies, incorporated) in the UK or any country which is a signatory to the Berne Convention on copyright (most countries).
- It must be original – not physically copied from another original work. It must involve original skill and labour but not necessarily thought. In the case of a limited edition of prints, each print qualifies as original because it is not a copy from another print.

- Under the old law, paintings, sculpture, drawings, prints and photographs are covered by automatically copyright protection. Other works (collage, montage, craftwork, artists' bookworks, body art, installations, laser and light works, mixed-media assemblages and holograms) under the old act are only covered if they can demonstrate they have 'artistic merit', ie the makers must have applied their skill and taste to its making with the intention to create a work which has aesthetic appeal. Such works are categorised as works of 'artistic craftsmanship'. After August 1, 1989, collages are elevated from works of 'artistic craftsmanship' to those that automatically qualify for protection. Holograms, as new technology, are covered in the new act by the new definition of a photograph – *'a recording of light or other radiation on any medium on which an image is produced or from which an image may by any means be produced and which is not part of a (moving image) film'.* Under the old act, prints made by a photographic process were classified as 'photographs', and prints employing traditional methods such as woodcuts, lithographs, engravings, silkscreen, etchings, not using a photographic process, were classified as 'prints'. Under the new law, all prints however produced are classified as 'graphic works'.

Copyright byline
Provided all three of the above tests are passed, copyright protection is automatic – neither of the laws require the maker to publicly claim or register copyright ownership or endorse the work for it to be protected in this country, but it is advisable to endorse all work to remind others of your copyright ownership. Endorsement is required for protection abroad. Endorsement involves indelibly marking the work with '©', the artist's name and the date it was created. Endorsement is a requirement for one of the new act's Moral Rights provisions (see below).

Copyright ownership

Both acts make a distinction between works made by a freelance artist (contract for services) and those made in the course of employment (contract of service). If a work is made by someone as part of their employment (unless the contract of employment states otherwise) the copyright owner is the employer. The situation is more complicated in the case of freelance artists, the new act tidying up anomalies in the old:

Works made by a freelance artist before August 1, 1989
The first owner of copyright is the maker except for the following 'artistic works' when the first copyright owner is the commissioner:

Who is the first copyright owner in artistic works?

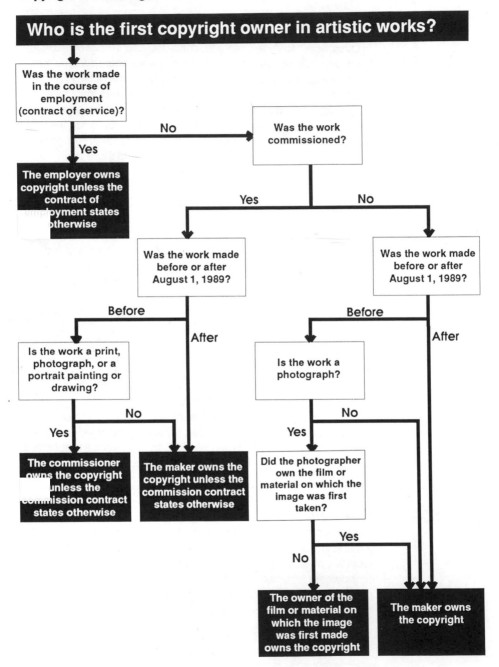

Was the work made in the course of employment (contract of service)?

No → **Was the work commissioned?**

Yes

The employer owns copyright unless the contract of employment states otherwise

Was the work commissioned?

Yes / No

Was the work made before or after August 1, 1989?

Was the work made before or after August 1, 1989?

Before / After

Before / After

Is the work a print, photograph, or a portrait painting or drawing?

Is the work a photograph?

No

Yes

The commissioner owns the copyright unless the commission contract states otherwise

The maker owns the copyright unless the commission contract states otherwise

No

Yes

Did the photographer own the film or material on which the image was first taken?

Yes

No

The owner of the film or material on which the image was first made owns the copyright

The maker owns the copyright

How long does copyright in artistic works last?

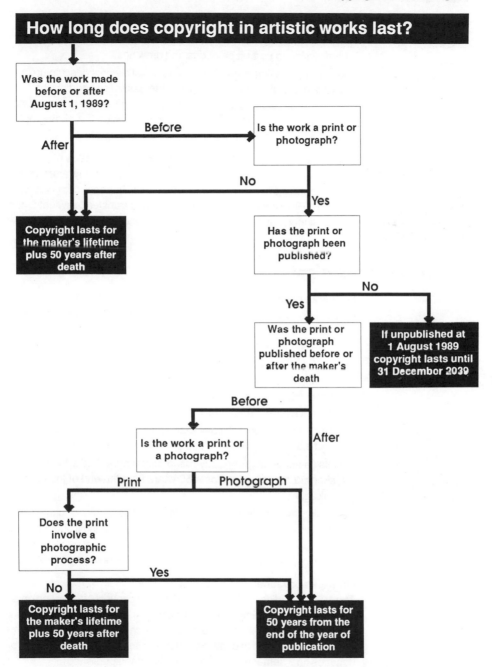

- commissioned prints
- commissioned photographs
- commissioned portrait paintings and drawings.

The maker is the first owner in any other artistic works or sculpture and any work of artistic craftsmanship whether commissioned or not.

The first copyright owner of an uncommissioned photograph is the person who owns the film or material on which the photographic image was first made – not necessarily the photographer.

Works made by freelance makers after August 1, 1989

The freelance maker is the first copyright owner of any artistic work (including photographs) irrespective of whether it has been commissioned or not. The freelance maker may be asked to transfer copyright to the commissioner, but this must be in writing signed by the maker.

Length of copyright

On works produced before August 1, 1989

Art work is protected for the maker's lifetime plus 50 years after death except for photographs and prints when length of copyright is determined from the date the work is published:

- unpublished photographs and prints: copyright lasts forever
- published photographs (including photographically made prints) whether they were published before or after the maker's death, copyright lasts 50 years from the end of the year of publication
- prints (ie not photographically made prints) published before the maker's death: copyright is for the maker's lifetime plus 50 years.
- prints (ie not photographically made prints) published after the maker's death: copyright lasts 50 years from the end of the year of publication.

'Publishing' here means issuing reproductions of a print or photograph to the public – not public exhibition of the original. Putting a photographic print, eg in a public exhibition does not qualify as publishing but reproducing it in a catalogue, on exhibition posters or postcards does.

On works produced after August 1, 1989

The 1989 law tidies up these anomalies and copyright protection on all artistic works (including prints and photographs) lasts for the maker's lifetime plus 50 years from the end of the calendar year in which the maker dies (ie length of copyright for prints and photographs no longer depends on whether and when they have been published).

Infringements

Copyright protects artistic works from the following 'restricted acts' without the authorisation of the copyright owner:

Infringements before August 1, 1989

- reproducing the work in any material form
- publishing the work
- including the work in a TV broadcast

Infringements after August 1, 1989

- reproducing the work in any material form – now including the use of electronic means
- putting into circulation copies of a work not previously put into circulation, in the UK or elsewhere
- including the work in a TV broadcast (including cable television)

The new law acknowledges new technologies and the ability to store and display images on computers; 'publishing' is widened to 'circulating' and 'elsewhere' is used to include all countries, not just those who are signatories to the Berne Convention.

Permitted copying

Copyright allows work to be copied for the following limited purposes:

Acts before August 1, 1989

- research or private study
- criticism or review provided it is accompanied by sufficient acknowledgement of the maker (and the photographer – both of whom may be copyright owners of the published photographic reproduction of a work)
- background use in TV and film (it must be part of the background setting and incidental to the main matter of the programme)
- judicial proceedings or reports of them
- use within educational establishments so long as a duplicating process is not used and for examination purpose whether or not a duplicating process is used
- sculpture or works of 'artistic craftsmanship' if permanently sited in a public place or in premises open to the public may be painted, drawn, photographed, filmed or televisually broadcast (not by cable), any reproductions may be published or televisually

broadcast without permission, no acknowledgement is required. A sculpture can't be made of another sculpture sited in public.

• artists who do not own copyright in their work can reproduce their original imagery in subsequent works so long as they do not repeat or imitate the main design of the original.

Acts after August 1, 1989

Much as before, except that reproductions may be used without copyright permission for the following additional purposes:

• advertisement of work for sale – allowing galleries and artists' agents to reproduce works in catalogues, posters or on television, but only if the purpose is to advertise the original work for sale. Museums and art galleries buying a work from an artist are not permitted to print and sell postcards of it without permission.

• copyrighted work, with the exception of photographs, can be used in reporting of current events, provided sufficient acknowledgement is given. Acknowledgement is not required in film or TV reporting. Photographs cannot be used without permission.

• artists are now permitted to use the copyright work of another artist provided it is incidental to the main image in the work.

• reproduction is now allowed for statutory functions such as Royal Commissions.

Also, reproduction for educational purposes whether within educational establishments or not, so long as it is either done by the person giving or receiving instruction and does not involve a reprographic process. Copying for examination questions is permitted however it is done. Reprographic process is defined as a process for making facsimile or multiple copies.

Reproduction licences

see 7 • Earning from reproductions

Only the copyright owner can give permission for reproduction. This can be a verbal agreement but a written document (a reproduction or copyright licence) is strongly advised. A licence should specify exactly how it can be reproduced, how many copies can be made, where they can be distributed, how much, when and how the copyright owner is paid. A licence can be exclusive, ie selling rights to only one person or organisation, or allow a number of organisations to reproduce the work.

Transferring copyright ownership

There is little change between the old and new laws – copyright ownership can only normally be transferred by a written document signed by both parties. Ownership of copyright and of the work itself are different legal entities. The sale of an artistic work does not transfer copyright to the new owner of the work. Copyright can be sold independently of the work itself. Thus the new owner of the work who does not also own copyright cannot give permission for its reproduction or copying.

Copyright heirs

If a copyright owner dies intestate (without a will) copyright is treated as part of the estate which will be distributed amongst the nearest kin. Copyright can be bequeathed to a named individual. Licences issued by the first copyright owner are binding on the new owner.

Bankruptcy

A copyright owner who becomes bankrupt may have their copyright taken in bankruptcy proceedings. The new owner, bank or other creditor, is permitted to use it by reproducing the work to pay off debts.

Remedies for infringement

Infringements before August 1, 1989 come under the old act, after that they come under the new act. You can take civil proceedings (in the County or High Court) to stop infringement and/or obtain damages. The infringer may also be committing a criminal offence. Legal action is often uncertain and could be expensive, so first deal directly with the infringer and try to get them to destroy, or remove from circulation, the copies. You might want to agree payment with them in return for you taking no action. But be clear what they are paying for. Don't make an agreement which see 23 • Contracts implies they can just go on making copies. If a direct approach fails take professional advice. Free legal advice is available from Citizens Advice Bureaux. The solicitor at an advice centre will not normally be a copyright specialist and can't act for you but it is a useful first port of call.

Moral rights

Whereas copyright seeks to protect the maker's economic rights, moral rights deal with the right to be recognised as the creator and prevent derogatory treatment of work. There are four moral rights: the right of identification, the right to object to derogatory treatment, the right to prevent false attribution, and the right of privacy.

Eligibility

All artistic works including works of artistic craftsmanship and of architecture are protected so long as it is original and of the author's own skill and labour though not necessarily thought. Copies or works which contain substantial elements of another original are not protected.

The right of identification

The maker of an artistic work has the right to be identified as such whenever the work is published commercially, exhibited in public or a visual image of it is broadcast, included in a cable programme, or a film including a visual image of it is issued to the public. The identification must be clear and reasonably prominent. This right is only valid if the maker previously asserts their right (see below).

The right to object to derogatory treatment

The maker has the right not to have their work subjected to derogatory treatment whenever it is published commercially or exhibited in public or a visual image of it is broadcast, including in a cable programme or in a film shown or issued to the public. 'Derogatory treatment' means any addition to, deletion from, alteration to, or adaption of the work which amounts to distortion or mutilation of it or is prejudicial to the honour or reputation of the maker. Destruction of a work is not likely to constitute 'derogatory treatment'.

False attribution

A person has the right not to be attributed as the maker of a work they did not make. This right is infringed whenever it or a copy is publicly exhibited, issued to the public, dealt with or possessed by someone knowing or with reason to believe it is falsely attributed. An artist also has the right to prevent anyone from dealing with a work or a copy which is attributed to the artist but has been altered without their permission. This right exists without the need for the maker to assert their rights.

The right of privacy

The new law also gives the right to commissioners of private or domestic photographs not to have copies put on public display.

Exceptions to moral rights

There are a number of exclusions to the moral rights of identification and objection to derogatory treatment. The main ones being when:

- the work is computer-generated
- the work is produced by the artist as part of employment
- the work is made for the purpose of reporting current events
- the work is made for, or made available for, publication in a newspaper, magazine or similar periodical or encyclopaedia, dictionary, yearbook or other collective work of reference
- the work is incidentally included in a film/TV or artistic work.

Assertion of rights

For the right of identification to be valid the artist must assert this right; appropriate wording needs to be included in all copyright assignments and licences and the name of the artist put on all original work (or authorised copies) on the frame or mount. Use a statement such as *'The right of (name of artist) to be identified as author of (identify work) has been asserted generally in accordance with sections 77 and 78 of the Copyright, Designs and Patents Act 1988'.*

Length of moral rights

Moral rights covering identification and derogatory treatment last for the same period as copyright and expire when that expires. Moral rights covering false attribution last for the maker's lifetime plus 20 years.

Transferral and waiving of moral rights

Moral rights cannot be transferred or assigned by the artist during their lifetime to anyone else. The maker still retains them even where both the original work and its copyright have been disposed of. On death, moral rights pass to the person named as beneficiary of them or if none, to the person to whom copyright passes. The artist may waive (ie give up) any or all moral rights conditionally or unconditionally, by a written signed statement, eg in a contract, or more informally under the general law of contact. All artists should beware of giving away their rights unknowingly.

Performing rights

Artists making live or time-based work may be protected by performing rights. These relate to performers and people owning recording rights to a performance. A recording means a film or sound recording made directly from the performance, from a broadcast, or from another recording of it. You own the recording rights on your own live art work provided it is a 'qualifying performance'. You can licence these to other people just as with copyright. A qualifying performance would be:

- a dramatic performance (including dance and mime)
- a musical performance
- a reading or recital of a literary work
- a variety act or any similar presentation.

You own the rights to your performance in any live art work, even if it is not of your devising. This means if you use other artists in a live work of your devising they own the rights on their 'performance'. If recording a performance your contract with the other performers should include an agreement to you using the recording, stating what it can be used for, where, when, etc. You may agree you can use a video of a work for your publicity, for showing privately, as part of an exhibition; but not that it can be broadcast on national TV without prior agreement, or payment.

Like copyright, you can take action against someone infringing your performing rights, for example by distributing illicit recordings. The permitted acts relating to copyright broadly relate to performing rights.

These rights last for 50 years after the performance takes place.

Conclusions

- Keep your copyright, only part with it if it is financially very worthwhile.
- When allowing someone to reproduce your work always have a written agreement or licence detailing what is being copied in what form, for how long, and for what fee.
- Always endorse your work on the back with the international copyright byline and assert your moral rights on all work, ie '©' artist's name, date of creation and 'All rights reserved'. Also assert your rights in all contracts and assignments of copyright.
- Detail your copyright and moral rights on all documents such as contracts of sale, exhibition contracts, loan forms for exhibitions.
- Check before signing contracts, including open exhibition submission forms, that you are not unwittingly signing away any of your copyright or moral rights.
- Make a will stating who your heir is to be in respect of your copyright and moral rights.
- Join the Design and Artists Copyright Society (DACS) who can act as your copyright policing and collecting agency.

25 • Contacts

Arts Councils & Arts Boards

Arts Council, 14 Great Peter Street, London, SW1P 3NQ, tel 071 333 0100

Arts Council Eire, 70 Merrion Square, Dublin 2, Eire, tel (010 353) 1 611840

Arts Council of Northern Ireland, 181A Stranmillis Road, Belfast, BT9 5DU, tel 0232 381 591

British Film Institute (BFI), 21 Stephen Street, London, W1P 1PL, tel 071 255 1444

Crafts Council, 44a Pentonville Road, Islington, London, N1 9HF, tel 071 278 7700

Crafts Council of Ireland, The Powers Court, Town House Centre, South William Street, Dublin 2, Eire, tel (010 353) 1 611840

East Midlands Arts Board, Mountfields House, Forest Road, Loughborough, LE11 3HU, tel 0509 218292

Eastern Arts Board, Cherry Hinton Hall, Cherry Hinton Road, Cambridge, CB1 4DW, tel 0223 215355

London Arts Board, Elme House, 133 Long Acre, London. WC2E 9AF, tel 071 240 1313.

North Wales Arts Association, 10 Wellfield House, Bangor, Gwynedd, LL57 1ER, tel 0248 353248

North West Arts Board, 4th Floor, 12 Harter Street, Manchester, M1 6HY, tel 061 228 3062

Northern Arts Board, 10 Osborne Terrace, Newcastle upon Tyne, NE2 1NZ, tel 091 281 6334

Scottish Arts Council, 12 Manor Place, Edinburgh, EH3 7DO, tel 031 226 6051

Scottish Film Council, Downhill, 74 Victoria Crescent Road, Glasgow, G12 9GN, tel 041 334 4445, fax 041 334 8132

South East Arts Board, 10 Mount Ephraim, Tunbridge Wells, TN4 8AS, tel 0892 515075

South East Wales Arts Association, Victoria Street, Cwmbran, NP44 3YT, tel 0633 875389

South West Arts Board, Bradninch Place, Gandy Street, Exeter, EX4 3LS, tel 0392 218188

Southern Arts Board, 13 St Clements Street, Winchester, SO23 9UQ, tel 0962 855099

Welsh Arts Council, Museum Place, Cardiff, CF1 3NX, tel 0222 394711

West Midlands Arts Board, 82 Granville Street, Birmingham, B1 2LH, tel 021 631 3121

West Wales Arts Association, 3 Red Street, Carmarthan, Dyfed, SA31 1QL, tel 0267 234248

Yorkshire and Humberside Arts Board, 21 Bond Street, Dewsbury, West Yorkshire, WF13 1AX, tel 0924 455555, fax 0924 400522

4 • Training

Arts Council of Great Britain, Personnel and Training Department, 14 Great Peter Street, London, SW1P 3NQ, tel 071 333 0100

Arts Management Centre, University of Northumbria, Squires Building, Newcastle upon Tyne, tel 091 232 6002

Arts Training Programme, De Montfort University, Scraptoft, Leicester, LE7 9SU, tel 0533 431011 ext 247

Arts Training South, CCE, University of Sussex, Falmer, Brighton, BN1 9Q1T, tel 0273 606755 ext 3602

Centre for Arts Management, Institute of Public Administration and Management, Roxby building, Liverpool University, Liverpool, L69 3BX, tel 051 709 6022 ext 2748

National Council for Voluntary Organisations, Local Development Unit, 26 Bedford Square, London WC1B 3HU, tel 071 636 4066 ext 2262

National Extension College, 18 Brooklands Avenue, Cambridge, CB2 2HN, tel 0223 316644, fax 0223 313586

Open University, Guide to the Associate Student Programme, PO Box 76, Milton Keynes, MK7 6AN

Training and Enterprise Councils (TECS), see telephone directory for details of your local office

9 • Residencies

Arts for Health, Manchester Polytechnic, Manchester, M15 6BY, tel 061 236 8916

British Health Care Arts Centre, Duncan of Jordanstone College of Art, 13 Perth Road, Dundee, DD1 4HT, tel 0382 23261, fax 0382 27304

Hospice Arts, 212 New London Rd, Chelmsford, Essex, tel 0245 358 130

The National Foundation for Arts Education, Department of Arts Education, University of Warwick, Westwood, Kirby Corner Road, Coventry, CV4 7AL, tel 0203 524175

see also Commissions and Arts Councils & Arts Boards

10 • Commissions

Art & Architecture Ltd, 19 Percy Circus, London, WC1X 9ES

Artangel Trust, 133 Oxford Street, London, W1R 1TD, tel 071 434 2887

Art in Partnership, 233 Cowgate, Edinburgh, EH1 1NQ

Artists' Agency, 16 Norfolk Street, Sunderland, SR1 1EA, tel 091 510 9318

Artworks Wales, 2 John Street, Cardiff, CF1 6EB, tel 0222 489543

AXIS, Leeds Polytechnic, Calverley Street, Leeds, LS1 3HE, tel 0532 8331215

British Health Care Arts Centre, Duncan of Jordenstone College of Arts, 13 Perth Road, Dundee, DO1 4HT, tel 0382 23261

Cardiff Bay Art Trust, The Exchange, Mount Stuart Square, Cardiff, CF1 6EB, tel 0222 488772

City Gallery Arts Trust, The Great Barn, Parklands, Great Linford, Milton Keynes, MK14 5DZ, tel 0908 606791

Common Ground, 45 Shelton Street, London, WC2H 9HJ, tel 071 379 3109

Contemporary Applied Arts, 43 Earlham Street, London WC2, tel 071 836 6693

Freeform Arts Trust, 38 Dalston Lane, London, E8 3AZ, tel 071 249 3394

Freeform North Tyneside, First Floor Offices, 61 Saville Street, North Shields, NE30 1AY, tel 091 259 5143

Glasgow Sculpture Studio, 85 Hanson Street, Glasgow, G31 THF

Hampshire Sculpture Trust, North Hill Close, Andover Road, Winchester, Hampshire, SO22 6AQ, tel 0962 846038

Partnership Art, Providence Mill, Second Floor, Alexandra Street, Hyde, SK14 1DX, tel 061 367 8640

Portland Sculpture Trust, 36 High Street, Fortuneswell, Portland, Dorset, tel 0305 823489

Public Arts, 24 Bond Street, Wakefield, WF1 2QP, tel 0924 295791

Public Art Commissions Agency, Studio 6, Victoria Works, Vittoria Street, Birmingham, B13 PE, tel 021 212 4454

Public Art Development Trust, 1A Cobham Mews, London, NW1 9SB, tel 071 2844983

Public Art Forum, The Administrator, Flat 1, The Priory, Webber Street, London, SE1 0RQ, tel 071 928 1221

Public Art Unit, Civic Offices, Euclid Street, Swindon, Wiltshire, SN1 2JH, tel 0793 295789

Scottish Sculpture Trust, 3 Bank Street, Inverkeithing, Fife, KY11 1LR, tel 0383 412811

11 • Project planning & fundraising

ABSA, Nutmeg House, 60 Gainsford St, Butlers Wharf, London, SE1 2NY, tel 071 378 8143, fax 071 407 7527

ABSA Northern England, Dean Clough, Halifax, West Yorks, HX3 5AX, tel 0422 344555

ABSA Northern Ireland, 181A Stranmillis Rd, Belfast, BT9 5BU, tel 0232 664736, fax 0232 661715

ABSA Scotland, Room 206, West Port House, 102 West Port, Edinburgh, EH93 9HS, tel 031 228 4262, fax 031 229 9008

ABSA Wales, 9 Museum Place, Cardiff, CF1 3NX, tel 0222 221382

British Council, Visual Arts Department, 11 Portland Place, London, W1N 4EJ, tel 071 398 3043

British Tourist Authority and English Tourist Board, Thames Tower, Black's Rd, London, W6 9EL, tel 081 846 9000

Calouste Gulbenkian Foundation, 98 Portland Place, London, W1N 4ET, tel 071 636 5313, fax 071 636 2948

Charities Aid Foundation, 48 Pembury Rd, Tonbridge, Kent, TN9 2JD, tel Tonbridge 771 333

Confederation of British Industry (CBI), Centrepoint, 103 New Oxford St, London, WC1A 1DU, tel 071 379 7400, fax 071 240 1578

Industrial Development Board for Northern Ireland, IDB House, 64 Chichester St, Belfast, BT1 4JX, tel 0232 233 233, fax 0232 231 328

Leverhulme Trust, Lintas House, New Fetter Lane, London, EC4, tel 071 822 5252

Mid-Wales Development, Ladywell House, Newtown, Powys, SY16 1JB, tel 0686 626965, fax 0686 622 499

Prince's Trust, 8 Bedford Row, London WC1R 4BA

Prince's Youth Business Trust, 5th Floor, 5 Cleveland Place, London, SW1Y 6JJ, tel 071 925 2900, fax 071 834 6494

Rural Development Commission, 14 Castle St, Salisbury, SP1 3TP, tel 0722 336255

Welsh Development Agency, Pearl House, Greyfriars Rd, Cardiff, CF1 3XX, tel 0222 222 666, fax 0222 390 752

see also **Arts Councils & Arts Boards**

12 • Strength in numbers

Acme Housing Association, 15 Robinson Road, Bothnal Green, London E2 9LX, tel 071 981 6811

African and Asian Visual Artists Archive, The Coach House Small Business Centre, 2 Upper York St, St Paul's, Bristol, BS2 8QN, tel 0272 244492

Art Workers Guild, 6 Queen Square, London, WC1N 3AR, tel 071 837 3474

Association of Artists in Ireland (AAI), Room 803 Liberty Hall, Dublin 1, tel 010 3531 740529, fax 010 3531 740529

Association of Illustrators (AOI), 29 Bedford Square, London, WC1B 3EG, tel 071 631 1510

Association of Photographers (AFAEP), 9-10 Domingo Street, London, EC1Y 0TA, tel 071 608 1441

Association of Visual Artists in Wales, Arts Workshop Gallery, Gloucester Place, Maritime Quarter, Swansea, Wales, tel 0792 652016

Autograph Association of Black Photographers, Unit 306, Bon Marche Building, London, SW9, tel 071 274 4000

Chartered Society of Designers, 29 Bedford Square, London, WC1B 3EG, tel 071 631 1510

Federation of British Artists (FBA), 17 Carlton House Terrace, London, SW1, tel 071 930 6844

International Association of Art (IAA/AIAP), 1 rue Miollis 75732, Paris, CEDEX 15, tel 010 33 1 45 66 57 57

National Artists Association (NAA), Membership Secretary, 12 Brookside Terrace, Sunderland, SR2 7RN

Panchayat, 8 Hoxton St, London, N1 6NG, tel 071 729 6273

Printmakers' Council, 31 Clerkenwell Close, London, EC1, tel 071 250 1927

SPACE, 8 Hoxton St, London, N1 6NG, tel 071 613 1925, fax 071 729 6273

Union of Scottish Art Workers, Crawford Arts Centre, 83 North Street, St Andrews, Fife, KY16 9AJ, tel 0334 74610, c/o Diana Sykes

WASPS, 26 King Street, Glasgow, G1 5QP, tel 041 552 0564

Women Artists Slide Library, Fulham Palace, Bishop's Avenue, London, CW6 6EA, tel 071 731 7618

15 • Abroad

Association of Commonwealth Universities, John Foster House, 36 Gordon Square, London, WC1H 0PF, tel 071 387 8572

British American Arts Association, 49 Wellington St, London, WC2H 9HJ, tel 071 379 7555

British Council, 11 Portland Place, London, W1N 4EJ, tel 071 930 8406

Carnegie UK Trust, Comely Park House, New Row, Dunfermline, Fife, KY12 7EJ, tel 0383 721445

Central Bureau for Educational Visits and Exchanges, Seymour Mews House, Seymour Mews, London, W1H 9PE, tel 071 486 5101, fax 071 935 5741

Commission of the European Communities, 8 Storeys Gate, London, SW1P 3AT, tel 071 973 1992, fax 071 973 1900

Commonwealth Foundation Fellowships, Education Division, Commonwealth Institute, Kensington High St, London, W8 6NQ, tel 071 603 4535 ext 300, fax 071 602 7374

Department of Education & Science, International Relations Division, Great Smith St, London, SW1P 3BT, tel 071 925 5000, fax 071 925 6000

Fulbright Award, UK Educational Commission, 6 Porter St, London, W1M 2HR, tel 071 486 7697, fax 071 224 4567

Kennedy Memorial Trust, 16 Great College St, London, SW1P 3RX, tel 071 222 1151, fax 071 222 8550

Rome Scholarships, British School at Rome, Tuke Building, Regents College, Inner Circle, Regents Park, London, 071 487 7403

The German Academic Exchange Service, 2 Bloomsbury Square, London, WC1A 2LP, tel 071 404 4065

United Nations Information Service, Ship House, 20 Buckingham Gate, London, SW1E 6LB, tel 071 630 1981

US/UK Educational Commission, 6 Porter St, London, WC1M 2HR, tel 071 486 1098

Winston Churchill Memorial Trust, 15 Queensgate Terrace, London, SW7 5PR, tel 071 584 9315

18 • Health and Safety

ArtSafe (UK), 33 Ruswarp Drive, Barrons Hill Lea, Tunstall, Sunderland, SR3 2BP

British Safety Council, 62-64 Chancellors Road, London, W6 9RS, tel 081 741 1231

Health and Safety Executive, Health & Safety, Baynards House, 1 Chepstow Place, Westbourne Grove, London, W2 4TF, tel 071 243 60000. Contact HSE Executive for the address of your regional office, or see telephone directory under 'Health and Safety'.

20 • Employment status & tax

Chartered Association of Certified Accountants, 29 Lincoln Inns Fields, London, WC2A 3EE, tel 071 242 6855

Institute of Chartered Accountants (England and Wales), PO Box 433, Chartered Accountants HallMoorgate Place, London, EC2P 2BJ, tel 071 628 7060

Institute of Chartered Accountants (Ireland), 11 Donegall Street, Belfast, BT1 5JE, tel 0232 321600

Institute of Chartered Accountants (Scotland), 27 Queens Street, Edinburgh, EH2 1LA, tel 031 225 567773

21 • Trading status

Charity Commission, St Albans House, 57-60 Haymarket, London, SW1Y 4QX, tel 071 210 3000, fax 071 930 9173

Companies Registration Offices
England: Companies House, 55 City Road, London, EC1

Wales: Companies House, Crown Way, Maindy, Cardiff, CF4 3UZ
Scotland: 102 George Street, Edinburgh, EH2 3DJ
Northern Ireland: 64 Chichester Street, Belfast, BT1 4JX

Co-operative Development Agency, Broadmead House, 21 Panton St, Haymarket, London, SW1Y 4DR, tel 071 839 2988

Industrial Common Ownership Movement, Vassalli House, 20 Central Rd, Leeds, LS1 6DE, tel 0532 461738, fax 0532 440002

24 • Copyright

British Copyright Council (BCC), 29-33 Berners Street, London, W1P 4AA, tel 071 359 1895

British Photographers' Liaison Committee, 9-10 Domingo Street, London, EC1 0TA, tel 071 608 1441

British Photographic Industry Copyright Association, Roxburghe House, 273-287 Regent Street, London, W1R 7BP

Chartered Institute of Patent Agents, Staple Inn Buildings, London, WC1V 7PZ, tel 071 405 9450

Committee on Photographic Copyright, c/o AFAEP, 9-10 Domingo Street, London, EC1Y 0TA

Copyright Licensing Agency Ltd (CLA), 90 Tottenham Court Road, London, W1P 9HE, tel 071 436 5931

Design & Artists Copyright Society Ltd (DACS), St Mary's Clergy House, 2 Whitechurch Lane, London, E1 7QR, tel 071 247 1650

Patent Office, Designs Registry, Cardiff Road, Newport, Gwent, NP1 1RH, tel 0633 814000

Performing Right Society Ltd (PRS), 29-33 Berners Street, London, W1P 4AA, tel 071 580 5544

Video Performance Ltd (VPL), Ganton House, 14-22 Ganton Street, London, W1V 1LB, tel 071 437 0711

26 • Further reading

General bibliography

A Code of Practice for Independent Photography, Vince Wade, AN Publications, 1989, ISBN 0 907730 06 X, £3.25, Includes a section on exhibiting.

Arts Council Directory of Media Education Resources, ed Margaret O'Connor with Diane Bracken, Arts Council, 1992, ISBN 0 9077330 19 1, £10.95 inc p&p. From AN Publications, PO Box 23, Sunderland SR4 6DG. Tel 091 567 3589.

Arts Address Book, ed Peter Marcan, Marcan (Peter) Publications, 1990. A comprehensive national and international listing of arts organisations, 31 Rowliff Rd, High Wycombe, Bucks HP12 3LD.

Artists Newsletter (annual individual subscription, £16). Monthly magazine relevant to all practice in the visual arts, craft and photography with 'live art' and 'film & video' opportunities columns, listings of live art events in the exhibitions section and articles. AN Publications, PO Box 23, Sunderland SR4 6DG. Tel 091 514 3600.

Eliminating Shadows - a manual on photography and disability, Ray Cooper and Ronald Cooper, London Print Workshop, 1990, ISBN 0 9506333 13, £12.95. Provides disabled photographers with a practical solution to photographic needs, 421 Harrow Rd, London W10 4RD. Tel 081 969 3247.

Running a Workshop: basic business for craftspeople, ed Barclay Price, Crafts Council, 1989, ISBN 0 903798 80 8. Aimed at craftspeople, the book looks at exhibiting along with selling, costing, premises, and other general topics. From AN Publications, PO Box 23, Sunderland SR4 6DG. Tel 091 567 3589.

The Artists Directory: A handbook to the contemporary British art world, A&C Black, 1988, ISBN 0 713630 39 6, £8.95. Includes a brief section on making an application and preparing for an exhibition. Art Guide Publications, A&C Black, 35 Bedford Row, London WC1R 4JH. Tel 071 242 0946.

2 • Looking at yourself

Life Skills Teaching, Barry Hopson & Mike Scally, McGraw Hill, 1981. Also Life Skills Teaching Programme 1-3 (1980, 82, 86). Life Skills Associates, McGraw House, Sheppenhangers Rd, Maidenhead. Tel 0628 23432.

4 • Training

Directory of Further Education, Career Research and Advisory Centre, Hobson Ltd. Lists courses in further and higher education. Available at main libraries and Careers Services, Bateman St, Cambridge CB2 1LZ.

Directory of Independent Training and Tutorial Organisation, Careers Consultants, 12/14 Hill Rise, Richmond, Surrey, TW10 6VA.

Directory of Opportunities for Graduates, New Opportunities Press, Yeomans House, 76 St James Lane, London, N1-0 3RD.

Film and Television Training, BFI, £4.75 inc p&p, BFI Publications.

Just the Job, Dept of employment, 1991, free. Guide to employment, training and enterprise, From local department of employment.

Opportunities for Expressive Arts Graduates, Brighton Polytechnic Careers Counselling Unit.

Paying for Training - a comprehensive guide to sources of finance for adult training, The Planning Exchange, 1988.

Second Chance - Annual Guide to Adult Education and Training Opportunities, National Extension College. Comprehensive - easy to follow. National Extension College, 18 Brooklands Avenue, Cambridge, CB2 2HN. Tel 0223 358295, Fax: 0223 313586.

Your guide to our employment, training and enterprise programmes, Department of Employment.

5 • Exhibiting

Artist Handbooks 5 – Organising Your Exhibition – the self-help guide, Debbie Duffin, AN Publications, ISBN 0 907730 14 0, £7.25 inc p&p. Covering finding space, finance, timetabling, publicity, promotion, framing, security and insurance, transporting work, hanging, private view, selling work and making the best of exhibition, AN Publications, PO Box 23, Sunderland SR4 6DG. Tel 091 567 3589.

Directory of Exhibition Spaces 3rd Edition, ed Richard Padwick, AN Publications, 1992, ISBN 0 907730 17 5, £13.99. The most comprehensive listing of over 2000 galleries and exhibition spaces in the UK and Eire, including public and private galleries, museums, libraries, arts centres, universities, theatres, heritage and community centres. AN Publications, PO Box 23 Sunderland SR4 6DG. Tel 091 567 3589

Guidelines on Exhibiting, Southern Arts Board, 1990. Free to makers in the Southern Arts region. Also available as a pack of three with the 'Publicity and Media Planning Guideline' and 'Guidelines to selling at trade and craft fairs' for £1.50. Aimed primarily at craftspeople, has information on selecting a venue, making an application to a gallery, arranging the exhibition and organising publicity. Southern Arts, 13 St Clement Street, Winchester, Hampshire SO23 9DQ. Tel 0962 55099.

Independent Photography Directory, ed Michael Hallett and Barry Lane, AN Publications, 1989, ISBN 0 907730 08 6, £5, Includes a listing of photography galleries and exhibition spaces plus other photography facilities and sources of information. AN Publications, PO Box 23 Sunderland SR4 6DG. Tel 091 567 3589

6 • Selling

Artists Handbooks – Selling, Judith Staines, 1993, AN Publications. The complete guide to selling, marketing, and pricing of artwork and craftwork. Available Spring 1993, AN Publications, PO Box 23, Sunderland SR4 6DG. Tel 091 514 3600.

Fact Pack 5: Craft Fairs, Kathyrn Salomon, edited by AN Publications, 1991, £1.85. Selected list of national and international fairs with advice on taking a stand etc. AN Publications, PO Box 23, Sunderland SR4 6DG. Tel 091 514 3600.

Running A Workshop - Basic business for craftspeople, Crafts Council, ISBN 0 903798 80 8. AN Publications, PO Box 23, Sunderland SR4 6DG. Tel 091 514 3600.

7 • Earning from reproductions

1992 Freelance Ilustrators Handbook, Carmel Hayes, Margaret Rose Press, £6.80. Advises on creating work for specialist fields, includes contact names and addresses. From AN Publications, PO Box 23 Sunderland SR4 6DG. Tel 091 567 3589.

Rights: The Illustrators guide to professional practice, ed Simon Stern, The Associations of Illustrators, 1989, ISBN 0 951 544 802, 1 Colville Place, off Charlotte Street, London W1P 1HN. From AN Publications, PO Box 23 Sunderland SR4 6DG. Tel 091 567 3589.

Survive, the illustrators guide to a profesional career, ed Aidan Walker, The Association of Illustrators, £10.75. Complete survival guide for illustrators, thorough and knowledgeable, or from AN Publications, PO Box 23 Sunderland SR4 6DG. Tel 091 567 3589.

9 • Residencies

Artist Handbooks 1 – Residencies in Education – Setting them up and making them work, Daniel Dahl, edited by Susan Jones, AN Publications, 1990, ISBN 0 907730 09 4, £7.25 inc p&p. As well as case-studies, has a comprehensive information section covering contracts, insurance, health & safety, training, resources, rates of pay for artists, arts organisations and funding. AN Publications, PO Box 23, Sunderland SR4 6DG. Tel 091 567 3589.

A for Arts: Evaluation, Education and Arts Centres, Saville Kishner, Arts Development Association, 1989, ISBN 0 948861 05 3, £5.95. Describes and assesses the evaluation which took place for 'The Magic Experience' and provides guidance for artists and administrators with evaluating their practice. **Note:** The Arts Development Association is no longer in existence.

Art & Healthcare, Linda Moss, Dept of Health, Health Building Directorate, ISBN 185195, £6, Intended for artists and organisations, showing how the arts work for hospitals. Includes how schemes were set up, case studies including artists in residence, funding, sponsorship and bibliography.

Artists and Schools, National Foundation for Arts Education, 1990, £5. Covers visual artists, verbal artists, textile artists and artists and cultural diversity. From NFAE, University of Warwick, Westwood, Kirby Corner Road, Coventry CV4 7AL. Tel 0203 524175.

Artists in Schools, Whitechapel Art Gallery, 1989, ISBN 0 85488 084 4, £3.95. An introduction to the gallery's artists in schools programme which has been running since 1979. Whitechapel Art Gallery, Whitechapel High Street, London E1. Tel 071 377 5015.

Artists in Schools, Caroline Sharp and Karen Dust, Bedford Square Press, ISBN 0 7199 1262 8, £10 inc p&p. Subtitled 'A Handbook for Teachers and Artists', it includes guidance on planning projects and advice on the role of artist plus an outline of funding possibilities. Harper & Row Distributors Ltd, Estover Road, Plymouth PL6 7PZ.

Engineers of the Imagination, edited byTony Coult and Baz Kershaw, Welfare State International, 1990, ISBN 0 413 52800 6, £8.95. Practical guide to creating processions, large scale puppets and sculptures, fixed structures, fire and ice technology, shadow puppets, processional theatre and dance music and celebratory food and feasts.

Just like an artist, edited by Mark Chapman, Schools Curriculum Development Committee, £24.17 minute video illustrates Suzanne O'Driscoll's school residency with 13-14 year olds. Useful for schools considering a residency. Dramatic Video (Distribution), 41 Stanhope Road, Reading, Berkshire RG2 7HW.

Kaleidoscope – arts work that works, edited by Nick Randell and Simon Myhill, Youth Clubs UK Publications, 1989, ISBN 090 7095 577, £5.95. It describes a wide range of arts in youth work settings in England and, as well as covering individual projects, it makes suggestions on how to start projects and initiate training programmes in youth clubs. Youth Clubs UK, 30 Peacock Street, Leicester LE1 5NY. Tel 0533 629514.

Media Education, Annual subscription, £7.50 (individual) or, £12.50 (institution). Published three times a year by regional arts boards in the South and East Anglia, is of interest to those involved in media and education. Lists courses, conferences, events, regional contacts, useful Information plus reviews and articles. Tower Arts Centre, Romsey Road, Winchester SO22 9PW.

Media Education Handbook, Kirklees Media Education Forum, £8.50. Descriptions of a range of media projects in schools. G Williamson, Curriculum Development Centre, Temple Road, Dewsbury, West Yorkshire WF13 3QD.

Primary Media Education – a curriculum statement, BFI, £7.25 inc p&p. Guide to teaching approaches in media education for primary teachers. BFI Publications, 29 Rathbone Street, London W1P 1AG.

Secondary Media Education – a curriculum statement, £8.50 inc p&p.

The Arts and the Education Reform Act 1988 – what teachers and artists need to know, Centre for the Study of Comprehensive Schools. Introduces the National Curriculum, ways in which assessment is likely to take place and at what ages, the links between artists and INSET courses and the possibilities for artists to work in schools. Contains a list of strategic organisations and publications. From CSCS, University of York, Heslington, York YO1 5DD. Tel 0904 433240.

The Arts in Schools – principles, practice and provision, Ken Robinson, Calouste Gulbenkian Foundation, 1982 and 1989, ISBN 0 903319 23 3, £6. Republished in 1989 with a new introduction, it is worthy of study by everyone concerned with the future of the arts in society. Calouste Gulbenkian Foundation, 98 Portland Place, London W1 4ET. Tel 01 636 5313.

The Art of Dying, Crimmin, Shand & Thomas, Kings Fund for London and The Forbes Trust, 1989, ISBN 1 85551 048 0, £6.50, It evaluates a project when two artists spent ten weeks in residence in a hospice in Lancaster. The general guidelines are of value to others wishing to work in similar ways. The Forbes Trust, 9 Artillery Lane, London E1 7LP. Tel 01 377 8484.

The Magic Exercise, Victoria Neumark, National Association of Arts Centres, 1989, ISBN 0 948861 03 7, £8.95, Based on twelve case studies of projects run in arts centres. It offers practical insights into creative partnerships between education, arts centres and professional artists, musicians, dancers and actors. Note: National Association of Arts Centre or the Arts Developmant Association as it became no longer exists.

Under the Rainbow – writers and artists in schools, David Morley, Bloodaxe Books in association with Northern Arts, ISBN 1 85224 112 8, £5.65. Sets out good practice from the Northern Arts region and from a two-day conference in 1988. Contains artists' experiences. Bloodaxe Books, PO Box 1SN, Newcastle NE22 1SN.

What the hell do we want an artist here for?, Sue Hercombe, Calouste Gulbenkian Foundation, ISBN 0 903319 411, £3.50. Looks at artists working in industry including a background to the subject – company and artists meeting, the needs of industries, the artists' viewpoint and the part played by arts administrators. From: Turnaround Distribution, 27 Horsall Rd, London N5 1HR.

10 • Commissions

Art in Public, what, why & how, ed Susan Jones, AN Publications, ISBN 0 907730 18 3, £9.99. Looks at the philosophy, relationships and practice involved in the public art sector. Definately not just another book on public sculpture, Art in Public takes a broad view of what artists are actually doing. With numerous examples, quotes and illustrations it will enable everyone working with art in public to develop a good practice based on real critical awareness of the context and value of art in public. AN Publications, PO Box 23, Sunderland SR4 6DG. Tel 091 514 3600.

Art & Craft Works – a step by step guide, Southern Arts, ISBN 0 9501228 4 X, £5.50. Containing a good commission contract checklist and examples of commissions from the Southern Arts region, Southern Arts, 13 St Clements Street, Winchester SO23 9DQ.

Art for Architecture, edited by Deanna PetherbridgeHMSO, ISBN 0 11 751794 1, £14.95. Subtitled a handbook for commissioning, this excellent book covers art in architecture with examples from this country and abroad; how to commission with models including one for artists initiating their own commissions; guidelines on commissioning for all parties; a bibliography and sample contract, Temporarily out of print.

Art for Public Places, Malcolm Miles, Winchester Press, 1989.

Art within Reach, edited by Peter Townsend, Art Monthly and Thames & Hudson, ISBN 0 500 97315 6, £6.95. Useful guide covers the implications of artists working in the public arena with details of contractual arrangements and legal and copyright considerations. Thames & Hudson 071 636 5488.

Mural Manual, Carol Kenna and Steve Lobb, Greenwich Mural Workshop, 1991, ISBN 0 907730 03 5, £5.40 inc p &p. Looks at the practicalities of setting up mural projects. From: AN Publications, PO Box 23, Sunderland SR4 6DG. Tel 091 514 3600.

New Milestones - Sculpture, Community and the Land, Joanna Morland, Common Ground, 1988, ISBN 1 870364 03 1, £5.95 inc p&p. Describes six sculpture commissions, section of practical information and an essay looking at how human activity has shaped and punctuated the landscape, Common Ground, 45 Shelton Street, London WC2H 9HJ. Tel 071 379 3109.

Percent for Art: a review, Phyllida Shaw, Arts Council, 1991, ISBN 07287 0628 8, £11 inc p&p. Review which examines projects in the USA, Europe and the UK, and offers recommendations for the future implementation of Percent for Art. From: AN Publications PO Box 23, Sunderland SR4 6DG. Tel 091 514 3600.

11 • Project planning & fundraising

ABSA/WH Smiths Sponsorship Manual, Mary Allen and Tom Stockil, ABSA, 1987, ABSA, Nutmeg House, 60 Gainsford St, Butlers Wharf, London SE1 2NY. Tel 071 378 8143.

Business in the Arts, ABSA. A leaflet on the ABSA scheme. ABSA Nutmeg House, 60 Gainsford St, Butlers Wharf, London SE1 2NY. Tel 071 378 8143.

Business sponsorship in the arts - a tax guide, Arthur Anderson & Co/ABSA, 1991. Aimed at sponsors but useful to those seeking sponsorship. ABSA, Nutmeg House, 60 Gainsford St, Butlers Wharf, London SE1 2NY. Tel 071 378 8143.

CAFE (Creative Activity for Everyone), 1989, Irish funding handbook. 23-5 Moss St, Dublin 2 Ireland. Tel 010 77 0330.

Crafts Council Publications: Setting Up in Business, Setting Up Scheme, Project and Exhibition Grants, Crafts Council, Crafts Council Bookshop, 44a Pentonville Rd, Islington, London N1 9HF. Tel 071 278 7700.

Development, Shelly Bancroft and John Murray, Producers Alliance for Cinema and Television, £7.50. The guide concentrates on developing an idea and seeing it through to the final production stages. PACT, Gordon House, 10 Greencoat Place, London SW1 1PH. Tel 071 233 6000.

Directory of Grant-Making Trusts, Charities Aid Foundation. Part 1 is a classification of charitable purposes which includes all the principle fields of interest for the allocation of donations made by grant-making trusts; Part 2 lists trusts who've made a donation for a specific purpose and amounts; Part 3 is an alphabetical register of grant-making organisations with basic information as supplied by the trusts; Part 4 contains indexes. Is usually available in major public and educational libraries.

Directory of Grantmaking Trusts in Scotland, M Saunders, Charities Aid Foundation. (see above)

Fact Pack 1: Rates of Pay, Susan Jones, AN Publications, £1.85, Annually updated listing of rates for commissions, residencies and other work undertaken by visual artists. AN Publications, PO Box 23, Sunderland SR4 6DG. Tel 091 514 3600.

Finding Sponsorship for Community Projects – a step-by-step guide, Caroline Gillies, Friends of the Earth and the Directory of Social Change, £9.45 inc p&p. Directory of Social Change, Radius Works, Back Lane, London NW3 1HL.

Funding Digest, Research Training Initiatives. Gives up-to-date information on new sources of money by scanning 140 key journals and analysing business sponsorship. Copies can be consulted at regional arts boards and other arts organisations.

Grants in Europe, Ann Davison, Bedford Square Press. Bi-monthly publication, 26 Bedford Square, London WC1B 3HQ.

International Foundation Directory 1991, Europa Publications. Provides international information. Usually available in main public libraries.

Key British Enterprises 5 Volumes, 1991. Britain's top companies, Available at good libraries.

Major Companies Guide, Mike and Nikki Eastwood, Directory of Social Change, 1991, ISBN 0 907164 63 3, £16.45 plus p&p. Information on 350 major companies with policies, arts sponsorship and advice on applying. Directory of Social Change, Radius Works, Back Lane, London NW3 1HL.

Practical Sponsorship, Stuart Turner, Kogan Page, ISBN 1 85091 245 9, £12.95. Looks at the issue from the sponsor's and the recipient's viewpoints, emphasising that both parties should be aware of the other's needs. Kogan Page, 120 Pentonville Rd, London N1 9JN.

Step by Step, Head to Head Communications, £35 inc p&p. Video and handbook aimed at those working on a limited budget. It covers commissioning expectations and outlines potential copyright problems and features six case studies. The handbook is a detailed guide to the production process. Concord Video and Film Council, 201 Felixstowe Road, Ipswich, Suffolk IP3 9BJ.

The Arts Funding Guide, Anne Marie Doulton, Directory of Social Change, 1992, ISBN 0 907164 27 7, £16.45 inc p&p. Contains practical advice and ideas for arts organisations on raising money from the Arts Councils, RABs and other official bodies with details of local authority funding, grant-making trusts and business sponsorship. Also information on funds available from Europe and USA. From: AN Publications, PO Box 23, Sunderland SR4 6DG. Tel 091 514 3600.

The Grants Register, MacMillan. Lists research and project grants, scholarships, fellowships, exchange opportunities primarily for postgraduate students for further professional or advanced vocational training. Usually available in main public libraries,

The Wales Funding Handbook, Clive Smithers, 1992, Wales Council for Voluntary Action.

Times 1000 - Worlds Top Companies. Address lists included, £399 to buy, so check local libraries first!

14 • Skill sharing

The Art Works Report, SHAPE London, 1987, £3.50. Produced as the result of a course for people with art training, to enable them to acquire skills in workshop techniques to use with community and special needs groups. SHAPE London, 1 Thorpe Close, London W10 5XL. Tel 081 960 9245

15 • Abroad

Across Europe – the artist's personal guide to travel and work, ed David Butler, AN Publications, 1992, ISBN 0 907730 15 9, £9.95. A first handbook for visual artists on Europe as a result of '1992 and all that'. Issues focused on include public funding, exhibiting, journals and agencies, changing trends, and finding studios etc, AN Publications, PO Box 23, Sunderland SR4 6DG. Tel 091 514 3600.

American Universities and Colleges, American Council on Education, Walter de Gruyter Inc, 200 Saw Mill River Rd, Hawthorne NY 10532. Tel 914 747 0110.

An Introductory Guide to Travel Opportunities for Black Art Practitioners, Susan Okokon, Arts Access Unit, Arts Council, £5 inc p&p. Lists organisations, trusts and educational opportunities. ACGB, 14 Great Peter Street, London SW1P 3NQ.

Art Guides, A&C Black. Guides to Paris, London, Glasgow, Amsterdam, Madrid, Berlin, New York and Australia with information on galleries, art fairs, magazines, art schools, art materials suppliers, restaurants, theatres, cinemas, hotels etc. Art Guide Publications, A&C Black, 35 Bedford Row, London WC1R 4JH Tel 071 242 0946.

Arts Networking in Europe, Arts Council, 1992, £10 including postage. Contact names, addresses and information of more than 140 European networks. ACGB, 14 Great Peter St, London SW1P 3NQ.

Information leaflets available free from HM Customs & Excise:

ATA Carnets, An International Customs Facilitation Scheme

ATA Carnets Europe Notice 756

ATA Carnets Notice 104 Non-EC Countries HM Customs and Excise, New Kings Beam House, 22 Upper Ground, London SE1 9PJ. Tel 071 6201313 or see telephone directory for your local office.

Fact Pack 10: Travelling, Selling & Working in the EC, Emma Lister, AN Publications, 1992, £1.85. Fact Pack giving basic contact list for all countries in the European Community. AN Publications, PO Box 23, Sunderland SR4 6DG. Tel 091 514 3600.

Handbook on US Study for Foreign Nationals, Institute of International Education, 809 UN Plaza, New York NY 10017 USA.

Making Connections: the craftspersons guide to Europe, Judith Staines, South West Arts Board, 1992, ISBN 0 95069 919 54.95, Award winning sourcebook for makers guiding you through the maze of 'Europaperwork'. Includes selective listings of contacts and organisations in 15 European countries and includes the World Crafts Council's Europe Directory. From AN Publications, PO Box 23, Sunderland SR4 6DG. Tel 091 514 3600.

Specialised Study Options USA: A Guide to Short-Term Programs for Foreign Nationals Vol 1 Technical Programmes, Vol 2 Professional Development, ed Marguerite & Edrice Howard Institute of International Education, 1986-1988.

Study Abroad-UNESCO, HMSO bi-annually. Includes details of grants and awards.

The Grants Register, Macmillan Biennial publication. Lists main sources of funding for UK citizens to study overseas; those available to artists and designers are relatively few, but worth checking out.

Who Does What in Europe, Rod Fisher, Arts Council, ISBN 0 7287 0603 X, £7.50 inc p&p. Gives information on the EC, Council of Europe, UNESCO, various foundations and other organisations. International Affairs Unit, ACGB, 14 Great Peter Street, London SW1P 3NQ.

16 • Publicity & promotion

A Basic PR Guide, Dorothy and Alastair MacIntosh, Directory of Social Change, £9.45 inc p&p. Advice on public relations, dealing with the media and organising publicity events. Directory of Social Change, Radius Works, Back Lane, London NW3 1HL.

Arts Council Press Contacts and Press Mailing Lists 1991, Arts Council, 1991, ISBN 0 7287 0618 0, £20. Two annually updated listings, one of arts press contacts in the press and media and the other of arts contacts throughout the UK arranged by artform and region. Press Office, ACGB, 14 Great Peter Street, London SW1P 3NQ. Tel 071 333 0100.

Fact Pack 2: Slide Indexes, Susan Jones, AN Publications, £1.85. Listing 36 indexes and registers nationally, some open to application. AN

Publications, PO Box 23, Sunderland SR4 6DG. Tel 091 514 3600.

Fact Pack 3: Mailing the press, David Butler, listings compiled by Caroline Lambert, AN Publications, 1991, £1.85. How to write an effective press release plus a comprehensive listing of national, international and regional press and art media. AN Publications, AN Publications, PO Box 23, Sunderland SR4 6DG. Tel 091 514 3600.

Fact Pack 4: Getting media coverage, AN Publications, 1991, £1.50. How to get your work/exhibitions in the media, with a listing of national and regional TV and radio companies. AN Publications, PO Box 23, Sunderland SR4 6DG. Tel 091 514 3600.

Film and Video Marketing, Michael Wiese, Focal Press, £13.95, Covers market research and product development through to promotion strategies and scheduling. It pinpoints common problems and offers practical solutions through case studies.

Publicity & media planning guidelines, Southern Arts, 1990, Free to makers in Southern Arts region. Also available as pack of three with 'Guidelines on Exhibiting' and 'Guidelines to selling at trade and craft fairs' for £1.50. Aimed primarily at craftspeople, contains useful advice for anybody planning a publicity campaign. Southern Arts, 13 St Clement Street, Winchester, Hampshire SO23 9DQ. Tel 0962 55099.

Willings Press Guide, Media Publications, Held by main libraries lists over 11, 000 UK publications including contact names and addresses, cost and circulation details.

18 • Health & Safety

Artists Handbook 2 – Health & Safety: making art and avoiding dangers, Challis & Roberts, AN Publications, 1991, ISBN 0 907730 10 8, Practical information and advice on health and safety for all involved in the creation of art and craftwork including substances, processes and equipment, AN Publications, PO Box 23, Sunderland SR4 6DG. Tel 091 514 3600.

'Electrical safety in welding', NC Balchin, Welding Institute Research Bulletin (18), 1977.

First Aid at Work, Health and Safety (First Aid) Regulations 1981 – Approved Code of Practice, HMSO, 1990, ISBN 011 885536 0, Her Majesty's Stationery Office (Books), Publications Department, PO Box 276, London, SW8 5DT.

Health and safety in welding and allied processes, PJR Challen, Welding Institute, 1983, ISBN 085300 146 4.

Health and safety in ceramics, Institute of Ceramics, Pergamon, 1980, ISBN 0 08 026173 6.

Health and safety in ceramics: A guide for educational workshops and studios, Institute of Ceramics, Pergamon, 1986, ISBN 0 08 033468 7.

Photographic chemicals: safety (ref J/931 h), Kodak, 1984. For further information about Kodak products, contact the Publications and Products Safety Advisory Service (PAPSAS) at A10B, Kodak Ltd, Kodak House, PO Box 66, Station Road, Hemel Hempstead, Hertfordshire HP1 1JU.

Printsafe: a guide to safe, healthy and green printmaking, T Challis, estamp, 1990, ISBN 1 871 831 02 4, £10.95.

Safety First, T Challis and J Tye, Dent, 1988, ISBN 0460 024922, £3.95. Paperback guide to the safety in the home and workshop.

Ventilation: a practical guide for artists, craftspeople and others in the arts, N Clark, T Cutter and J Mcgrane, Lyons & Burford, 1987, ISBN 0 94 1130 44 4, A complete guide to choosing suitable ventilation systems.

19 • Benefits

DSS information leaflets available free from your local office or from some libraries:
A Guide to Family Credit Booklet NI 261.
A Guide to Maternity Benefits Booklet NI 17A.
Babies and Benefit Leaflet FB8.
Cash help while you're working Leaflet FB4.
People with small earnings from self-employment Form N1 27.
Self-employed? - A guide to your National Insurance and Social Security benefits Leaflet FB30.
Sickness Benefit Booklet NI 116.
Social Security Benefit Rates and Contributions Form NI 196.
Social Security Benefit Rates Form N1196.
Statutory Sick Pay - Check Your Rights Leaflet NI244.
Unemployed - A guide to benefits to make ends meet Leaflet FB9.
Which Benefit? Leaflet FB2.

20 • Employment status & tax

Artists Handbooks 3 – Money Matters, the artist's financial guide, Deeks, Murphy and Nolan, AN Publications, £7.25 inc p&p, Gives advice on keeping accounts, VAT, and taxation and contains an accounting system. AN Publications, PO Box 23, Sunderland SR4 6DG. Tel 091 514 3600

Croner's Reference Book for the Self-Employed and Small Business. *See 21 • Trading status.*

DSS information leaflets available free from your local office or from some libraries:
Class 2 N I Contributions Form NP18
More than 1 job? Your class 1 contributions Form NP28.

More than one job? Class 1 Contributions Form NP28
National Insurance for employees Form NI 40.
National InsuranceContributions Class 2 Form NP 18.
Should I be registered for VAT? Form 700/1/91. HM Customs & Excise, free.
Starting and Running Your Own Business, Dennis F Millar, Department of Employment, free.
Starting in Business booklet IR28, Inland RevenueFree, Contains form 41G which you need to complete and return on becoming. self-employed.
Thinking of Working for Yourself? IR 57, Inland Revenue, free.

21 • Trading status

Croner's Reference Book for the Self-Employed and Small Business, Croner Publications Ltd, Loose-leaf book that is updated monthly with new information on legislation, regulations affecting the self-employed. Tel 081 547 3333.
Starting Your Own Business, Hodder/Consumers' Association, 1992, Strong on practical information and addresses of other organisations that may be able to help. Looks at various aspects of self-employment from mall order to market trading and franchising, Consumers' Association, 14 Buckingham Street, London, WC2N 6DS.
Voluntary but Not Amateur, National Council of Voluntary Organisations, £7.95, Guide to the legal aspects of running a small organisation, including fund raicing and aocounting. 26 Bedford Square, London WC1B 3HU.

22 • Insurance

Fact Pack 6: Insurance, Chris Mcready, AN Publications, 1991. Advice on insurance for artists. Available by mail order only from AN Publications, AN Publications, PO Box 23, Sunderland SR4 6DG. Tel 091 514 3600.

23 • Contracts

Artists Handbooks 4: Copyright, Roland Miller, AN Publications, 1991, ISBN 0 907730 12 4, £7.25, Includes an example of a copyright licence. *See 24 Copyright.*
Contracts Factpacks, Nicholas Sharp, AN Publications. A series of model contracts with alternative wordings to allow the user to tailor them to their needs. This will gradually build to a comprehensive series covering all areas of visual arts practice. Contact AN Publications, PO Box 23, Sunderland SR4 6DG for details on contract factpacks currently available. Tel 091 514 3600.
Rights, Simon Stern, includes standard Association of Illustrators' contract. *See 7 • Earning from reproductions*

Small Claims in the County Court. A guide to procedures on how to sue and defend actions without a lawyer. Available from your local county court.

24 • Copyright

Applying to register a design (temporary revision August 1989), The Patent Office, 1989. Available from The Patents Office, Designs Registry, Cardiff Road, Newport, Gwent NP1 1RH. Tel 0633 814000.
Artists Handbooks 4: Copyright, Roland Miller, AN Publications, 1991, ISBN 0 907730 12 4, £7.25. Looks at the effect and use of copyright legislation in the visual arts. Advice on exhibiting, performance, photography, videoreproductions, promotional material, fees, infringements, moral rights. AN Publications, PO Box 23, Sunderland SR4 6DG. Tel 091 514 3600.
Copyright, basic facts, The Patent Office, 1990, DTI/Pub 232/30K/2/90.
Copyright, Designs and Patents Act 1988, HMSO, 1988, ISBN 0 105 448 885.
Photocopying from books and journals: A guide for all users of copyright literary works, edited by C Clark, British Copyright Council, 1990, ISBN 0 901 737 062.
Photographers Guide to the Copyright Act, 1988, British Photographer's Liaison Committee, 1989, ISBN 0 951 467 107.British Photographic's Liason Commitee, 9-10 Domingo Street, London EC1A 0TA.
Registered designs, basic facts, The Patent Office, 1990, DTI/Pub 230/30K/2/90. Available from The Patents Office, Designs Registry, Cardiff Road, Newport, Gwent NP1 1RH. Tel 0633 814000.
Rights, Simon Stern, looks at copyright agreements for illustrators. *See 7 • Earning from reproductions*
What is intellectual property?, The Patent Office, 1990, DTI/Pub 233/30K/2/90.

27 • Advertisers index

Eastern Arts Board

The Board's mission is to develop a wide range of arts activities of the highest quality, to stimulate artistic innovation and creativity and to extend involvement in the arts among all sections of the regional community.

The Visual and Media Arts Department works to support and develop activities in visual art, craft, film, video, photography and live art. We welcome submissions to our Slide Directory which is an unselected showcase for the work of regional visual and media arts practitioners. It is a central part of our information and advisory services on all aspects of the visual and media arts in the region.

Eastern Arts Board, Cherry Hinton Hall, Cambridge, CB1 4DW, telephone 0223 215355. We are the Regional Arts Board for Bedfordshire, Cambridgeshire, Essex, Hertfordshire, Lincolnshire, Norfolk and Suffolk.

Eastern Arts Board is committed to equality of opportunity in all its work.

East Midlands Arts
Support for Artists, Craftspeople and Photographers

Following the recent restructuring of East Midlands Arts, the new board has continued to emphasise its commitment to the support of the individual artist.

In recognition of this, the new **Media, Publishing and Visual Arts Department** offers grants, information, advice and encouragement to individual practitioners living and working in the region. Grants available to individuals still include the nationally recognised 'Start-up' grant aimed at artists, craftspeople and photographers in the early stages of their career.

KEEP IN TOUCH by registering on the 'Art Index' an information and promotion service for all practitioners living in the region.

For full details of all schemes and services, contact the Media, Publishing and Visual Arts Department, East Midlands Arts, Mountfields House, Forest Rd, Loughborough, Leicestershire LE11 3HU. Telephone: 0509 218292.

East Midlands Arts is an equal opportunities organisation which welcomes applications from any artists regardless of age, class, disability, race, religion, sex or sexual orientation.

WEST MIDLANDS ARTS

West Midlands Arts offers support to artists through the provision of funding, advice and information. Priority is given to activities which

- extend access to the arts

- sustain innovation

- encourage the best possible standards

- develop artistic and managerial skills

Call 021 631 3121 to find out about Grant Schemes and the full range of services available.

West Midlands Arts is the Regional Arts Board for Hereford & Worcester, Shropshire, Staffordshire, Warwickshire and the Metropolitan Districts of the West Midlands.

CLEVELAND ARTS

CLEVELAND ARTS OFFERS INFORMATION AND SUPPORT SERVICES FOR ARTISTS, CRAFTSPEOPLE, FILM AND VIDEO MAKERS, PHOTOGRAPHERS, EXHIBITION ORGANISERS AND ARTS ORGANISATIONS

For more information please contact:

The Administrator
Cleveland Arts
PO Box 12
Marton House
Borough Rd
Middlesborough
Cleveland TS4 2YP
Tel: 0642 211347
Fax: 0642 251209

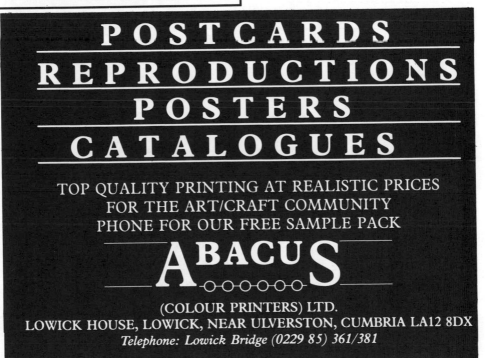

29 • Index

Page numbers in italic are references to illustrations.

Essential reading for artists, makers & photographers

AN Publications produces a whole range of publications on the visual arts. They can be bought from good bookshops, or by mail order from us. Many are listed below, but for further information or a catalogue, please contact us at

PO Box 23, Sunderland, SR4 6DG, 091 567 3589, fax 091 564 1600. Credit card order line 091 514 3600.
(Please add 10% tp prices to cover postage unless you subscribe to *Artists Newsletter* in which case postage is free.)

Residencies in Education:
setting them up and making them work
Daniel Dahl

"...explores the best ways of developing the mutual understanding and collaboration that are essential to get the most out of placements and residencies."

Mailout

Artist-in-education projects always begin with enthusiasm but can fail through poor co-ordination. *Residencies in Education* considers six different projects to help artists, organisers and teachers.

124 pages, illustrated £7.25

Health & Safety:
making art & avoiding dangers
Tim Challis & Gary Roberts

"It is in the interest of all artists to study the contents of this handbook."
Leisure Painter

Making art can be dangerous. Artists and makers now use substances and processes which can damage human health and the environment. This unique handbook covers all art and craft forms to help you protect people and the environment, and prepare your COSHH assessment.

144 pages, illustrated £7.25

Organising Your Exhibition:
the self-help guide
Debbie Duffin

"A do-it-yourself guide designed to help... artists to get their work on the wall with the minimum of agony."
Wideangle

"...detailed advice on pitfalls ranging from dealing with printers to buying wine."
Art Monthly

The revised and updated edition of Debbie Duffin's invaluable practical guide offers excellent advice on finding space, finances, publicity, insurance, framing and hanging work, private views, and selling. The essential sourcebook on setting up and running any exhibition.

116 pages £7.25

Copyright:
protection, use & responsibilities
Roland Miller

"...a comprehensive guide."
Portfolio Magazine

Essential advice on negotiating rewarding copyright agreements; exploiting the earning and promotional potential of copyright; and dealing with infringement of copyright. Designed to help *you* make the most of copyright.

128 pages, illustrated £7.25

Money Matters:
the artist's financial guide
Sarah Deeks, Richard Murphy & Sally Nolan

"...recommended".
Ceramic Review

Reliable user-friendly advice on: tax, National Insurance, VAT, keeping accounts, pricing your work, grants, insurance, dealing with customers, suppliers and banks, and much more. Features an accounting system specially devised for artists.

134 pages, illustrated £7.25

Directory of Exhibition Spaces 93/94

(3rd edition) ed Richard Padwick

"No self-respecting artist who wants to show and sell work should be without it."

Working for yourself in the Arts and Crafts

A comprehensive listing of over 2000 galleries in the UK and Eire to help you find the right exhibition space. Details when and how to apply, type of work shown, space, facilities, and the financial deal with artists. An indispensible reference for everyone in the visual arts.

256 pages, illustrated £13.99

Across Europe:

the artist's personal guide to travel and work
ed David Butler

"... a much needed sourcebook."

Sam Yates, Crafts Council Bookshop

A combination of artists' first-hand experiences and hard facts gets under the Eurospeak to show what '1992-and-all-that' could mean for you. Over 20 European nations are covered, giving information on: organisations, funding, magazines, agencies and other sources of information. A must for everyone interested in selling, exhibiting, working or training in Europe.

168 pages, illustrated £9.95

Art in Public:

new

what, why and how
ed Susan Jones

Available November 1992

An exciting variety of arts and crafts are now being commissioned for public places. This unique handbook looks at the radical development of art in public over recent years. It also acts as a practical handbook of valuable information and advice for all artists and commissioners involved in the creation of public artworks.

176 pages, illustrated £9.95

Independent Photography Directory

ed Michael Hallett & Barry Lane

"If you tale photography seriously this is an essential"

Untitled Magazine

Over 250 organisation working in independent photography listed with details of: history, funding, exhibition and education policy, space, opening hours and darkroom facilities. Also Arts Council policy and support schemes, awards, fellowships, competitions, training and careers, and press lists.

244 pages, illustrated £5.00

Live Art

ed Robert Ayers & David Butler   *"an inspiration"* Live Art Listings

What is live art? How far does it overlap and integrate with other art forms? However you define your art, if it involves live or non-permanent elements this book is for you. It includes advice on putting a performance together, touring work, copyright, contracts and documentation, with examples of live art through photographs and comments by artists. For everyone who wants to develop, earn from, or promote live art.

178 pages, illustrated £9.95